Helion & Company Limited
Unit 8 Amherst Business Centre
Budbrooke Road
Warwick
CV34 5WE
England
Tel. 01926 499 619
Email: info@helion.co.uk
Website: www.helion.co.uk
Twitter: @helionbooks
Visit our blog http://blog.helion.co.uk/

Published by Helion & Company 2023
Designed and typeset by Farr out
    Publications, Wokingham, Berkshire
Cover designed by Paul Hewitt, Battlefield
    Design (www.battlefield-design.co.uk)
Cover photo by courtesy of the Airborne
    Assault Museum

ISBN 978-1-804513-72-9

British Library Cataloguing-in-Publication
    Data
A catalogue record for this book is available
    from the British Library

We always welcome receiving book
proposals from prospective authors.

CONTENTS

ABBREVIATIONS

2PARA	2nd Battalion The Parachute Regiment		**MRAF**	Marshal of the Royal Air Force
APU	Anguilla Police Unit		**NATO**	North Atlantic Treaty Organisation
ASC	Army Strategic Command		**OD**	Defence and Oversea Policy Committee
BBC	British Broadcasting Corporation		**PAM**	People's Action Movement
BIO	British Information Officer		**PM**	Prime Minister
C-in-C	Commander-in-Chief		**Psyops**	Psychological Operations
Comcen	Communications Centre		**PWD**	Public Works Department
Coy	Company		**RAF**	Royal Air Force
D-Notice	Defence Notice		**RAMC**	Royal Army Medical Corps
DWS	Diplomatic Wireless Service		**RE**	Royal Engineers
FCO	Foreign and Commonwealth Office		**SBO**	Senior British Official
HMG	Her Majesty's Government		**SNOWI**	Senior Naval Officer West Indies
HO	Home Office		**SPG**	Special Patrol Group
ITV	Independent Television		**UDI**	Unilateral Declaration of Independence
LPD	Landing Platform Docks		**UHF**	Ultrahigh Frequency
LPH	Landing Platform Helicopter		**UK**	United Kingdom
MoD	Ministry of Defence		**UN**	United Nations
MP	Member of Parliament		**US**	United States

ACKNOWLEDGEMENTS

To my grandparents, Maurice and Monica Lord

I would like to thank my editors at Helion & Company, Tom Cooper, Bill Norton and Andy Miles for their help and encouragement during my writing of this book. In particular, Tom showed faith and interest in this project and its neglected historical subject matter from the outset and gave me the space to approach it in my own way. Furthermore, I am also grateful to Andy for allowing me to use photos from his collection of military training manuals. I have also appreciated the publication advice provided by my former dissertation supervisor at the University of Leeds, Professor Edward Spiers. His considerable publication record and knowledge of military history have always been a source of inspiration to me. Moreover, I would like to thank Professor Helen Parr of Keele University for her support, especially in advising about the Parachute Regiment and its archives.

I appreciate, once again, the assistance of the UK National Archives staff at Kew, who are always helpful and efficient. Furthermore, I am very grateful to Ben Hill and his archival team at the Airborne Assault Museum, Duxford. They made my first visit to this museum and archive very pleasant, and their research advice proved very useful. I thank the Airborne Assault Museum also for granting me permission to use numerous photos in this book. Similarly, I am most grateful to Albert Grandolini for allowing me to use photos from his collection in this book.

As always, I appreciate the support and interest of my families in Lancashire and Yorkshire. My grandfather, Maurice Lord, regularly asks 'haven't you finished writing that book yet?' His questioning and enthusiasm for my projects always keeps me focused and aware that an eager consumer of my research is waiting for the completed monograph. Finally, and most importantly, I am incredibly grateful to my partner, Christina, for her support throughout this project since its commencement in 2020. I regularly natter on and on to her about my interests in military history and international relations and she listens with patience, attentiveness, and curiosity (feigned or otherwise). As always, I am grateful for her love, companionship, and sense of humour.

INTRODUCTION

In the morning darkness of 19 March 1969 British soldiers and marines clambered aboard the Gemini dinghies, boats and Westland Wasp helicopters of HMS *Minerva* and HMS *Rothesay*, anchored off the coast of Anguilla. Following a series of dramatic and fast-moving political events in the Caribbean island, this taskforce had been dispatched by the Labour government of Prime Minister Harold Wilson to restore law and order. As the troops neared the shorelines of Road Bay and Crocus Bay, the tension was palpable aboard the two frigates as navy and army officers scanned the horizon. They had, after all, been told to expect resistance from Anguilla's 'defence force', a group of men and boys of uncertain number predicted to be armed with an assortment of firearms. The defenders were commanded by J. Ronald Webster, the supposed 'President' of the new Republic of Anguilla, who had led a two-year revolt against the island's union with St Kitts and Nevis, both located around 70 miles to the south-east along the Leeward Islands chain. As this union, or 'Associated Statehood', had been created by the British to help dismantle their Caribbean empire, residual commitments arguably obliged London's intervention to restore law and order. Webster's regime was also rumoured to be supported by mysterious figures from the American Mafia, further persuading Whitehall to take action to suppress the growth of organised crime believed to be on the island.

Charles Douglas-Home, reporting for *The Times* aboard *Minerva*, noticed that Royal Navy gunners anxiously gripped their gun mounts tightly as they observed a battery of flashes light up the distant beaches of Road Bay. 'Peering into the darkness, they first saw two cars, headlights blazing, racing down a hill towards the landing parties. Then came a barrage of flashes which officers thought was the opening of a gun battle.'[1] Fortunately, these flashes turned out to come from the bulbs of journalists' cameras, eager to capture the first shots of a British military intervention in the Caribbean. As British troops hit Anguilla's beaches, therefore, they must have been confronted with an atmosphere of tense expectation alongside surreal anti-climax. Indeed, these initial moments of 'Operation Sheepskin' – the invasion of Anguilla – were emblematic of the much wider surreal episode in British military history now unfolding, often characterised, according to the journalists who reported upon it, by farce, blunder and embarrassment.

The fact that the island was subsequently occupied by the taskforce that day without any casualties or much resistance soon exposed the Wilson government to ridicule by the full spectrum of the British and international media. *The Guardian* marvelled that 'we can all glory once again at the splendid sight of the British sledgehammer, coming down unerringly on a colonial nut'.[2] Comparing the episode with President John F. Kennedy's failed Cuban invasion of 1961 the *Daily Mail* asked, 'Is this Wilson's Bay of Piglets?'[3] In the United States (US), the *Washington Post* concluded that 'London looks silly' in its handling of the crisis, whilst the *Chicago Tribune* more scathingly exclaimed that '[to] the long and lustrous record of British arms [roll the muffled drums to the names of Blenheim, Ramillies,...Waterloo and Omdurman] add now the famous victory at Anguilla'.[4] The tone of this criticism, focusing on the perceived anachronistic gunboat diplomacy of a crumbling former imperial power that had totally misjudged the situation in Anguilla, would come to colour the lens through which the crisis was viewed for decades to come. Indeed, whilst there were some early attempts to assess the intervention dispassionately, this comedic or tragic narrative often continues to dominate memory of Operation Sheepskin, if this event is remembered at all outside of the Caribbean.[5]

This interpretation was somewhat projected by Donald E. Westlake's *Under an English Heaven* (1972), which constituted the first extensive study of the invasion. Arguing that, rather than seeking independence through revolt, Anguillians preferred to return to British colonial rule to escape union with St Kitts-Nevis and that this was ultimately the outcome of Operation Sheepskin, Westlake wrote that 'this was a military expedition doomed by its presumptions to plunge into defeat, humiliated rather than slaughtered, but resoundingly trounced for all that'.[6] More recent academic studies by Spencer Mawby and Don E. Walicek have added further to academic understandings of various aspects of Operation Sheepskin. Mawby has considered both the long-term policy assumptions and short-term events that spurred the British government into launching the invasion. Stating that Whitehall thinking about Caribbean decolonisation was influenced by 'the assumption that colonial subjects were peculiarly prone to corrupting external influences', Mawby argued that intensified fears

about Mafia infiltration persuaded senior members of the Labour government about the need to intervene militarily. Furthermore, the coinciding onset of violence in Anguilla in early 1969 added further justification for those policymakers arguing that Britain needed to restore law and order. Ultimately, Mawby argued that the British government's 'action in authorizing the invasion demonstrates the dramatic animating effect of this kind of portrayal of politics in the colonial periphery'.[7] Whilst his study is useful for assessing the British decision-making process in the weeks prior to invasion, he does not consider in depth the military's implementation of Operation Sheepskin or the experience of occupation for either Anguillians or the British forces.

Walicek's study has, however, helped to restore the much-neglected Anguillian voice in the retelling of Operation Sheepskin, using interviews to consider the experience and memory of ordinary islanders under military occupation. In so doing, he paints a generally negative picture of the British Army's performance, including violent search operations and a flawed Hearts and Minds public relations campaign. According to Walicek's analysis, therefore, the operation was characterised by 'controversy, violence, and infractions on freedom'.[8] His fascinating interviews with islanders adds an additional layer to academic understandings of Anguillian identity and complements the accounts of the invasion by more prominent island leaders. These include Ronald Webster himself, whose continual media interviews across 1967–69 and more recent memoirs – *Scrap Book of Anguilla's Revolution* (1987) and *Revolutionary Leadership* (2011), provide excellent resources for understanding the Anguillian revolutionary perspective.[9]

Apart from these excellent studies, historical analysis of Operation Sheepskin and the Anguillian Revolution remains limited. This is especially the case regarding the British military experience. Details of operations on the island during the initial landings and long-term military occupation, which lasted until September 1971, are very minimal in historical accounts. The reasons for this neglect could be numerous. Certainly, the seemingly uneventful course of this bloodless invasion could have dissuaded military historians from detailed study of the operation. Upon closer examination of surviving military and political records, however, the mistakes within operational planning and implementation – particularly regarding intelligence gathering, communications and psychological operations (psyops) – prove of considerable interest. Moreover, the relative success of the British occupation force – Force Anguilla – in establishing good relations with the islanders over a course of months and years constitutes a rare triumph of British internal security operations in the 1960s and 1970s.

Collectively, therefore, the significance of Operation Sheepskin for the military historian and general reader has been underestimated. This fact is especially true when considering that the invasion of Anguilla in March 1969 constituted the first military intervention of Harold Wilson's premiership. Whilst his Labour government had inherited a range of military commitments East of Suez from the Conservatives, such as the Indonesian Confrontation (1962–66) and Aden Emergency (1963–67), Operation Sheepskin would be the first test of Labour's willingness to use force prior to the onset of Operation Banner in Northern Ireland in August 1969. Anguilla is therefore important for understanding the nature and culture of Labour's decision-making in the field of military intervention. The embarrassment that the Anguilla intervention caused the Wilson government may explain why it was forgotten so quickly and comprehensively. As Mawby has noted, Cabinet ministers who took the decision to intervene mention this episode only briefly or not at

Harold Wilson was leader of the UK's Labour Party between 1963 and 1976. He was Prime Minister from 1964 until 1970 and would later serve another term in the same office between 1974 and 1976. (Open source)

Denis Healey was the British Defence Secretary at the time of Operation Sheepskin and had overseen a radical review of British defence policy that saw a drastic cut in commitments 'East of Suez' and a refocussing upon Britain's commitment to NATO and the Central Front in West Germany. (Open source)

all in their subsequent memoirs or published diaries.[10] The extent to which Operation Sheepskin was soon overshadowed by the much larger deployment in Northern Ireland perhaps also explains why this episode was forgotten so quickly.

Nevertheless, Anguilla is peculiarly distinctive in occupying the curious hiatus between the end of active military operations East of Suez in November 1967 and the onset of military commitments in the Irish Troubles. An examination of Anguilla, therefore, helps to bridge the gap between two important chapters in postwar British military history. The Healey defence reforms of 1968, accompanying the decision to pull troops back from East of Suez, changed the strategic system through which Britain projected military force into the wider world outside of NATO commitments. Anguilla would, therefore, be the first test of this new system, demonstrating Britain's willingness to act as a global power in a post-imperial world. The fact that this intervention would occur in the Caribbean also makes this episode distinctive for the military historian. Despite the extent of British military commitments in this region during the 1960s and 1970s, literature on postwar campaigns rarely examine the military experience in the Caribbean.[11] Analysis of the Anguillian crisis therefore goes some way towards helping to restore historiographical awareness of this region and its importance to recent British military history.

The Anguilla crisis also has historical significance outside of military considerations. It reveals much about the nature of British decolonisation in the Caribbean and the evolution of local island identity in the aftermath of empire. As Rafael Cox-Alomar – a leading expert on the decolonisation of the Eastern Caribbean – argues, the process of imperial retreat in this region was especially intricate and 'evolved from the complex, intimate and dynamic interaction of ever-changing variables'.[12] Indeed, he emphasises the 'arbitrariness and unpredictability of the decolonizing process' in the Leeward and Windward Islands.[13] Anguilla would prove to be emblematic of this, as the British were forced to accept the unravelling of their carefully made plans and agree to the eventual restoration of long-term colonial rule over the island.

This episode also adds to understandings of Cold War tensions in the Caribbean. With the Bay of Pigs (1961) and Cuban Missile Crisis (1962) only recent memories, the region was at the centre of East-West tensions. As Mawby has stated, this Cold War dimension and other factors such as the relationship between US race relations and Caribbean movements, meant that crises in the

British decolonisation of this region were of particular interest to Washington DC and retained considerable American media coverage.[14] This was perhaps even more understandable given that *The New York Times* estimated that more Anguillians lived in New York City than did on the island itself.[15] Moreover, at just over 1,200 miles distant from Florida, the close proximity of the island allowed easy access for American journalists. In a year when US headlines were dominated by events such as the quagmire of the Vietnam War, the excitement of the Apollo 11 Moon Landings or Senator Edward M. Kennedy's Chappaquiddick crash, Anguilla offered a colourful news scoop of anachronistic British gunboat diplomacy with a Cold War regional flavour. Regular discussion of the Anguilla crisis at the United Nations (UN) also ensured interest from elements of the Non-Aligned Movement, the Commonwealth and the Communist world. Despite its size and comedic value, therefore, Operation Sheepskin was truly an international talking point.

Opening with a contextual study of Anguilla's history and place within the wider process of decolonisation in the Anglophone Caribbean, analysis will then move to the initial phase of rebellion against the Bradshaw government in 1967. Attention will then move to the diplomatic negotiations that produced, upheld and experienced the collapse of the Interim Agreement of 1968. The deteriorating political circumstances in Anguilla culminating in the notorious Whitlock affair of March 1969 will then be covered, leading to the descent into military intervention. Attention will then be particularly focused on the planning, implementation and evaluation of Operation Sheepskin before progressing to examine the longer-term military occupation and series of political settlements that defused the crisis.

My intellectual curiosity about Operation Sheepskin was initially sparked by reading a brief recollection of the 'ultimate absurdity' of paratroopers dispatched to Anguilla in Simon Winder's book *The Man Who Saved Britain*.[16] Examining how the sting of imperial retreat was cushioned within 1960s British culture by the James Bond phenomenon, Winder appears to suggest how Sheepskin was a symptom of the strange new world in which Britain found itself by 1969. I hope this book encourages others to continue exploring the smaller, often ignored, military deployments and garrisons at the end of empire.

1

SECURITY AND DECOLONISATION IN THE ANGLOPHONE CARIBBEAN

In the fast-fading evening light of 29 January 1935 chaos engulfed Buckleys Estate on the outskirts of Basseterre, the capital of St Kitts. Around 6pm the local 'defence force' or colonial militia had joined the police in attempting to dislodge a large crowd of strikers protesting near the estate house.[1] Unrest had broken out on the previous day, generated by the declining wages and working conditions of sugarcane cutters on the island resulting from the wider international collapse of commodity prices. After a tense standoff, the Riot Act was read, and orders given for the security forces to move in on the strikers. Suddenly, they were hit by a bombardment of stones from the crowd, 400 to 500 strong, which intensified the sense of a situation spiralling out of control. The command was thus given to fire upon the key ringleaders, resulting in three dead, eight wounded and the eventual dispersal of the crowd.[2] Fearing further riots, the colonial government called for what would become a familiar pattern in British policing of the Caribbean over subsequent decades: the deployment of a Royal Navy warship carrying troops to bolster local security patrols. HMS *Leander* arrived off the Kittitian coast, sending Royal Marines to briefly police the island until it was clear that the industrial unrest had ended.

Whilst the spark of labour rebellion on St Kitts had been snuffed out almost immediately, these events proved to be the first signs of much wider unrest throughout Britain's Caribbean colonies. On 21 October 1935 another British warship was requested to bring colonial forces to suppress a revolt against customs duties in St Vincent. Within weeks, yet another ship was sent to St Lucia to quell a coal strike and Royal Marines extensively patrolled the island. Violence also erupted in Barbados in 1937 and Jamaica in 1938, whilst other industrial disputes developed in British Guiana, Trinidad and Tobago during these troubled years.

Historians concur as to the crucial significance of the 1935 unrest in influencing British government policy and neuroses for decades to come about the potential for further rebellion and the collapse of colonial authority in the Caribbean. Mawby argues that the riots made government officials 'alert to any evidence of local demagoguery or external subversion which might set off a new insurrectionary movement in the region'.[3] Coincidingly, however, he states that the unrest constituted a 'crisis of imperial legitimacy' that underlined the need for colonial reform in the Caribbean.[4] Richard Hart has also claimed that the 1930s revolts were of 'tremendous significance', initiating a 'new upsurge of working class protest and organizational activity in the British colonies'.[5] Indeed, the unrest indicated that future anti-colonial resistance would be dominated by labour organisations and many of the Caribbean's pro-independence leaders would emerge from these groups. Ultimately, therefore, the seeds of Caribbean decolonisation and accompanying British security fears that would influence postwar decades had been planted by the late 1930s.

British security policy in the Anglophone Caribbean

As Britain emerged battered and bankrupt from the Second World War there was an increasing realisation that the forces of anti-colonialism across the empire could not be ignored forever. Whilst the British Raj was quickly dismantled in India and Pakistan, there was a general consensus in Whitehall that decolonisation would be a much slower process in other regions. This attitude was certainly applied to the Caribbean where, as Mawby notes, London policymakers adopted a 'developmentalist view which portrayed the achievement of independence as analogous to a child's attainment of maturity after a period of careful schooling'.[6] With Britain undertaking a 'paternal role which necessitated disciplinary action in cases of insubordinate behaviour' in its colonies, this outlook dominated thinking about imperial defence and security in the Anglophone Caribbean.[7]

On the one hand, security policymakers feared internal destabilising forces, commonly perceived as militant workers' unions and incendiary demagogue politicians who might mobilise anti-colonial rebellions. These fears were demonstrated when the Grenada Manual and Metal Workers Union, led by the firebrand Eric Gairy, launched a general strike in early 1951. With memories of 1935 still fresh, London responded to the growing violence on Grenada, which islanders named 'red sky' due to the number of burning plantations, by sending the light cruiser HMS *Devonshire* to deploy Royal Marines in March.[8] With instability failing to subside over subsequent months, 'B' Company of the 1st Royal Welch Fusiliers was then sent to restore order in May 1951.

Coincidingly, the British feared the destabilisation of their colonies by external influences. With Cold War tensions growing in the 1950s at a time when the British were launching democratic reforms in the Caribbean in preparation for eventual independence, London feared communist subversion and the overthrow of colonial authority. This was particularly apparent in British Guiana where the electoral success of Cheddi Jagan's People's Progressive Party in April 1953 led to Whitehall hysteria that the colony was about to fall under Soviet influence. Having suspended the recently created constitution, the Churchill government decided to intervene militarily under the codename Operation Windsor. On 8 October a large force of Royal Welch Fusiliers and Royal Marines embarked on the frigates HMS *Bigbury Bay* and *Barghead Bay* from the cruiser HMS *Superb*, the latter being unable to approach the shores of the colony due to its extensive mudbanks.[9] The troops then proceeded by air and sea to occupy key sites throughout the colony and conduct internal security operations. The fusiliers were then relieved by a battalion of Argyll and Sutherland Highlanders who, based at Georgetown, New Amsterdam and the US airbase at Atkinson Field, patrolled coastal areas and the capital extensively. They were then replaced by the Black Watch in October 1954.[10]

As David French has noted, this episode proved to be 'the insurgency that never was', with the British intervening to forestall a perceived impending communist takeover rather than reacting to an actual one.[11] The similarities of this intervention with events that would unfold more than 15 years later in Anguilla are striking. The British media greeted the military operation with astonishment, assessing that there was no security threat to quash.[12] Consequently, a lack of accurate intelligence and the potency of hysteria had both played some part in persuading Whitehall to commit troops perhaps unnecessarily. Moreover, as Mawby has noted, the initial plan for Operation Windsor had counted on the element of

The events of the Cuban revolution and its aftermath deeply shook many governments in the Western world, particularly those with a direct interest in the Caribbean. Here Cuban revolutionaries are seen in the Havana Hilton in 1959. (Open source)

Fidel Castro, seen here in the late 1950s, cast a long shadow over events in the Caribbean during the Cold War. (Open source)

Revolution of 1958–59. There was growing tension between Havana and London over the threat posed by anti-Castro groups operating out of the Bahamas. The existence of many uninhabited islands in this territory proved useful for storing weapons for operations against Cuba and for helping refugees escape the Castro regime. As an article in *Military Review* noted, in late 1962 a gun battle had broken out between Cuban vessels and exiles within Bahamian waters. Moreover, following an incendiary speech by Fidel Castro whereby he warned that Cuba had the means to attack any British islets harbouring the exiles, tensions reached a peak when Cuban forces captured a group of exiles in Anguilla Cays in the Bahama Banks on 13 August 1963.[14] As events escalated, therefore, the Royal Navy launched the 'Bahamas Patrol' to curb the activities of anti-Castro groups. This operation was still underway and yielding results years later, with two arms caches identified in August 1967.[15]

The Cuban threat, combined with geographical proximity, ensured that British internal security and defence policies, combined with the timing of decolonisation in the Caribbean, were also deeply influenced by the United States. Indeed, Cox-Alomar argues that there is 'a robust correlation between the islands' constitutional evolution and the geopolitical worries of the Anglo-American alliance' meaning the process of imperial retreat should be viewed through a transatlantic 'triangle' of influences centred on London, Washington and the colonies.[16] During the 1960s the Royal Navy cooperated with the US coastguard in policing anti-Castro elements in the Bahamas and also with US anti-submarine forces in the area.[17] At a time when transnational movements such as Black Power and Rastafarianism were increasingly viewed as security threats, there was also concerted efforts by London and Washington to curb their influence. For instance, as the *Military Review* noted, in 1960 British troops in Jamaica engaged in a shootout with Rastafarians and helped to round up their leadership, whilst police in New York City simultaneously arrested Jamaicans who had established a paramilitary organisation in the US.[18] Moreover, as a UK Naval Intelligence Report of 1968 stated, '[it] is frequently suggested that Black Power will also flourish in the [Caribbean] area but it is a movement difficult to define...Nevertheless, there is undoubtedly widespread sympathy for the Negro movements in the US which may be reflected in time by hostility towards whites as a whole.'[19] The Caribbean was therefore a region where British security concerns and US race relations somewhat intersected.

The complex interplay of security interests in London, Washington and the Caribbean could also collide into bitter disagreement which could destabilise the decolonisation process. Perhaps the most notorious episode in this regard occurred over US control of the

surprise, which had been subsequently lost due to rumours in the media.[13] Collectively, the military intervention in British Guiana demonstrated how sensitive London was to communist subversion in the Caribbean and the extent to which it was willing to act militarily to stop this perceived incursion. Troops would again be committed to maintain stability in the run-up to Guyanese independence between 1962 and 1966.

Alongside imagined Communist threats to their colonies, the British had to deal with more tangible ones following the Cuban

Perhaps one of the most iconic images of the Black Power movement in the 1960s is this photograph taken at the 1968 Olympic Games in Mexico when Tommie Smith and John Carlos made their protest on the podium for the 200 metres medal ceremony. The events surrounding Operation Sheepskin would unfold only a few months later. (Open source)

Chaguaramas military base in Trinidad. The base had been handed to the Americans during the 'destroyers for bases' agreement in the Second World War. However, Caribbean politicians planning for the creation of the new West Indies Federation in the late 1950s demanded that their new federal capital be situated at Chaguaramas, much to the irritation of the Eisenhower administration. London was inevitably torn between its Special Relationship with Washington and its plans for the West Indies Federation. According to Mawby, 'this was one of the main issues which dominated the short life of the federation', with Trinidadian politician Dr Eric Williams launching an unsuccessful four-year campaign for the return of the base.[20] US influence over UK security policy and the decolonisation process could, therefore, be both complementary and counterproductive.

Regardless of the specific security threat, the Anglophone Caribbean tended to be a theatre naturally dominated by the Royal Navy. As a UK Naval Intelligence Report of 1968 stated, 'Since the time of Drake, Britain has been involved in the Caribbean and a considerable part of our maritime history has been written there. Today, Britain continues to have many interests, political, commercial and defence in the area which is widely dispersed and essentially maritime in character.'[21] This naval emphasis was reflected in Britain's military organisation in the region, although these structures were evolving over post-war decades. In the interwar period, the job of maintaining internal security and protecting trade had been allotted to a cruiser squadron, but by the 1960s this naval presence consisted of two large frigates.[22] Moreover,

the Royal Air Force (RAF) retained no significant presence in the area.[23] Until October 1956 naval forces had been overseen by the Commander-in-Chief, America and West Indies Station, based in Bermuda. Under this C-in-C, the post of Senior Naval Officer West Indies (SNOWI), occupied by a commodore (second class), had been created in 1951 to oversee the navy's Caribbean commitments more closely, although officially still based in Bermuda. Following the abolition of the C-in-C role, SNOWI became the most senior military officer in the region.

The British Army also retained a sizeable presence in the Caribbean during the early postwar decades. The Army's 'Headquarters Caribbean Area', based in Kingston, Jamaica, was formed in 1948 from wartime headquarters in the Northern and Southern Caribbean. Upon Jamaican independence in August 1962, it then merged into the new joint service Headquarters British Forces Caribbean Area in Nassau, Bahamas. Separate Garrison Headquarters also existed in British Guiana until independence in 1966 and British Honduras (Belize) more permanently.[24] According to the Naval Intelligence Report, the Belize garrison was the last British Land Force permanently stationed in the region in 1968, consisting of a Lt. Colonel and staff, an infantry company and stockpiles to support a larger force if necessary.[25] The *Chicago Tribune* estimated this garrison strength to be around 250 soldiers.[26]

As London initially pulled its colonies into the West Indies Federation between 1958 and 1962 in an effort to grant independence to a larger state, this had also affected the organisation of local military units. The West Indies Regiment, disbanded in 1927, had been reconstituted in January 1959 mainly by absorbing the Jamaica Regiment, although notable quantities of recruits would also join from Trinidad and Tobago, alongside others from the Leewards and Windwards. As Humphrey Metzgen and John Graham have noted, the new regiment would 'serve throughout the region – a means of introducing the troops to islands other than their own and building friendships between the Caribbean public and their soldiers'.[27] The subsequent breakup of the Federation in 1962 caused the disbandment of the regiment and its dispersal into the independent Jamaica Regiment, Trinidad and Tobago Regiment and Barbados Regiment. Other islands with volunteer forces would also establish regular units after their independence, such as the St Kitts and Nevis Defence Force established in 1967 as the Anguilla crisis unfolded. Militia forces had been established in both St Kitts and Nevis from the 1860s onwards following the withdrawal of an imperial garrison in 1852. Its three companies were responsible for internal security in Basseterre, the Kittitian districts and Nevis respectively.[28] The long-term neglect of their Anguillian partner in this defence arrangement perhaps partly explains the hostility of Anguillians to Basseterre's security forces during the crisis of 1967–69.

Collectively, whilst British security policy in the late imperial Caribbean was increasingly tailored to meet the needs of decolonisation, it was consistently dominated by fears of internal unrest and external subversion. The use of short-term military interventions, usually involving Royal Navy ships deploying troops to assist colonial police in conducting internal security operations, became commonplace. As will be demonstrated in the next section, the plans drawn up in Whitehall across the 1950s and 1960s for the independence of Britain's Caribbean colonies would reflect these security concerns.

Decolonising the Anglophone Caribbean

As the prospect of Britain's eventual retreat from the Caribbean entered policy discussions in Whitehall's corridors of power and in colonial governor's residences during the late 1940s, the natural inclination of many officials was for the islands to be federated. This strategy followed wider trends around the empire, whereby the British recognised that economic, political and military stability would be best ensured by larger postcolonial states that were better able to fend off the familiar threats of internal rebellion and external subversion. Federations were thus established in Central Africa, Malaysia and South Arabia. Moreover, the geographically isolated and economically underdeveloped nature of many British Caribbean colonies meant that they were perceived by policymakers to be particularly vulnerable to these threats, making a federation especially attractive.

Early planning for the West Indies Federation was evident in the creation of the University College of the West Indies in 1948. However, political union was only passed into law under the British Caribbean Federation Act of 1956 leading to the creation of the federation in 1958 with its capital based at Port of Spain, Trinidad. The partnership involved almost all of Britain's Caribbean colonies apart from the Bahamas, British Guiana and British Honduras. Its constitution established an Executive Governor-General, Prime Minister, Cabinet and bicameral legislature, whilst other institutions were created across the federation's lifetime including a civil service.[29] The 1960s would, however, witness the collapse of most of Britain's federal projects around the empire. One British official remarked to *The New York Times* with somewhat resigned humour that 'I guess we just don't do federations very well'.[30] This conclusion was certainly true of the West Indies Federation which collapsed in 1962.

Historians continue to debate the reasons for this failure. Mawby has argued that Caribbean politicians realised that the federal project, instead of offering a quick route to independence, was actually slowing the process down due to Britain's strict planning of guarantees for regional security.[31] As he notes, '[efforts] to inhibit the potentially irresponsible behaviour of nationalist politicians in their new regional forum by retaining elements of colonial control encumbered the federation with a constitution which was less advanced than that of the unit territories and this, in turn, contributed to its demise'.[32] The security restrictions placed on federal independence were certainly influenced by American interests in the region. Indeed, Cox-Alomar emphasises how Washington's enthusiastic support for the federation was based on fears of political fragmentation which could encourage further communist infiltration in the region.[33] The security priorities of the UK-US alliance were, however, counterproductive as, by slowing down the decolonisation process, they made federal independence less appealing than island independence, thus generating the fragmentation which policymakers had sought to avoid.

The lack of a coherent sense of regional identity and unity among the islands also contributed to federal collapse. Political culture in the Anglophone Caribbean often centred around island nationalism and this was perhaps enhanced by the considerable distances between each population. The disparities in economic development between these islands added further to political calculations as it became clear that the larger economies of Jamaica and Trinidad and Tobago would likely be supporting the smaller islands under federal independence. Subsequently, when Jamaica voted 54.11 percent to 45.89 percent to leave the West Indies Federation in a referendum of September 1961, the impending independence of the largest partner of the union quickly initiated the unravelling of the federal project.[34] At each stage of this collapse, the political, infrastructural and economic viability of each island were key factors in determining whether they could sustain individual independence. Thus, Trinidad-Tobago broke away from the federation and lowered the Union Jack in August 1962.

Despite this major setback in British planning, the concept of a federation for the remaining 'Little Eight' colonies of the Eastern Caribbean – St Kitts-Nevis-Anguilla, Barbados, Dominica, St Lucia, Grenada, St Vincent, Antigua-Barbuda and Montserrat – remained appealing to Whitehall policymakers.[35] However, negotiations for a new federation between 1962 and 1965 fell victim to the same British unimaginativeness and local island conditions that had hindered the larger West Indies Federation. Economic inequality and mutual suspicion between the islands affected movement towards a settlement. Moreover, British security planning and miserliness in financial aid to the proposed federation also quelled enthusiasm for the plan. With evident déjà vu, Barbados – blessed with the largest economy of the remaining Little Eight and a good island infrastructure – saw the benefits of individual independence over supporting its neighbours in a restrictive federation.[36] It too therefore became an independent state in November 1966.

The question of what to do with the remaining islands, known as the 'Little Six', after Barbadian independence caused an almighty headache in London. By the mid-1960s, as Westlake notes, 'the British were temporarily weary of West Indies Federations' following their demise in the Caribbean and also in Africa, Asia and the Arabian Gulf.[37] New solutions were therefore sought to the old problems of how to grant independence to islands perceived as incapable of sustaining economic viability and defence against internal and external threats. Whitehall mandarins soon focused on a new concept of independence accepted in 1960 as permissible by the United Nations known as Associated Statehood. Under this arrangement a territory could retain links with the colonial power, whilst obtaining full autonomy over the development of its own constitution. Moreover, the territory could elect to end its association with the colonial power whenever needed.[38] Associated Statehood could also be permanent or, as Westlake noted, 'a temporary way station on the road to complete independence'.[39] Cox-Alomar has highlighted several reasons for the appeal of Associated Statehood for the Little Six, among them its acceptability to the UN after years of criticism about British colonial policy and both flexibility and extra time in London's planning for possible independence.[40] Most importantly, the British could prevent the security threats feared to be potentially caused by each island deciding to go their own way.

St Kitts, Nevis and Anguilla

For many Anguillians the prospect of Associated Statehood in union with its distant neighbours, St Kitts and Nevis, was unacceptable. Anguilla, an island of about 35 square miles, had a population of around 6,000 in the late 1960s. One of the most northerly of the Leeward Islands, it was situated closer to Franco-Dutch St Maarten eight miles to the south and was also separated from St Kitts and Nevis by 60 miles of ocean and several French and Dutch islands.[41] Geographical distance from its neighbours also coexisted alongside economic distance, Anguilla having always been the long-term poor relation of St Kitts and Nevis. This wealth disparity was partly due to geography, with fertile and volcanic St Kitts contrasting with Anguilla's low-lying limestone platform covered with scrub and low bush, the latter island thus having suffered from poor agricultural production.[42] Unemployment was a persistent problem in Anguilla, assessed to have reached 40 percent of those on the island by the early 1970s and forcing many to rely on remittances from family working abroad.[43]

Poor living standards amongst Anguillians could, however, be blamed on more than just geographical factors. Although centuries of British colonial neglect played a major role, many blamed underinvestment in the island instead on the hostility of the St Kitts administration. This mistrust was longstanding and mutual. Resentment had grown with the gradual loss of Anguillian political autonomy to St Kitts, beginning in 1822 when London instructed that an Anguillian representative sit in the Kittitian assembly to pass laws for the island despite Anguilla having governed itself for decades. Tensions grew yet again in 1871–72 when the Leeward Islands Act incorporated Anguilla further into a union with St Kitts and Nevis under the Federal Colony of the Leeward Islands, thus losing its seat in the Kittitian assembly. In each instance, the British preference for collectivised and centralised colonial rule thus undermined an Anguillian political culture which craved autonomy. Furthermore, each successive union enflamed Anguillian resentment towards St Kitts, whom it blamed for much of its economic woes. Kittitians, according to George C. Abbott, regarded the Anguillians 'as poor and not particularly grateful brothers whom they have had to subsidize continually'.[44]

By the 1960s Anguilla still lacked most essentials of modern infrastructure. As Westlake listed, '[no] general electricity. Three hundred and fifty children in a one-room schoolhouse. Less than a mile and a half of paved road. Medical facilities that frequently had operations performed by the light of a hurricane lamp'.[45] Additionally, Westlake notes that the Basseterre government had removed the archaic telephone system from Anguilla following a hurricane and failed to replace it, whilst also – according to the Anguillian perspective noted by Westlake – diverting funds specifically allocated for building a cargo pier on Anguilla in order to construct one on St Kitts.[46] As the discussions over Associated Statehood got underway in London between February and May 1966, Anguillians faced the prospect of permanent union with St Kitts and the gradual removal of Britain's colonial oversight, regarded as the only protection against Basseterre's perceived misrule.

Anguillian hostility towards St Kitts was embodied in the figure of the Chief Minister, Robert Llewellyn Bradshaw. Born of humble Kittitian origins in 1916, Bradshaw ascended into the political sphere – as did many of his contemporaries – through trade unionism, having worked as an apprentice machinist in a sugar mill. He was elected to the Leeward Islands Legislative Assembly in 1946 before progressing to represent his islands in the federal parliament for the duration of the West Indies Federation between 1958 and 1962, also gaining a Cabinet position.[47] Following the federation's collapse, he became Chief Minister of St Kitts, Nevis and Anguilla in 1966. Famed for his upper-class vowels, preference for military uniforms, prominent moustache and yellow Rolls Royce, his eccentric exterior hid a more complex personality. Mawby states that 'Bradshaw's sartorial dandyism, oenophilia and antiquarianism made him vulnerable to charges of being one of Naipaul's 'mimic men', whose attempts to emulate English aristocratic culture transformed them into comical figures. Despite these affectations, Bradshaw's political hegemony in St Kitts was founded on a remarkable achievement'.[48] Dyde viewed him as a man of diverse reputations. He notes that Bradshaw's working class Kittitian supporters viewed him as a pioneering Martin Luther King-style liberation figure, whilst the Anguillians often regarded him as an authoritarian dictator and the British viewed him as 'a stiff-necked obstructionist cum rabble-rouser too big for his boots'.[49] It would be Bradshaw who would assume both a prominent role in the discussions over Associated

Statehood in 1966 and as arch-antagonist of the Anguillians during their revolution of 1967–69.

Bradshaw had done little to reassure the Anguillians in the run-up to statehood. Facing opposition from the island over the constitutional settlement, he is said to have notoriously pledged that 'I will not rest until I have reduced that place to a desert'.[50] Westlake attributes Bradshaw's uncompromising stance over Anguilla's autonomy to his perception of himself as father of the new nation and Anguilla as a wayward child in need of correction.[51] Bradshaw's comments greatly influenced Anguillian public opinion against Associated Statehood. As the Wooding Report (1970), commissioned by the British government in 1969, emphasised, '[the] Anguillans, almost to the last child, seem honestly convinced not only that Mr. Bradshaw said that he would turn Anguilla into a desert, but that he would do it if he could.'[52] Whilst Bradshaw could not avoid the long-established sense of hostility and mistrust between Anguilla and St Kitts which partly set the Associated State up to fail even prior to independence, some of his words and actions across 1967–69 would serve to deepen and prolong the crisis. Tensions had already begun to worsen following the general election of July 1966 in which Bradshaw's Labour Party won seven of the 10 seats in the Basseterre assembly, whilst the opposition People's Action Movement (PAM) – including the sole Anguillian assembly representative Peter Adams – won the remainder.[53]

Anguillian politicians had appealed directly to London twice across 1966 requesting that their union with St Kitts and Nevis be dissolved.[54] However, the British remained committed to implementing the vision of Associated Statehood following the collapse of their previous routes to imperial retreat. Moreover, as Cox-Alomar notes, the fact that most islands were finally 'on a similar wavelength' to Whitehall about the desirability of this form of constitutional relationship meant that the London discussions of February to May 1966 'unlike the federal discussions, did not amount to full-scale negotiations'.[55] Under the final agreement legalised through the West Indies Act 1967, Britain retained control over the defence and foreign policies of the Associated States of St Kitts-Nevis-Anguilla, St Vincent and the Grenadines, Antigua-Barbuda, Dominica, Grenada and St Lucia. Their respective governments, overseen by a Governor and Prime Minister, retained full control of their domestic policies and constitution. To assuage Anguillian fears of Kittitian domination, the agreement also provided for the creation of two councils for Anguilla and Nevis with a Commonwealth Office officer sent from London to assist in establishing these institutions. However, when plans were finally released in January 1967, the powers allocated to the councils were nowhere near those needed to reassure the opponents of Bradshaw on Anguilla and, moreover, these institutions could be dissolved by Basseterre at any time.[56] The British and Kittitians emphasised that the Anguillian representative at the talks, Peter Adams, had agreed to the settlement. Adams, however, argued that the document he signed had merely proposed various constitutional ideas for further exploration, rather than a strict agreement.[57] Ultimately, as the Associated State moved closer to the date set for Association Day – 27 February 1967 – many Anguillians remained totally hostile to participation in the new nation.

One such Anguillian, a businessman named J. Ronald Webster, was gradually rising to prominence amid the tension and dismay. Born in a fishing village on the north-east coast of the island in 1926, Webster had moved to neighbouring Dutch St Maarten in 1936 to seek employment. As he himself recollected, his time on the island became a "rags to riches' story'.[58] Having served three years in the

Ronald Webster. (Albert Grandolini collection)

Dutch colonial army and reaching the rank of corporal, he went on to work for over 27 years on the Mary Fancy's Estate owned by a Dutch settler, D.C. van Romondt. Webster claimed that by early adulthood his employers 'were treating me like an adopted son' and his loyalty was rewarded in 1958 when he inherited the entire estate of 300 acres, worth around $1.5 million.[59] This fortune made Webster the wealthiest man in Anguilla when he returned to his home island in 1960. According to his recollection, he was immediately astounded by how underdeveloped the island was in contrast to St Maarten, claiming 'Anguilla was in a very backward condition – the basics such as roads, water, electricity, communications, schools, hospital facilities and so on, were all badly lacking. And unlike on St. Martin, there was no tourism at all.'[60] Webster subsequently contacted Bradshaw's government in September 1966 and offered to fund electricity and road systems but, according to his account, '[on] both occasions that I went up to St. Kitts, the government couldn't find time to see me. I was just referred to a secretary, and, naturally, I felt frustrated and insulted.'[61]

Similar to Bradshaw, Webster possessed a complex personality that frequently led commentators to diverse conclusions. To his Anguillian supporters, he was a freedom fighter and father of the nation who led the island to freedom from Basseterre's domination.

Webster's own conception of himself was somewhat influenced by a sense of divine calling and destiny. As he recollected,

> I heard the call to lead the people of Anguilla. I sat up in utter amazement and total disbelief. The voice was so distinct and real that I could not doubt my hearing. It was no figment of my imagination. I was convinced it was a divine call and that its fulfilment lay somewhere in the uncertain future.[62]

This sense of identity reflected Webster's deep religious faith as a Seventh-Day Adventist. It perhaps also helped to shape his unshakable commitment to Anguilla's separation from the Associated State. In the words of Westlake, '[a] short and slender man, with long-fingered hands, Ronald Webster gives an impression of wiry strength under rigid control. In photographs he looks mild and meek, and some interviewers have come away describing him as shy'.[63] For instance, *The Times* branded him as a 'soft-spoken and deeply sincere man'.[64] As Westlake emphasised, however, this shyness was curiously mixed with 'an absolute and total sense of conviction'.[65] British officials who dealt with Webster during the occupation viewed him through a twin lens of belittlement and respect. The commander of the Anguilla Police Unit (APU) reported that Webster's 'intellectual, personality and character limitations' meant that he was manipulated by 'unscrupulous individuals'. Nevertheless, the report continued, '[it] must be acknowledged, however, that Webster is sincere and has the best interests of the people of Anguilla genuinely at heart'.[66] Whilst the extent to which he was in control of events in Anguilla would be sometimes questioned, no other figure had so much influence over the course of the Anguillian Revolution.

Having experienced Anguilla's neglect first hand, Webster soon became a prominent critic of Associated Statehood. When Bradshaw visited Anguilla in late 1966 to hold a series of public meetings on the constitutional settlement, Webster and his growing supporters disturbed each event by blowing conch shells and making 'a lot of noise'.[67] The ingredients were now in place to ignite the tinderbox. As the day of statehood approached, Britain remained unwilling to listen to Anguillian demands for separation, Bradshaw remained insensitive to Anguillian fears and the islanders themselves were beginning to launch more provocative demonstrations against the new government and its constitutional settlement. As Webster recalled, '[tempers] began to flare up on all sides. It became very clear to me that drastic measures would have to be taken if we were to achieve our wishes. The revolution did not start in 1967. Tempers flared in '66.'[68]

2

ASSOCIATED STATEHOOD AND REBELLION

At 4am on 14 February 1967 the Royal Navy frigate HMS *Salisbury* landed a large party of St Kitts police and Royal Marines at Island Harbour, the most prosperous region of Anguilla situated in the northeast.[1] This force had been requested from London by the Bradshaw government following significant unrest over the preceding 10 days initiated by Anguillians protesting Associated Statehood. The situation had begun to deteriorate on 4 February when Anguilla had held a Beauty Queen contest at the

Secondary School in The Valley – the main settlement and heart of administration in the centre of the island – in preparation for sending the winner to the statehood celebrations in St Kitts. Consequently, the event was viewed as an effort to encourage unity between the islands and hence regarded as in need of disruption. Webster and his followers first protested outside the school before some went on to shut down its electricity. The small number of police on the island – all of whom were from St Kitts – then dispersed the protesters with tear gas. Webster even claimed that 'there was an exchange of gunfire and missiles' during this chaos which ultimately cancelled the pageant.[2]

According to Brian Dyde this incident was the first warning sign which made Basseterre take notice of the depth of Anguillian hostility to Associated Statehood and thus police reinforcements were sent to the island.[3] The situation escalated further on 6 February when these reinforcements arrived at Anguilla's airfield and were confronted by protesters. According to Webster, the opposition which the police faced was such that they sped to their barracks and 'forgot all their ammunition at the airport!'[4] The bullets were duly seized. Moreover, the threat posed by the protesters – who were gradually evolving into insurgents – was further confirmed when shots were fired at police in the East End, thus driving them out of the area. As law and order in Anguilla deteriorated, Bradshaw called for British military assistance.

When the Royal Marines came ashore on the morning of 14 February they wore steel helmets rather than their distinctive green berets, clearly expecting serious resistance from islanders who had recently ejected police from positions using small arms fire. However, mirroring more dramatic military events two years later, *The Sunday Times* reported that '[to] their great surprise, the islanders met them [the Marines] on the beach, all smiles. The invaders' arms were returned to the ship, and the invaders themselves came back for a swim.' Indeed, relations between the Royal Marines and the islanders was so good that '[a] longboat was sent back to the ship to fetch sweets for the children, and when the ship finally weighed anchor the entire population of Island Harbour stood on the beach and sang "God Save the Queen" for the British sailors.'[5]

This brief military intervention is shrouded in some mystery. The precise number of Kittitian police deposited by the Royal Marines is contested: Webster claimed 69 in his memoirs of 1987, *The Times* reported only four in 1967 whilst *The Sunday Times*, writing in 1969, estimated 40.[6] Moreover, according to *The Sunday Times* report, a British government spokesman – Lord Beswick – denied in the House of Lords that British troops had landed on Anguilla two days after the intervention. The article went on to claim further that the story of the British military landing 'has never been admitted by British government spokesmen in London, [and] is supported by the testimony of dozens of eye witnesses, including Royal Navy personnel.'[7] *The Sunday Times* concluded that this military intervention underlined the longstanding animosity of Anguillians towards Bradshaw; their quaint British patriotism and the shocking deficiencies of Whitehall's intelligence about the island.[8] Two additional lessons could arguably be added to this assessment. Firstly, the extent to which London was supportive, at this stage, of Bradshaw and his determination to retain Anguilla inside the Associated State even through force of arms. The British did, of course, have a general responsibility to uphold law and order prior to statehood and acted upon this when Anguilla seemed to be slipping into chaos. Secondly, this episode underlines the complexity of Anguillian nationalism; an identity which was becoming increasingly isolationist from the Associated State and yet desired continuing colonial links with Britain. As will be demonstrated, Anguillian identity was forced to become increasingly flexible under the strain of their revolution.

Association Day to State of Emergency

Although Bradshaw's government had been surprised by the scale and passion of Anguillian hostility to statehood as manifested in the events of February 1967, there had been plenty of warning signs since the constitutional settlement in London. Anguillians had

Anguillians protest against Associated Statehood.
(Albert Grandolini collection)

directly appealed to the British government in June and October 1966 requesting direct rule from London and on both occasions had been ignored.[9] Bradshaw had also visited the island in the later months of 1966 to hold four public meetings about statehood, all of which had been disrupted by Webster's supporters. Further discontent was registered when, as per the constitutional settlement, the Commonwealth Office sent their local government expert – Peter Johnston – in January 1967 to assist in setting up the Anguilla council. Although the London agreement had also stipulated the need for a committee to be established to discuss the local council, this body had only been created in October 1966 and had met infrequently and at short notice by the time Johnston arrived.

When he landed at Anguilla's airfield on 27 January Johnston was met by a crowd of around 400 carrying placards stating, according to the Wooding Report, 'We don't want Statehood we want England', 'Seeking the choice of Mother's care' and 'God save The Queen'.[10] The crowd then followed him to a meeting at the Court House whereby Johnston discussed the local council proposals with island leaders. According to Webster, '[the] meeting ended abruptly when a large crowd of angry Anguillians stormed the Court House.'[11] Following yet more failed negotiations between Peter Adams, Dr W.V. Herbert – the leader of the opposition PAM – and the Bradshaw government in early February, Herbert and Adams travelled to London to register Anguillian fears with the Minister of State for Commonwealth Affairs. During this visit, Basseterre made further public assurances that the local council plan would be implemented, but neither this nor a visit to Anguilla by H.P. Hall – Under-Secretary at the Commonwealth Office – was enough to assuage the increasingly entrenched grievances of the islanders.

With the date of Association Day still fixed on 27 February 1967 the time in which to reassure the Anguillians had largely run out by the end of Hall's visit. On 24 February Arthur Bottomley, Wilson's Minister for Overseas Development, arrived in St Kitts to celebrate statehood. When he visited Anguilla two days later, he was greeted with crowds, placards and a general atmosphere of resistance similar to those which had met previous British diplomats over recent weeks. The degree of hostility that existed to the new union on Association Day itself may perhaps be symbolised in the flag raising ceremony which occurred without public attention at 4am. Vincent Byron, Warden of Anguilla, raised the new flag – a black triple palm tree on a tricolour of green, yellow and light blue – at Government House surrounded by police. According to Westlake, '[he] was wearing his pajamas at the time, and after hoisting the flag he yawned and went into the house for breakfast.'[12] Webster claimed that later in the day Anguillians tore the flag down, an act of defiance which was followed by a procession in which mourners walked behind a station wagon 'carrying a coffin draped in black, symbolizing the death of Statehood in Anguilla'.[13]

The Wooding Report detailed a sharp upsurge in violence towards symbols of government authority in the months following Association Day. On 8 March Government House burned down with the

The rebel dolphin flag of Anguilla flies at the airport. (Albert Grandolini collection)

warden only just managing to escape the flames through an upstairs window. Webster denied claims that the fire was deliberately started, believing that an 'electrical short' had caused it and stating that '[actions] were taken against the Warden's car, by throwing stones, as a political protest. We did not burn down the house.'[14] A series of shooting incidents then occurred across March, April and May 1967. The police station was fired upon on four separate occasions. An Anguillian member of Bradshaw's Labour Party, David Lloyd, had his hotel shot at twice, the latter incident seeing the building peppered by more than 50 rounds whilst the Acting Warden was a guest at the hotel. Moreover, on 29 May the Customs house was also damaged by gunfire.[15] Webster claimed that several shooting incidents were committed by the police themselves in order 'to get a bigger police force sent over'.[16]

Tensions ultimately reached boiling point on the day in which the Customs house was attacked. At a meeting arranged by Webster and chaired by Adams in Burrowes Park, a crowd of around 300 voted to expel the police from Anguilla. The crowd then descended on the police station, where Webster informed Acting Assistant Superintendent Charles Edgings that the 17-man force 'must leave the island by sundown the following day'. 'Hundreds' of protesters subsequently returned to the building on 30 May to ensure that the police left, whilst Webster's followers seized the police arsenal upon their departure.[17] Webster also claimed that his men dismantled the police communications equipment, although media reports later stated that the police did this themselves.[18] The weapons windfall included 17 rifles – probably bolt action .303 Lee-Enfields, although one NATO automatic rifle likely to be a 7.62mm L1A1 Self-Loading Rifle was also mentioned – plus 1,200 rounds of tear gas and 200lbs of gelignite.[19] Adding this collection to the ammunition already stolen from the police at the airport in February and potentially other firearms, Webster now had a fairly notable arsenal for repelling the very small police force and militia of the Associated State security forces.[20] To further deter Bradshaw from sending more police, Webster's supporters placed heavy construction equipment on the airstrip, thus making an airborne landing impossible.

The consequences of these events were seismic, raising the situation to the level of a crisis. Webster labelled it the 'point of no return' for Anguilla.[21] The ejection of the police – Basseterre authority personified – confirmed to Bradshaw that the island was now in a state of armed rebellion. On 30 May he declared a state of emergency which vested his office with new powers. Moreover, he cut off mail to Anguilla, froze Anguillian bank accounts and banned all financial transactions with the island.[22] With the dismantling

An Anguillian pulls down the tattered Associated State flag from The Valley police station. (Albert Grandolini collection)

of police communication equipment and the previous removal of telephones from Anguilla, the island was now truly isolated. One of the few outlets through which the Anguillians could now project their message to the outside world was through the media. Fortunately for the Anguillians, the dramatic events of May 1967 had attracted more and more journalists to covering the crisis and the islanders would, in turn, become increasingly adept at using them. As Webster recalled, the police expulsion 'immediately catapulted [Anguilla] into the headlines of the world press'.[23]

The Times provided fairly even coverage, noting Bradshaw's decision to request British military intervention to suppress the uprising alongside mentioning Peter Adams' letter to the UN Secretary-General, U Thant, declaring that 'Anguillans prefer death to the oppression of St. Kitts'.[24] The *Daily Mail* called the situation a 'mini crisis' whilst, rather more sensationally, the *Daily Mirror* claimed that the police arsenal had been seized by '[about] 250 rebels, armed with guns' and reported Bradshaw's claims that he expected 'some kind of action within two days'.[25] On the international front, the *Chicago Tribune* focused on the Anguillian act of rehoisting the Union Jack in place of the Statehood tricolour after the police

Ronald Webster and colleagues. Note the Anguillian policeman wearing an imported American police cap, following the ejection of the Associated State police from Anguilla. (Albert Grandolini collection)

U Thant, UN Secretary-General at the time of the events of Operation Sheepskin. (Open source)

departure and covered Adam's UN letter in detail.[26] As the reportage of Adams' letter demonstrates, the other main outlet through which Anguilla could transmit its message was the UN. In time, both the Anguillians themselves and sympathisers from around the world would use this platform to keep the crisis under the international media and diplomatic spotlight.

Immediately following the police expulsion, Adams, Webster and other island notables established a 15-man Peacekeeping Committee to maintain order on the island and guard against potential invasion. Webster became responsible for defence and set about arming a 'defence force' of volunteers – usually men and boys – with the weapons accumulated over preceding months. According to Webster, this group comprised of 22 men with a further 120 on call if needed. Furthermore, a new police unit was created under the command of a retired Anguillian police sergeant.[27] Coincidingly, Basseterre began to increase its arsenal which included, according to some rumours, reactivated eighteenth century cannons at the fort on Brimstone Hill.[28]

The threat of invasion loomed large within Anguilla's history. Following the English colonisation of the island in 1650, their settlements had been devastated by the French in both 1666 and 1688. During the War of Austrian Succession (1740–48) France had sent yet another force in May 1745 in reprisal for the British capture of French St Maarten. A naval expedition under the command of Commodore de la Touche landed a force of around 700 men at Crocus Bay, a site on the northern coast where British forces would

land over two centuries later during Operation Sheepskin. Conch shells, which would be used again by Webster's men when guarding against invasion during the 1960s, were blown by slaves to raise the alarm.[29] Ultimately, the militia repelled the invasion with almost 60 French killed or wounded.[30] A final French invasion occurred in November 1796 during the Revolutionary Wars (1792–1802). Four hundred men landed at Rendezvous Bay on the southwest coast and proceeded to destroy the settlements at South Hill and The Valley. On this occasion the island militia were pushed back to the fort at Sandy Hill in the east and, low on ammunition, they were only saved from defeat by the arrival of HMS *Lapwing* which compelled the French to withdraw.[31] Despite this long history of invasion, successive colonial administrations had made no subsequent effort to strengthen Anguilla's defences. As previously mentioned, the Kittitian volunteer militia originally established in the 1860s and subsequently reorganised around 1896, had been stationed in St Kitts and Nevis.[32]

Raid on St Kitts

As the invasion threat of 1967 loomed, the Peacekeeping Committee decided upon a highly bold, even farcical, course of action. With Bradshaw having rejected the demands of an Anguillian delegation on 31 May for separation from St Kitts and restoration of British colonial administration, Anguillians decided to launch a raid on Basseterre, the Kittitian capital. Webster claimed that the 'main purpose of the raid' was to abduct Bradshaw and his deputy, Paul Southwell.[33] Westlake further alleged that '[the] ransom was to be Great Britain's acknowledgement of Anguilla's secession from St. Kitts', explaining the raid as being the Anguillian way of 'trying to attract the donkey's [Britain's] attention'.[34] However, whether this plan was likely to force the Wilson government into conceding to Anguillian demands is debatable. Moreover, the chances of seizing Bradshaw from right under the noses of his security forces were slim. Another objective of the raid can also be gleaned from Webster. As he explained, '[what] we really wanted was to keep the battle away from Anguilla. We felt that by attacking St. Kitts we would give them less incentive to come here. They'd have to try to guard their own place, attack being the best defence'.[35] Given the limited size of the Kittitian security forces and this unanticipated show of Anguillian gung-ho, Bradshaw would certainly be given food for thought when making any further plans to invade his troublesome neighbour.

The role of the PAM opposition in the raid has been the subject of some debate. Webster noted that the raiding party 'were supposed to link up with Dr Herbert (who founded the PAM opposition in St. Kitts), but somehow it didn't work out that way'.[36] In the aftermath of the raid, the Bradshaw government would claim that the attack constituted a PAM coup attempt and arrested Herbert and several of his friends.[37] Kittitian historian Whitman Browne appears to have suggested that some collaboration between the Anguillians and PAM took place, stating that:

> The Anguillians wanted to be rid of Bradshaw and his government, but so too did the PAM politicians. That attack on St Kitts was carefully planned between Kittitians and Anguillians to overthrow the Labor Government. The Anguillian rebellion became a useful tool in the hands of desperate politicians on St Kitts willing to trade treason for political power.[38]

Westlake, on the other hand, argued that allegations of PAM involvement in the attack were nonsense. Noting that Herbert and 'PAMs other legal whiz kids' were 'very sophisticated people', he argued that 'if they were going to pull a *coup d'état*, they would probably behave a little more effectively than the gunmen of June 9'.[39]

Webster's fishing boat, carrying 13, landed a raiding party at Half Way Tree on the southern coast of St Kitts – a significant distance from Basseterre – on the night of 9/10 June 1967 following a confused voyage. The precise number of raiders deployed on the island is unclear. According to a statement by Diana Prior-Palmer, a British-born American citizen who was in St Kitts during the raid and subsequently deported by Bradshaw, eyewitnesses had 'reported that the attack was carried out by three Anguillians, possibly accompanied by three 'Mercenary' Americans'.[40] Webster subsequently stressed that these Americans were 'volunteers' and 'just people sympathetic to our struggle and were definitely not mercenaries'.[41] Having landed a distance from Basseterre, the raiding party suffered from a lack of transport and only reached the capital in the early hours of 10 June. Having then failed to locate Bradshaw, Dyde claimed that the raiders chose to change objectives and shoot up key locations associated with government authority. These included the Police and Defence Force headquarters, plus the electricity station where a Kittitian soldier was wounded in the attack. Bradshaw later claimed in a radio address that the assault had been made with 'automatic weapons, rifles, explosives, tear gas and other weapons. Shots were fired at the homes of the Director of Public Prosecutions…the Attorney General, the Senior Crown Counsel and private homes'.[42] Furthermore, it has also been claimed that Radio Station ZIZ and the gasoline depot at Ponds Pasture in Basseterre were additionally attacked.[43]

How far the raid can be considered a success is open to question. On the one hand, the party failed to achieve their main objective of locating and abducting Bradshaw and Southwell. Moreover, five of the raiders were arrested which, considering the small numbers involved in the attack, was a significant capture rate.[44] Others, including the Americans, managed to escape with the assistance of Webster's friends in Dutch St Eustatius, having stolen a boat in Helden's Bay to reach the island.[45] On the other hand, St Kitts never did launch an invasion of Anguilla throughout the remaining years of crisis, so Webster's tactic of attacking as the best form of defence may have been effective. There may, however, have been other reasons for Bradshaw's potential hesitance to invade, including the small size of his own forces and the refusal of other Caribbean states and Britain to lend significant military assistance. Regardless of this inaction, it is worth noting that Bradshaw increased his demands for a military solution to the Anguillian rebellion following the raid, rather than being deterred by the attack.[46]

The raid had, nevertheless, underlined to Basseterre its own defence vulnerabilities. The government arrested 22 people in St Kitts who were suspected of either participating in the raid or assisting it. Only three of the suspects were ever brought to trial and all were eventually acquitted.[47] The raid and the wider Anguillian crisis also provided Bradshaw's government with the justification to significantly reform and expand the Associated State's military forces. D.E. Phillips has noted how many Eastern Caribbean states, of which St Kitts was a prime example, 'felt particularly vulnerable to internal threats and destabilization from external sources' as the 1960s progressed, and that St Kitts' largely ceremonial 'minimilitary units' did not have the clout to suppress mass disorder.[48] The Anguilla crisis had underlined this vulnerability further, contributing to what Whitman Browne described as 'a new, Caribbean-orientated militarism, as against the prior militarism which was an expression of European nationalism in the Caribbean area'.[49]

In July 1967 around 20 soldiers from the old volunteer force were selected for special training under Geoffrey Ellis, a former captain in the British Army. The course ran from August to November and, according to Browne, focused on 'invasion tactics, security work, special skills and arms'.[50] These men would form the embryo of a new, more professional and regular military unit under the command of Captain Erroll Maynard. The new regiment within the St Kitts and Nevis Defence Force officially came into being in January 1968, although there were doubts amongst many Kittitians about both the desirability and legality of the new force. Some opponents argued that Section 41, Chapter 181 of the Revised Laws of Federation 1961 did not allow for the creation of a separate unit detached from the police.[51] Despite the persistence of this legal question throughout Bradshaw's tenure in office, the defence budget would grow significantly from $90,000 (East Caribbean) to $172,000 in 1972 and $425,000 in 1981.[52] Around this period of reform, the British replaced the old Lee-Enfield bolt-action rifles of both the police and army with L1A1 Self-Loading Rifles and, over subsequent years, the new defence force would purchase a range of further British weaponry, including armoured cars and automatic weapons.[53] The militarisation of St Kitts security also had implications for Bradshaw's own political image. Always known as a flamboyant dresser, he now became colonel of his regiment and 'put on a khaki uniform complete with Sam Browne belt and holstered pistol'.[54]

The Barbados Conference

Although Britain and the Anglophone Caribbean had refused Bradshaw's requests for military assistance following the Anguillian attack, numerous states – Jamaica, Trinidad-Tobago, Guyana and Barbados – established a team to try to negotiate a settlement. Following a series of talks in late June 1967, both St Kitts and Anguilla agreed to attend a multi-national conference in Barbados at the end of July. Perhaps aiming to send a clear message at this upcoming conference about the scale of support for separation from the Associated State, the Anguillian Peacekeeping Committee announced on 7 July that a referendum would take place four days later. Islanders were asked whether they desired separation and whether they approved of the creation of an interim government with powers to create a constitution and hold elections.[55] The Committee demonstrated their awareness of the importance of favourable media coverage and projecting a message of democratic values on the international stage by inviting journalists to observe the referendum process and announce the results to the world. Subsequently, the results amounted to 1,813 votes in favour of separation and five opposed.[56] Moreover, 1,794 to five voted in favour of creating a new Council to move preparations for secession forward.[57]

Harvard Professor Roger Fisher, who would later be involved in bringing peace to important conflicts including the Iranian Hostage Crisis, El Salvador and apartheid South Africa, was present in Anguilla during the referendum. He had been approached by an Anguillian-born New Jersey-based businessman in June who had requested that Fisher become Anguilla's legal representative and he had accepted.[58] Following the Unilateral Declaration of Independence (UDI) announced to the Anguillian people after the referendum results, Fisher set to work drafting a constitution for the island which established a Council of seven members. This institution would include Webster, responsible again for defence, alongside Adams and other island notables such as Walter Hodge and Emile Gumbs. Having apparently broken away from the

Associated State through the UDI, the Anguillian leadership sent a telegram to London on 12 June requesting that options for a new bilateral relationship with Britain be explored.[59]

The businessman who had recruited Fisher to the Anguillian cause was Jeremiah Gumbs, a man who would become famous for his defence of Anguilla on the international stage. Born the son of a fisherman in 1913, Gumbs had left Anguilla at the age of 11 to work in the sugar cane fields of the Dominican Republic before moving to New York at the age of 25. He then gained American citizenship after serving in the US Army during the Second World War.[60] Having become a successful businessman in the post-war decades, by the late 1960s he owned a domestic central heating company in New York, plus Anguilla Airways and a hotel at Rendezvous Bay in Anguilla.[61] He had, however, never forgotten his roots and had thus been involved in philanthropic activities to develop the island. When Anguilla jumped onto the international stage following the ejection of the police in May 1967, therefore, he had been contacted by Wallace Rey, at the behest of Webster, to help the cause. Subsequently, assisted by Fisher, Gumbs would be responsible for making Anguilla's case to the UN in New York.[62] He was described by *The Times* as 'bear-like' and by Westlake as '[a] big bearish man, with a strainingly sincere expression of face and a deep, mellow, slow-moving voice'.[63] Webster would speak highly of Gumbs in his memoirs, describing him as 'a kind of roving Ambassador for Anguilla, in and out and always ready and willing to help'.[64]

It was amid the intensified climate of secession generated by the 11 June referendum that the belligerent parties – combined with representatives from Britain, Trinidad-Tobago, Barbados, Jamaica, and Guyana – descended on the Barbados conference for an initial sitting between 25 and 29 July. The Anguillian team were led by Peter Adams, who had assumed leadership of the island Council, whilst Bradshaw represented his own government and the British sent Lord Shepherd, who became Minister of State for Commonwealth Affairs during the conference. Described in Parliamentary tributes as 'wily', 'shrewd', 'respected' and 'authoritative', Shepherd would be responsible for driving Britain's efforts to achieve a diplomatic solution to the Anguilla crisis across mid-1967.[65]

According to a Foreign and Commonwealth Office (FCO) report about the Barbados conference, 'it was agreed that there should be an immediate return to constitutional rule in Anguilla. The St. Kitts Government would amend their draft legislation providing Councils for Nevis and Anguilla so as to give them increased responsibilities in local affairs, and would secure its early enactment.'[66] Moreover, no prosecutions would take place for political actions taken by Anguillians between 31 May and 31 July. New government administration of Anguilla would take the form of a five-member Interim Advisory Committee until the new council could be formed, whilst a new Warden from outside the Associated State would also be appointed. Although a new St Kitts police detachment would be posted to Anguilla, stability would be guaranteed initially by a peacekeeping mission composed of police contributed by Jamaica, Trinidad-Tobago, Barbados and Guyana. To sugar the pill, Britain pledged £50,000 for the Associated State to spend on Anguilla and Nevis.[67] Once the conference report was signed, the British and Caribbean governments also negotiated how the logistics of the peacekeeping operation would be implemented. It was agreed that a British military force would initially escort the St Kitts police to Anguilla and would suppress any resistance encountered. Once the commander of the Caribbean peacekeeping team had satisfied himself that the island had been secured by the

British military, his force would then depart Antigua for Anguilla to take over peacekeeping duties.

Any agreement, however, was quickly undermined. Adams' delegation flew back to Anguilla during a brief adjournment between 29 and 31 July to explain the deal to the islanders. Webster was immediately opposed to the settlement, recalling that:

> I was convinced that Anguillians would never accept a return to St. Kitts. I was also aware that the tense situation in Anguilla would worsen with the presence of outside police [peacekeepers] who had the same powers as the St. Kitts police. The freedom of the island was much more precious to the Anguillians than the EC$240,000 offered by the British Government.[68]

Webster, Gumbs and other associates opposed to the deal therefore flew to Barbados for the second stage of the conference, intent on voicing their objections. Webster recollected that, when in the conference room, 'I bluntly refused to sign the conference document. I was so infuriated that I tossed the document across the table.'[69] According to Dyde, 'after the conference had ended it soon became obvious to Bradshaw and the rest of those who had signed that the stance which had been taken by Webster and his colleagues had the approval of virtually the entire Anguillian population', thus reducing quickly their faith in the agreement.[70] Moreover, members of the Anguillian council issued a statement on 7 August claiming that the island's four delegates who had signed the Barbados agreement had done so under duress.[71]

Despite these setbacks, the Anguillians had not explicitly rejected the agreement and the British remained willing to uphold their own role in implementing the peacekeeping operation.[72] Additionally, in the days following the conference, Guyana confirmed its willingness to uphold the agreement whilst Basseterre sent its formal invitation to London to dispatch a Royal Navy frigate and party of marines or naval personnel to escort its police back to Anguilla. The British, therefore, proceeded with preliminary military planning. The Senior Naval Officer West Indies, Commodore Townley, diverted HMS *Mohawk* to Antigua in preparation for undertaking the transportation of Associated State police.

As estimates of the potential opposition to the peacekeeping operation varied 'from nil to fairly considerable' – reflecting a lack of intelligence about the island which would continue to hamper British planning in the future – SNOWI also requested Royal Marine reinforcements to prepare for all eventualities.[73] As a message from the Commonwealth Office to the Ministry of Defence (MoD) of 6 August 1967 explained, it was crucial 'that the initial operation to re-establish control is completed quickly so that the Commonwealth peace-keeping team can move in without delay. If adequate forces are not made available, the rebels might be encouraged to resist and, in those circumstances, the peace-keeping team might be reluctant to go in.'[74] To avoid the need to request another frigate with reinforcements to complete the British operation if serious resistance was encountered – which could, in turn, also weaken the Royal Navy's Bahamas Patrol – reinforcements to HMS *Mohawk*'s marine detachment were asked for including one company HQ, a rifle troop, an assault engineer section and company radio operators.[75] It was estimated that the initial British military operation would last around 48 hours before the peacekeeping team of 60 police entered Anguilla. Alongside supressing any opposition from islanders, the Royal Marine operation would secure the airfield, seize illegal firearms and establish a radio link.[76] Then, following the British military transfer of security duties to the peacekeeping team, HMS

Mohawk would remain offshore for up to two weeks depending on the level of unrest in Anguilla.[77]

The momentum behind implementing the operation slowed to a crawl, however, over the assembling of the Caribbean peacekeeping team. As a report to Harold Wilson's Foreign Office private secretary observed, 'we have found ourselves bogged down on the question of the Caribbean peace keeping team of police…There seems to be some misunderstanding, particularly in Jamaica, about the part HMG is prepared to play in implementing the Barbados agreement.' It noted further that the Caribbean governments had thus requested another meeting in Jamaica to discuss the operation.[78] Whilst these talks took place in August their outcome was, according to the incoming Secretary of State for Commonwealth Affairs, 'negative'. Moreover, he noted that following the 'repudiation' of the Barbados agreement by the Jamaican Prime Minister, British diplomats had attempted to salvage the deal with the remaining three Caribbean states but that these efforts had ultimately led to nothing.[79] Britain's first international initiative for solving the Anguilla crisis had thus petered out into failure. London was, moreover, unwilling to act unilaterally at this stage in undertaking the entire peacekeeping operation by itself. The MoD wrote to the Commonwealth Office reporting the Defence Secretary's 'serious misgivings about any thought of British forces going it alone with the St. Kitts' police'.[80]

As with much of the Anguilla crisis, the humiliation of Britain's diplomatic defeat was very public. Almost immediately after the Barbados settlement was concluded, *The Times* reported that '[some] doubt is felt in London about the permanence of the agreement'.[81] Within weeks both this newspaper and the *Sunday Telegraph* had reported a state of 'deadlock' in the diplomatic efforts to solve the crisis.[82] The *Daily Mail* similarly reported that whilst a Royal Navy frigate was waiting to pick up the Caribbean peacekeepers, this force was 'unlikely ever to land on Anguilla, for Guyana and Jamaica are markedly unenthusiastic'.[83] Likewise, *The Guardian* observed that it 'seems probable that nothing will be done about sending a peacekeeping force' before arguing that, whilst administrative difficulties had been blamed for the delays, 'it is likely that they [the Caribbean states] are perturbed by signs that the Anguillans intend to resist a landing by the force'.[84] The *New York Times* similarly reported Anguillian confidence that their Caribbean neighbours would not join the peacekeeping operation, stating that the 'expression of popular will [against the Barbados agreement] is believed to be the principal deterrent to forceful action by the other Caribbean islands'.[85] Just as publicly embarrassing, Britain's acting chief of its UN delegation, Sir Leslie Glass, was forced to resist pressure from a subcommittee of the Special Committee on Decolonization (the Committee of 24) which had been hearing petitioners from Anguilla, insisting that the crisis was an internal problem of the Associated State and therefore outside the sub-committee's purview.[86] This international scrutiny, occurring in mid-August just as the Barbados agreement was unravelling, may have added to the general atmosphere of defeat.

The aftermath of the Barbados agreement's collapse, alongside being characterised by a sense of deadlock, witnessed the emergence of new public narratives surrounding events in Anguilla. On his return to London from Barbados in early August 1967, Lord Shepherd had alerted the media that American organisations had attempted 'to set up posts for gambling and drugs and frankly making money'. The *Telegraph* article in which his comments were reported further claimed that these mysterious organisations had tried to disrupt the Associated State of St Kitts-Nevis-Anguilla for 'commercial purposes' and that they 'appeared to be at the root of

recent disturbances in the East Caribbean'.[87] *The Guardian* appeared to sketch some of these groups in more detail, describing them as 'American gambling and drug rings, and the Mafia has been mentioned as one of them. Competing American interests wanted a completely independent Anguilla, which would be financed by them and would in turn allow them to set up a casino.'[88] Moreover, *The New York Times*, perhaps indicating that some legitimate businesses were also involved in cheering on the independence movement, had later asked Webster whether Anguilla had been 'encouraged to secede by real estate operators'.[89] Shepherd would again return to the theme of criminal activity when addressing the media whilst licking his wounds after the failure of the Jamaica talks. This time he claimed that Anguilla was now 'wide open to strong-arm influences'. *The Telegraph*, again reporting on his comments, went on to summarise that 'there were interested bodies whose names he [Shepherd] would not mention. Money was to be made within the group'.[90]

According to Westlake, Bradshaw had been the first to advocate the notion that Anguilla could be potentially dominated by American organised crime groups and Lord Shepherd was, accordingly, the first British diplomat to publicly voice this idea.[91] American organised crime had a long history of activity in the Caribbean, most notably the gambling empires expelled from revolutionary Cuba and the subsequent Mafia involvement in attempts to assassinate Fidel Castro. As Westlake notes, Trinidadian Prime Minister Eric Williams had observed that 'if the Mafia or any other sort of American crooks are not already in Anguilla, they soon will be. They are everywhere else in the Caribbean'.[92] Alongside potential investment by legitimate businesses, the prospect of dubious businessmen investing in an independent rebel Anguilla was, therefore, certainly not beyond the realms of possibility. However, no credible leads of Mafia influence were ever produced or proven. As will be demonstrated, this did not prevent the rumours of a gangster takeover gaining traction in the years to come and ultimately playing an embarrassingly prominent role in the British decision to invade Anguilla.

Beyond sustaining the island's place in worldwide media headlines, the failure of the Barbados agreement also had a tangible impact upon Anguilla's political leadership. Whilst the more radical figures such as Webster and Harrigan had been willing to serve previously under the leadership of Peter Adams, who had undertaken the difficult task of representing his island across the preceding years of political uncertainty, Adams' participation in the Barbados agreement persuaded them that new leadership was required. According to Webster, when Adams returned from the conference he and his colleagues were 'very unpopular, and several Anguillans wanted to attack them'.[93] In early August at a public meeting, Webster recalled, 'I had been proclaimed to replace Peter Adams as President. He had been requested by the people after the Barbados Conference to step down for "selling out Anguilla to St. Kitts."'[94] Political clout therefore shifted decisively towards Webster following the collapse of Barbados and this, combined with the deteriorating economic conditions in Anguilla, led to a new sense of boldness in decision-making amongst the revolutionary leadership.

Towards an 'Interim Agreement'

Around the time that Webster assumed full political control on 6 August 1967, Jerry Gumbs was again pressing the island's case to the UN. When reporters asked him about Anguilla's economic situation, which remained under the heel of Basseterre's sanctions, Gumbs claimed that offers to develop the island had 'poured in from all over the world' since UDI and suggested that Anguilla could print 'Free Anguilla' stamps, mint 'metallic currency' and 'sell flags' to raise

Ronald Webster at home. (Albert Grandolini collection)

not a casino.'[102] Webster would later recollect the rumoured Onassis offer in his memoirs, claiming that a reporter who had been talking recently with Onassis had told Webster that the magnate 'was looking for some little country where he could register his ships. I told the reporter that I was not much interested, since we first had to get our new nation recognised internationally. Only then could we consider any trade deal.' Indeed, Webster seemed uncertain about the provenance of the offer, retelling that '[perhaps] the reporter's idea was just to get a news story, but some short time later three chaps flew here and brought a similar offer, as if it came from Onassis himself. I never really knew if Onassis sent them.'[103]

revenues for sustaining the rebel government.[95] Offers of assistance had indeed reached the Anguillian leadership from diverse quarters across mid-1967. Webster had himself sold some of his property on St Maarten to help the Anguillian treasury.[96] Most notably, however, the Anguillian leadership had accepted the support of a peculiar organisation known as the San Francisco Group. Some members of this organisation were ideological followers of Dr Leopold Kohr of the University of Puerto Rico, who advocated the political, economic and social benefits of creating small city-states and saw great potential in Anguilla to practice his theories. When Kohr visited the island in mid-1967, according to Webster, he 'offered his ideas on having Anguilla remain in a very simple lifestyle, without cars, electricity or any modern conveniences.'[97]

The group which formed around Kohr subsequently helped the Anguillian leaders raise funds, devising methods similar to those mentioned by Gumbs. They arranged for honorary passports and flags to be created, plus the minting of 'Anguilla Liberty Dollars', all of which were offered to readers of The New York Times in return for donations to the Anguillian cause, published in a full-page advert in the newspaper on 14 August.[98] As Webster recalled, 'The New York Times ad got us a lot of attention and quite a number of people responded with donations of money.' Indeed, he acknowledged that the San Francisco Group's efforts 'raised quite a bit of money, which helped keep everything paid for'.[99] The relationship, however, did not last. Among various other resentments, Westlake observed that once Webster's government showed an interest in promoting tourism on the island, members of the San Francisco Group realised that the Anguillians were not committed to Kohr's theories and, consequently, their relationship's 'downhill plunge was steep and bumpy'.[100] Westlake does, however, acknowledge that the relationship had been built on long-term misapprehensions from both sides.[101]

Offers of assistance also allegedly came from another quarter. The New York Times reported on 18 August that Webster had claimed to have rejected a $1 million offer from Greek shipping magnate Aristotle Onassis, who would later marry the widowed American First Lady Jacqueline Kennedy. According to the article, 'Webster said that Mr. Onassis had indicated an interest in using the new red and green flag of the "Republic of Anguilla" as a flag of convenience for his ships'. The article went on to say that '[later], Mr. Webster said, he heard that Mr. Onassis was also interested in a hotel with a gambling casino. Mr Webster said a hotel would be acceptable, but

Despite some successes in saving the island from economic collapse, Webster's regime still faced a political crisis that showed no signs of abating in the later months of 1967. In September Bradshaw visited the United Kingdom for 10 days, during which time he made a television appearance, spoke to newspaper reporters and Caribbean groups and discussed with Whitehall the next steps following the failure of Barbados. In a report to Prime Minister Harold Wilson the Secretary of State for Commonwealth Affairs, George Thomson, claimed that Bradshaw's British public relations initiatives were 'an endeavour to improve the bad public image which he has here'. Thomson went on to summarise that the government talks had been 'fairly cautious' but somewhat productive, focusing on the possibility of sending a Parliamentary delegation to investigate the crisis and a temporary British administrator to govern Anguilla whilst a settlement was decided.[104]

Illustrating how far the Commonwealth Office was still wedded to the idea of continued union between Anguilla and St Kitts, Thomson raised the worrying possibility that the delegation might recommend political separation and stated that this was 'a solution which we may be driven to if all else fails but which we would prefer to avoid if possible in view of likely repercussions elsewhere [amongst other former colonies]'. He also raised other potential difficulties, including the prospect of a 'closer British commitment' to the crisis, international accusations of 'neo-colonialism' and 'loss of face for Mr. Bradshaw' if a British administrator was sent to Anguilla. Moreover, Thomson also acknowledged the difficulties entailed in gaining Anguillian agreement to these proposals. He noted that the British were 'unwilling to negotiate with the Anguillans in a way which might imply recognition of their so-called "republic"'. Reflecting upon the recently failed talks of July and August, he also noted 'the risk that any agreement reached in discussion with Anguillan representatives outside their island may be disavowed at a later stage.'[105] The British therefore faced a range of considerable challenges in endeavouring to reach a settlement during the later months of 1967.

The month of September also witnessed the birth of Anguilla's new newspaper, The Beacon, under the editorship of Webster's comrade Atlin Harrigan. Harrigan, an electrician who became disenchanted with Anguilla's underdevelopment, had been aligned with Webster since early in the revolution, galvanising the island to reject Associated Statehood through a letter to *The Democrat*, a Kittitian newspaper, in which he argued for separation from St Kitts. As Anguillian historian Colville Petty summarised '[with] those words, the Anguillian people were spurred into action. Atlin had lit the flames of the Revolution…Having lit the flames, Atlin was one among those who ensured that they kept on burning.' Consequently, Petty judged that '[if] Ronald Webster is the father of modern Anguilla then Atlin Harrigan was its mother.'[106]

According to *The Beacon*'s first issue, the newspaper offered an outlet through which 'the people of Anguilla, and the world outside Anguilla can learn what is happening on the island, and whereby they can voice their opinions.'[107] Consequently, the newspaper offered a rare glimpse into ordinary island life and Anguillian voices during the revolution. The first edition also illustrated that the island's republican leanings only ran so deep. Although perhaps only projecting one political viewpoint in this instance, the newspaper confidently announced that 'all Anguilla asks for is that here [sic] secession from St Kitts be recognised, and that at least an administrator be appointed by Britain to run the affairs of this island, and to end the present deadlock'.[108]

London's diplomatic fortunes improved when a Parliamentary delegation consisting of two MPs, Nigel Fisher and Donald Chapman of the Conservative and Labour parties respectively, arrived in the Eastern Caribbean in December 1967 to seek solutions to the crisis. Perhaps illustrating the sense of political stasis which both Webster and Bradshaw must have felt by the final months of the year, both sides agreed to the 'Interim Agreement' negotiated by the delegation. The belligerents agreed to invite a British civil servant to advise the Anguillian Council during an interim period of one year, during which time this Crown representative could impose a degree of legality on the rebel island whilst a longer-term settlement could be negotiated.[109] In essence, therefore, the Interim Agreement merely bought the British more time in which to secure a lasting agreement, rather than producing a major breakthrough in the dispute between Basseterre and the Anguillians.

Nevertheless, the agreement also anticipated some economic relief for Anguilla. In his letter endorsing the Fisher-Chapman delegation's plan and pledging that 'efforts will be made in good faith by all to restore friendship and harmony', Premier Bradshaw encouraged the allocation of British development aid to Anguilla and agreed that 'normal trade and other services as may be agreed will be restored', alongside the mail service.[110] Correspondingly, the Anguillian leadership also similarly pledged to seek a restoration of 'friendship and harmony', whilst inviting the new Senior British Official (SBO) – as the civil servant was to be known – to 'help work towards an agreed long-term solution for Anguilla'. Accordingly, the island council 'would not act without seeking his advice' and he would be 'invited to sit with the Council at all its meetings, and would have access to all papers and documents'.[111]

As 1967 drew to a close, therefore, the dispute between Anguilla and Basseterre remained deep and had the potential to sputter on. The Interim Agreement did, nevertheless, provide a ray of hope that the two sides were open to discussion and a potential agreement. The year had been a whirlwind ride for the Anguillians, who had ascended from the obscurity of colonial neglect to the subject of extensive front page media headlines and international attention. The British had swayed from initial relative indifference to Anguilla's plight when ushering in the new Associated State to being forced to confront the embarrassing inadequacies of its Caribbean decolonisation plans posed by the Anguilla crisis. The conflict continued to be viewed, to a significant degree, through a regional strategic lens. British policymakers remaining concerned that Anguillian independence would encourage wider fragmentation of the Associated State system throughout the Caribbean and, accordingly, wanted to encourage the survival of the Kittitian, Nevisian and Anguillian union if at all possible. Whilst showing signs of short-term compromise, Bradshaw remained adamant that Anguilla should remain inside the Associated State. The fate of all sides now rested on whether a lasting agreement could be reached over the next year. If not, then the conflict could easily re-emerge with renewed intensity.

3
THE INTERIM AGREEMENT AND THE WHITLOCK AFFAIR

The civil servant selected to become the Senior British Official in Anguilla during the interim period was Anthony Lee. Colin Rickards of *The Times* described Lee as 'a tall and solidly built figure…He is soft spoken and appears quiet and diffident, with an upper-class self-effacing habit of hugging himself while engaging in small talk.'[1] Having served in the Royal Navy during the Second World War, Lee had subsequently pursued a career in the colonial administrations of Tanganyika and South Arabia. In December 1967 Lee had helped to manage the Fisher-Chapman delegation's mission to the Eastern Caribbean before being selected as the British representative in Anguilla for the interim year. Unless further extensions were requested, this timeframe would last from the moment of Lee's arrival in Anguilla on 8 January 1968 until 9 January 1969.

Implementing the Interim Agreement

From the outset, the Anguillians approached the interim period as an opportunity to demonstrate their ability to govern themselves effectively and therefore further their cause of separation from St Kitts. Atlin Harrigan's editorial in a January 1968 edition of *The Beacon* highlighted that '[during] this interim period, we are being watched and tested by those who have faith in us, and even more closely by those who have scoffed at us. We are going to be judged as to how we take over the responsible task of governing ourselves. We shall be judged by our ability to work together…our ability to treat one another with justice and fair play'.[2] Webster also viewed the interim period as an opportunity to show the Anguillian capacity for self-government. He recalled that 'I felt the longer Anguilla continued to function as a de facto independent government, the more the status quo would tend to operate in the island's favor [sic].'[3] Indeed, he summarised 1968 as:

... a period of time when we had to express our responsibilities though at times tempers flared up, and I had to keep things under control. We very well knew that at the end of the one-year period a report had to be made on the Anguilla situation, as to whether or not we could govern ourselves.[4]

The Island Council, therefore, maintained friendly – if perhaps cautious – relations with Tony Lee during his tenure as SBO. One of the few notable disagreements encountered between the Council and Lee occurred over an element of the islanders' self-government. In July 1968 the original Island Council elected in October 1967 was dissolved and the Anguillians decided to hold fresh elections. The Associated State legislature in Basseterre had, however, passed a Local Government Act in November 1967 outlining the responsibilities of the island councils, according to its own constitutional stance, and the Anguillian desire to hold an election did not conform to this Act. Indeed, according to Webster's memoirs, Bradshaw had declared that the election would be illegal unless held under the Act.[5] Consequently, as detailed in a letter from Webster to the British Under-Secretary of State for Commonwealth Affairs dated 15 July 1968, Lee had argued that if Anguilla decided to hold the election under the Act then the British government could recognise the Council; the UN Committee of 24 and international opinion would be satisfied and Bradshaw's bluff would have been called, forcing him to accept the election.[6] However, when the Anguillians decided to press ahead unilaterally regardless, Lee demonstrated his cooperative spirit and acted as Returning Officer for the election. The Anguillians decided to proceed for numerous reasons, including – as detailed in Webster's letter – a desire not to take instructions from St Kitts and to not divide Anguillian public opinion through a controversial election and thus cause instability.[7]

Webster recalled that relations with Lee were 'okay to the end of December '68…When Lee was sent we felt glad to know we had someone to assist us with the burdens we were encountering at the time.' He further asserted that 'Lee sat in with us during our meetings and pretended to be fully with us. But, reading between the lines, we knew very well that he had been engaged by Britain and St. Kitts. His real loyalties rested there, and he had to communicate with both.'[8] Tony Lee was, in fact, in a difficult position. Westlake argues that, whilst London seemed intent on playing 'a game of Masterly Inactivity, waiting for the Anguillans to calm themselves and march obediently back to St. Kitts' during the interim period, Lee recognised that this would never happen and continued to inform his political masters in Whitehall of this fact.[9] As London's man on the ground, therefore, he had to represent Britain – following its somewhat disinterested stance over Anguilla – and at the same time engage with the island's interests, concerns and priorities.

British sluggishness during the interim period certainly constituted a missed opportunity to find a concrete and lasting settlement. At first glance, it may appear surprising that London adopted this approach following the diplomatic disappointments of mid-1967. It was, however, perhaps symptomatic of a longer-term mind-set that had repeatedly ignored the political desires and realities of Anguilla in favour of Britain's neat federalised exit strategy from the Caribbean. Mawby has noted how far Britain's approach to Anguilla was based on long-standing colonial assumptions about the 'political immaturity' of such islands and hence the need to fuse them together into larger political groupings rather than allowing them to go their own separate ways.[10] Consequently, Whitehall continued to insist on the deep undesirability of Anguillian independence and clung to the hope that islanders would see reason and return to

what the British believed to be the best option of union with St Kitts and Nevis as though, as Westlake summarised the British attitude, Anguillian concerns 'were simply a case of hysterics'.[11]

Scepticism about the Interim Agreement and its lack of results soon emerged in Harrigan's editorial column in *The Beacon*. Marking two months since the arrangement was accepted, the newspaper praised that 'with the presence of Mr Tony Lee on the island, we realise that there is no longer a danger of overt hostile action being taken against us, and life is returning to normal'. It also expressed gratitude for a visit in early February by a British Overseas Development Team to assess the island's infrastructural needs. However, Harrigan went on to list a number of grievances that remained unaddressed and which, he argued, 'hindered' Lee's objectives of assisting in the governance of Anguilla and finding a long-term solution to the wider conflict with Basseterre. Firstly, he stated that Anguillian savings in St Kitts remained frozen, 'causing an ever increasing hardship'. Moreover, he complained that Anguilla's share of the British grant to the Associated State for 1967 had never reached the island and insisted that this be remedied.[12] Two editions later and *The Beacon* somewhat continued its theme of scepticism about the Interim Agreement by reprinting an article by Lord Lambton in the *London Evening Standard*. Lambton, a politician who had recently visited Anguilla and St Kitts, argued that the agreement would not help solve the crisis, '[for] conflicting impressions are held [about the meaning of the deal].' He went on to assess that 'Anguilla believes that its independence has been established. St Kitts believes that Anguilla will be returned to it by the British Government at the end of the year. A settlement based on such a misunderstanding will do more harm in the long run than a clear unpopular decision would have done now.'[13]

Despite these political difficulties, some progress was being made in the realm of infrastructural development through the operations of the British Development Division based in Barbados. A prefabricated school was purchased for Anguilla, alongside hospital equipment, a cold store and ice factory. Some roads were also improved.[14] Furthermore, around 110 feet of the airfield's runway was paved during the Interim Agreement, but Anguillians would have to wait until 1974 before the entire runway of 3,600 feet was completely paved.[15] Just how generous the development project of the Interim Agreement was is open to interpretation. A total of $250,000EC was spent across 1968, compared with the $500,000EC that would be spent in 1969 following the British invasion.[16] Both figures were significantly in excess of the funds allocated to Anguilla during the late colonial period. Nevertheless, if Britain had wanted to illustrate to Anguillians the tangible benefits of the Interim Agreement and, ultimately, remaining part of their Associated State, a larger development budget could perhaps have been allocated in 1968.

Despite Anguillians gaining an improved sense of security through the Interim Agreement, the two belligerents of the crisis did not entirely abandon their defensive postures following the endorsement of the agreement. Both Anguilla and Basseterre formally created their own defence forces in January 1968. The St Kitts and Nevis Defence Force – consisting of a regular corps, reserve corps and cadet corps totalling around 175 men – was now commanded by Captain Errol Maynard, one of the regulars selected for professional training under ex-British Army officer Geoffrey Ellis in 1967. Whilst training would continue to come from the British military over the coming years, the new Associated State force would also receive advisors from Jamaica, Guyana and Trinidad-Tobago. Although Whitman Browne claimed that the defence force was never intended as an invasion force for Anguilla, he also noted the guidelines for defence force conduct established by Guyanese Captain Oscar Pollards: to maintain internal stability; preserve the government under all circumstances apart from after an election defeat and, if forced to take a side, to prioritise the will of the people.[17] It could perhaps be argued that restoring Basseterre's constitutional rights over Anguilla could have fallen within the realm of internal stability and protecting the government. On the other hand, however, the recent Anguillian raid against St Kitts had illustrated the serious weakness of the state's security infrastructure and, accordingly, Browne may have been correct in his assessment of Bradshaw's purely defensive intentions. Moreover, the small size of the St Kitts and Nevis Defence Force would perhaps also have reduced the likelihood of a successful invasion and occupation of Anguilla.

Whether intended to mirror Basseterre's militarisation policy and demonstrate its self-perception as an independent state, or else simply to institutionalise Webster's armed followers, Anguilla swore in its own Defence Force on 2 January 1968. According to a subsequent report written by Detective Inspector R.F. Williams, around 100 people gathered outside the Administrative Building to watch the swearing in ceremony. The report estimated that 'a group of 46 people is the maximum that the Defence Force and 'volunteers' ever mustered and represent all who patrolled during May 1967–March 1969. However, some lost interest and others moved away for work, so Webster could at no time have called upon more than about 25 to defend [the] island.'[18] As will be demonstrated, Webster would later significantly over-exaggerate his military strength as the threat of an invasion increased, in the hope of deterrence. Williams concluded that the Anguilla Defence Force 'does seem to have been ill-organised and ill-led with individuals taking their own actions as they saw fit'. The unit's firepower also seemed very limited, with Williams assessing that '[it] is likely that at no time could Webster have called upon more than 25 weapons for his Defence Force.' Although efforts were made to purchase weapons from Puerto Rico and the United States, and one American citizen allegedly did land supplies of some nature in mid-1968, most attempts to obtain weapons from overseas seem to have been unsuccessful.[19] As Williams summarised:

> Whether Webster was successful in purchasing arms from abroad or not is debateable but it seems most likely that had he done so he would have been only too eager to tell the outside world, and in particular St Kitts, in order to gain the maximum publicity for his Force. It may also help in assessing the overall position to point out that the Defence Force patrolled in the main with worn out, unserviceable weapons.[20]

Despite its limitations, the instituting of the Anguilla Defence Force was one of several developments across 1968 whereby the Island Council asserted its sovereignty. As Walicek notes, Anguilla increasingly acted as an independent state as the year drew on, including printing their own stamps and preparing to sell government-owned land.[21] According to the Wooding Report, Webster and his colleagues also made several tours to important regional political centres including the UN in New York, Jamaica and Barbados. Furthermore, funds from sympathetic friends overseas continued to assist the revolutionary government.[22]

The Interim Agreement of 1968 was, collectively, a strange interval in the Anguilla crisis. On the one hand, its initial negotiation constituted an achievement of sorts. Following the diplomatic dead-ends encountered in mid-late 1967, the concept of a political breathing space was a logical next step and allowed Webster and Bradshaw to show good will in desiring a political settlement. Additionally, some sorely needed infrastructure improvements were made in Anguilla under British development projects. On the other hand, however, in terms of concrete political achievement, the interim year can be judged as a political failure and, indeed, a wasted opportunity on the part of the British. As Westlake summarised, '[in] 1968, in the political life of Anguilla, nothing grew.'[23]

The reasons for this are manifold. Westlake partly blames Lee for not advocating the Anguillian perspective loud and clear enough for London to recognise the irreconcilability of the two belligerents. Indeed, he claimed that '[Lee] knew from early in the Interim Agreement Year that nothing would ever reattach Anguilla to St. Kitts, yet he failed to communicate this awareness to his superiors. Perhaps nobody could have broken through their complacence and their obtuse determination to live theoretically, but the point is that Tony Lee didn't.'[24] Perhaps more importantly, 1968 was wasted due to the disconnected stance of Whitehall. Their inability to comprehend and act upon the wishes of the Anguillians reflected a longer-term disregard for island nationalisms and a tendency to prioritise their federal projects. Behind this mentality lay a fear of political disintegration and a colonial lens that questioned the capacity of smaller islands for self-government and development. Finally, the Interim Agreement failed due to the intransigence of the Anguillians and Basseterre, combined with their mutual tendency to see radically different possibilities in the agreement. The former viewed it as a step towards independence, whilst the latter saw it as a route through which it could reabsorb Anguilla back into the state. If anything, by the end of 1968 the two sides had moved further away from each other, rather than advanced towards common ground. Both sides had invested in their military preparedness. Bradshaw had also returned to his public narrative that Anguilla could be seized by gangsters, which could result in embarrassment for Britain and the US.[25]

Collapse of the Interim Agreement

In the second half of 1968 Whitehall gradually recognised that no political progress had been made so far under the Interim Agreement and belatedly attempted to get negotiations moving. Consequently, William Whitlock – Labour MP for Nottingham North and Parliamentary Under-Secretary of State for Foreign and Commonwealth Affairs – invited Webster and Bradshaw to London in October for talks. The son of a dock worker, Whitlock had served extensively in the military during the Second World War before becoming a long-serving trade unionist. He soon established a reputation in the Labour Party for his 'organising skills, loyalism and persuasive manner', whilst achieving success when he notably supported the right of Ugandan Asians to settle in Britain from Uganda in 1968.[26] Having been elected an MP in 1959, he worked extensively in the Treasury and HM Household department through the 1960s before becoming Parliamentary Under-Secretary at the Commonwealth Office in July 1967 and Parliamentary Under-Secretary at the Foreign and Commonwealth Office upon the ministry's creation in October 1968.

It would be the Anguilla crisis, however, for which Whitlock would be remembered in political circles. He readily admitted that before the talks with Webster and Bradshaw between 4 and 23 October 1968 he had known 'very little about the St. Kitts/Nevis/Anguilla problem'; however, as the talks progressed, he 'learned just how strong is the feeling of the Anguillans towards St. Kitts'.

Whilst Whitlock acknowledged that he could 'have done business' with Webster's legal representative during discussions, he concluded that any hopes of a settlement were 'frustrated by Webster's periodic statement that it would be political suicide for him to go back with any other agreement than that of U.K. recognition of Anguilla either as a U.K. colony or as a separate Associated State'.[27]

According to a Commonwealth Office spokesman, quoted by Reuters, '[the] purpose of the talks, which are purely exploratory, is to discuss what is to take place of the present interim settlement when it expires next January.'[28] Webster claimed that, in terms of proposals for a long-term settlement, a range of options were presented at the talks, all of which maintained the links to Basseterre alongside varying degrees of autonomy for Anguilla. According to a statement issued by him after the talks, the Anguillian delegation 'considered favourably the possibility of a loose federal association with St Kitts' with enhanced devolved powers for the island. Webster claimed that Bradshaw rejected these proposals.[29] However, if Whitlock is to be believed, Webster was also generally uncompromising on the need for Anguillian independence from St Kitts, which would also have reduced the chances of the talks reaching an agreement. Ultimately, as the Anguillians were, according to Webster's memoirs, 'strictly interested in complete separation from St. Kitts', whilst Bradshaw and the British continued to pursue union, the talks soon reached deadlock.[30] The evolving tone of the talks was reflected in the composition of the meetings, which descended from an initial direct discussion between Webster and Bradshaw – their first ever face-to-face political discussion – to a series of separate meetings with more junior British officials. As this new phase of discussions developed, Webster 'told them [the British] that definitely they would not be able to settle our affairs by meetings of this kind'.[31]

Ultimately, therefore, the London talks of October 1968 ended in deadlock. Although the prospect of extending the Interim Agreement – a decision which needed the consent of both belligerent parties – was discussed, no agreement was reached. According to Webster's post-talks statement, '[the] delegation felt that although in principle there was no objection to the extension of the interim agreements', this continuation would be 'easier to sell' in Anguilla if certain financial and legal grievances were addressed.[32] These grievances included the frozen Anguillian savings in St Kitts, the withholding of pensions to retired Anguillian civil servants and the inability to legally transfer titles of land in Anguilla due to the need to register deeds in St Kitts. Although these issues were discussed further in an effort to resolve them, no final solution was reached and, accordingly, no agreement on extending the Interim Agreement was achieved.

With the interim year due to end in January 1969, both Webster and Bradshaw returned from London to face a relapse into diplomatic stalemate and an uncertain future. Some efforts were made to put positive spins on the situation which suited the agendas of each side. Bradshaw apparently praised having 'broken the ice' with his opponents and expressed his desire to visit Anguilla.[33] Harrigan's editorial in *The Beacon* judged that '[the] time spent has not been wasted, and Mr Whitlock will have gained a deep knowledge of the personalities and problems involved…We also know that our aspirations have been taken seriously, and not just brushed aside as they have in the past in St Kitts.'[34] Letters from the public to *The Beacon* remained belligerent and uncompromising on the issue of independence. One correspondent, based in St. Thomas, praised Webster's leadership and gratefully acknowledged that '[the] way you represented us at the London Talks has thrilled us.'[35] Another letter stated that '[we] are quite capable of becoming a nation. What

has Anguilla gained by interim? What will she gain by an extension? What will happen at the end can happen now. Anguilla will have no alternative but to go independent. Act now.'[36]

Webster did, however, attempt to sustain dialogue with Bradshaw and London following his return from the October talks. On 7 November he wrote a letter outlining Anguilla's conditions for extending the Interim Agreement which included many of the financial and legal grievances discussed in Whitehall. According to Webster's recollection, Bradshaw responded that these 'demands were essentially the same as what I had proposed in London, and he would like for me to come to St. Kitts for discussions, refrain from obstructing the continuation of the interim agreement, and dispel any thoughts or rumours of Anguilla's independence'.[37] With discussions making little headway and the end of the current agreement in view, Webster appealed to the British government, writing to Lord Chalfont – Minister of State for Foreign and Commonwealth Affairs – on 30 December 1968 reaffirming Anguilla's absolute independence but also requesting that the interim agreement be extended for an indeterminate period.[38]

Chalfont had, earlier in 1968, been faced with somewhat similar circumstances of an island colony fearing its postcolonial future outside of Britain's orbit in the case of the Falkland Islands. During his trip to this British territory in the South Atlantic, Chalfont could offer no reassurances to the islanders that Britain would not relinquish sovereignty in favour of Argentina. Indeed, as Calum Thomson has stated, Britain would begin negotiations with Buenos Aires about the future of the islands in the late 1960s and 'according to Foreign Office papers had accepted in principle the renunciation of British sovereignty over the islands under certain conditions'.[39] In this instance, Britain again seemed to be prioritising wider regional priorities over the self determination of an island people. In the case of Anguilla, the British response to Webster's letter was to reject the proposed extension of the Interim Agreement. Consequently, the interim year ended on 9 January 1969. Tony Lee, whose office of SBO was abolished, was instructed to take up a new role on the staff of the British Government Representative in Castries, St Lucia. Webster, meanwhile, announced that Anguilla was independent of the Associated State and severed all ties with the British Crown.[40] Anguilla accordingly returned to the position it had emerged from in December 1967: one of deep political and economic uncertainty about the future.

UDI and Webster's American advisors

The collapse of the Interim Agreement did not simply mean the end of the political breathing space created since December 1967. It also meant a halt to British development projects aimed at improving Anguilla's infrastructure and the restoration of Basseterre's economic sanctions. The first few months of 1969, therefore, perhaps proved the most acute time of immense challenges and uncertainty for Webster and the Island Council. Facing no end in sight to the turmoil that had engulfed the island since the beginning of the revolution almost two years previously, it was perhaps unsurprising that Anguillian society began to fragment in early 1969 into those who favoured the pursuit of continued negotiations and links with Britain and those who desired a more complete and radical independence. Prominent US citizens on Anguilla, including Jack Holcomb, the Haskins family, Pastor Freeman Goodge and Anguilla-born Jerry Gumbs all tended to favour independence and increasingly appeared to carry Webster towards their mode of thinking. Atlin Harrigan, Webster's long-time ally and editor of *The Beacon*, favoured a more moderate approach of continued dialogue with London.

The Americans who surrounded Webster in this last stage of Anguilla's rebellion were a diverse mix of individuals with colourful backgrounds. The key figure who captured the imaginations and concerns of British policymakers was Jack Holcomb who, according to The New York Times, had been 'variously described by them [members of the Island Council] as lawyer, police officer and developer'. Much of Holcomb's intentions and identity, however, remained shrouded in speculation. In an interview with his wife featuring in the same article, Mrs Holcomb 'described him as an investment and real-estate broker and a former police commissioner of Sea Branch Lakes [Sea Ranch Lakes, Florida]. He is not a licensed attorney, but he has "an extensive law library"'.[41] According to Westlake, Holcomb had been involved in the manufacture of surveillance devices in Florida before becoming a police commissioner, a job from which he had been dismissed over the discovery of a narcotics charge from his youth.[42] In his role as a businessman interested in construction materials, Holcomb had travelled to Anguilla in 1968 and proposed a business deal to the island leadership involving, according to Westlake, 'a guarantee that he would be the sole supplier of all building materials on the island for twenty-five years…[Additionally] he wanted it tax-free.'[43] Although the proposal fell through, Holcomb retained a considerable interest in the island and travelled regularly to Anguilla across early 1969.[44] Accordingly, speculation about Holcomb increased in the media and in Whitehall as his influence over Webster seemed to grow.

Another American, Lewis Haskins, was also an influential colleague of Webster intent on Anguillian independence from Britain. Having moved to the island in 1960, he had established an electronics components plant on the island which had provided a rare source of employment for Anguillians. Described as 'a ruddy-faced, husky man from Worcester [Massachusetts]' by the Los Angeles Times, Haskins claimed to have manufactured rifle parts during the Second World War.[45] As a deterrent to any invasion threat, the Anguillians claimed that Haskin's current plant was an arms factory. According to the article, he had become a 'principal adviser to the seven-man Anguillan ruling council, and over the years one of the closest men to Ronald Webster'. The degree of his influence over the island was also suggested by the Los Angeles Times which noted that 'Haskins, many say, more than any other person, "has been putting thoughts and words in the mouths of Anguillans" and pushing hard for an independent Anguilla for the past three years.'[46] His sons, Raymond and Sherman, also had militant reputations on the island, Westlake claiming that they had 'been hanging around with the rougher young people from the beginning, and of course that group inevitably favored [sic] whatever decision was likeliest to start a fight.'[47]

The growing tension between Harrigan and the more radical island leaders was evident in December 1968 as the expiration of the Interim Agreement came into view. In his newspaper editorial of 14 December Harrigan questioned the wisdom of an immediate declaration of independence from both Basseterre and Britain upon the termination of the interim year. Claiming that '[the] solution of the Anguilla problem is a matter for experts, a matter of high diplomacy, of playing the right card at the right time', he judged that the decision to pursue another UDI had apparently 'been taken without the consultation and the advice of these experts'. He proposed that the experts included Professor Roger Fisher – who had helped draft the 1967 constitution – Anguilla's lawyer at the London talks, Hudson Philipps, and Tony Lee, who Harrigan described as a 'true friend of Anguilla' who would 'hate to see us make false step at this juncture'. In concluding, Harrigan advised Anguilla's leaders to

avoid taking any hasty actions and instead '[let] some one else take the next step. The declaration of unilateral independence is much more powerful as a threat, than it could work out in practice.'[48]

In a subsequent issue of The Beacon, published on 28 December 1968, Harrigan's editorial focused on the political attacks made against his newspaper since the previous December within public debates and by various members of the Island Council. Detailing the most recent incident, he claimed that at a public meeting held by Wallace Rey and Webster it had been 'insinuated that the Editor was being used as a stooge in preventing Anguilla from attaining what the people wanted'. Defending himself, Harrigan claimed that the Anguillian crowd at the meeting agreed 'that all Anguilla wanted was secession from St. Kitts only and not from England.' He continued that 'this [argument] is all that the Beacon has been saying, and it says so with the firm support of the majority of the Anguillans'.[49] Webster also noted the increasingly divergent positions taken by The Beacon and his government in his memoirs. He stated that '[from] the beginning The Beacon started off with proper guidance. After a while it started shifting slowly from its real target of secession from St. Kitts and support for the struggle and began to deal with personalities.' Although Webster claimed to have not approved, some militants organised the seizure of the printing press at one point, Webster stating that '[those] who did it said it was more damaging for Anguilla to have bad news or incorrect news than no news at all.'[50]

Despite Webster's immediate declaration of independence following the end of the Interim Agreement, it would be the events of February 1969 that brought the international spotlight and, subsequently, British attention back to Anguilla. On 2 February Webster announced that a referendum would be held four days later posing two options for the Anguillian public: either association with St Kitts or a second UDI.[51] Somewhat mirroring the overwhelming results of the original referendum of July 1967, the outcome of 6 February 1969 was 1,739 voters in favour of UDI and four opting for continued union.[52] Unlike the 1967 referendum, however, the new UDI severed all links with Britain as well as St Kitts and led to the drafting of a more American-style republican constitution by Holcomb. Webster now became 'President-elect' of the new republic, whilst a national election was to be held within 60 days and timetabled for 6 April.[53]

Lee reported on the UDI in detail. Whilst it contained many grand notions derived from the US Constitution, including '[man's] right of dignity, and his inalienable right to life, liberty and the pursuit of happiness', it also expressed many grievances and declarations distinct to Anguillian identity.[54] It criticised the centuries-old British colonial neglect which had left islanders 'without paved roads, electricity, water, telephones, a port facility, or any other forms of elementary advancement commensurate with other societies of the world'. Furthermore, it highlighted the British political ignorance from which the Associated State had spawned, which 'failed to consider geography, similarity of interests, population distribution or safeguards of democratic process, and thereby produced a form of government inconsistent with the enjoyment of ordinary human rights'.[55] In a separate report to the FCO on 6 February, Lee recognised how damaging the UDI had been for British interests. He predicted that Webster 'will have complete powers to do what he wants and he will take his orders from Holcom'. Moreover, Lee saw no chance of Webster being ousted from power, whilst the pro-British moderate islanders were 'ham-strung' with fear.[56] Ultimately, Lee concluded that 'Holcom and friends are going to get into action very quickly and that their plans are made to this end. Therefore I would expect to encounter stronger opposition from the regime in future.'[57]

This latest development within the Anguilla crisis once more made media headlines. British newspapers focused on the republican direction of Webster's move. Both *The Times* and *Daily Telegraph* printed a *United Press International* report which announced the severance of ties with Britain and the creation of an 'American-type constitution'.[58] In a subsequent edition, the *Daily Telegraph* observed that '[more] in sorrow than in anger, it seems, the Anguillians have now concluded that Britain has abandoned them and feel that they must go-it-alone as a republic. Their constitution calls for a president and vice-president, an 11-man legislature, a Bill of Rights, provisions preventing compulsory trade union membership and a clause disestablishing the Church of England.'[59] The *Daily Mirror* rather cynically joked that '[declaring] independence is becoming almost a national industry for the tiny island of Anguilla' and highlighted how Anguillians had been 'swift to see the commercial possibilities of political action' in the form of producing highly collectable independence stamps.[60] Viewing the UDI from the wider strategic perspective of Caribbean political fragmentation that had terrified Whitehall for years, *The Guardian* wrote six days after the referendum that 'if Anguilla gets away with independence, it's rumoured that another islet, Barbuda, will secede from the State of Antigua'.[61]

Concern about how far the Anguilla crisis appeared to be spiralling out of control certainly intensified amongst British officials around the referendum. Moreover, the perceived evolving nature of political leadership in Anguilla, including whether Webster was still the driving force behind the revolution or increasingly under the influence of American advisors, was the source of growing concern. On 6 February, Whitlock estimated that 'the influence of Jerry Gumbs…would be at work either to overthrow Webster or to use him as the front man of the extremists. My assessment has unfortunately proved correct: Webster appears now to be making common cause with these extremists and American speculators'.[62] Perhaps indicating continued confidence and agency on Webster's part, Tony Lee concluded soon afterwards that:

> Webster's personal standing is strengthened since 15 January. His method has been to denounce any opposition to him as treason to the cause of liberation from St. Kitts. Opposition by moderates has ceased although their unease persists. Webster's primary motivation is this cause and sees himself as almost divinely ordained to it. In Holcom's case and Webster's inner circle (with exception of Haskin) motivation is applicability to profit, and the essential pre-requisite "Independence."[63]

The increasing concern of British policymakers about the advisors surrounding Webster also allowed for the gradual return of the rumours that had circulated in 1967 about the vulnerability of Anguilla to criminal exploitation. Whilst Bradshaw had been one of only a few voices advocating this view originally, this threat was now being voiced by an increasing number of commentators and officials, thus strengthening the chances of it gaining traction within policy discussions.

As Westlake notes, the first British newspaper to explore a criminal narrative in depth was *Private Eye* which, on 17 January 1969, claimed that '[the] controversy between plucky little Anguilla and the tyrant Brandshaw [sic]…has its roots in the American underworld, notably in the so-called Mafia, led by Meyer Lanksy in Florida'.[64] Lansky, known as the 'Mob's Accountant', had risen to power in the 1930s and established a lucrative empire of illegal casinos from New York to Florida, additionally helping to create the National Crime Syndicate.[65] The *Private Eye* article went on to state that Lansky's colleague, Dino Cellini, had visited Anguilla in 1967 with an offer to build a casino there. The article also claimed that '[the] "independence movement" is, in the main, financed by Lansky and is believed to be not entirely a question of freedom.'[66]

With no British representative remaining in Anguilla, it became difficult for London to ascertain the truth of rumours about organised crime. Consequently, Tony Lee's periodic trips to the island as part of his role of helping to discharge Britain's responsibilities for the external and defence policy of the Associated State were important for offering some assessment of the situation. As a FCO note explained:

> The British Government feel they must…be in a position to satisfy themselves that undesirable elements are not establishing themselves on Anguilla – a development which would be a matter of concern to other Governments in addition to the British Government. In the judgement of the British Government periodic visits to Anguilla by Mr. Lee are the only way to do this.[67]

One of the 'other Governments' was the United States. On 31 January the FCO wrote to the US State Department in Washington DC asking for their 'assessment' of Jack Holcomb and requesting that they discourage him from interfering in Anguillan constitutional affairs at such a sensitive time.[68] Indeed, the degree to which Holcomb was a particular source of British fears was confirmed during one of Lee's trips in early February. Lee 'asked Webster what he thought worried me most about Anguilla, to which he [Webster] replied "Your cool reception". My reply was "Holcom", which of course he po-poed.'[69] In the same report of his trip, Lee summarised bleakly that:

> Webster is completely out of his depth and his sense of proportion and reasoning has deserted him; he has the emotional support of the mass of the people while moderate men recognise that he is no longer rational. They are fearful of the trouble into which he is leading them and Anguilla, which they see as deriving from exploitation by a few Americans; this will enrich a few Anguillans but will lead, they say, to the spoilation of the island and physical conflict between Anguillans.[70]

Whilst British concerns about the spiralling crisis were growing in early February 1969, the pressure to undertake further and decisive steps by Britain towards ending the crisis were also rising. A communique emerging from the Fifth Conference of the Heads of Government of Commonwealth Caribbean Countries, which was held in the Trinidad Hilton Hotel from 3 to 6 February, stated that '[the] Conference called upon the Government of the United Kingdom to take all necessary steps in collaboration with the Government of the State to confirm the territorial and constitutional integrity of St. Kitts-Nevis-Anguilla.'[71] This statement soon became much debated by British policymakers eager to assess the thinking of Commonwealth Caribbean governments about the Anguilla crisis and Britain's possible options for taking action.

Sir G. Peter Hampshire, British High Commissioner to Trinidad-Tobago, judged that '[there] is nothing new or surprising in the document' and specifically noted that the '[the] paragraph on Anguilla can presumably only be helpful to us as an authoritative statement of Commonwealth Caribbean support for the constitutional solution which we continue to pursue'.[72] Another British diplomat, Mr Murray based in Kingston, had sought out the opinion of James Lloyd, a Jamaican politician who had served as the first black Administrator of Grenada, about the communique. According to Murray, Lloyd regarded the communique 'as being deliberately vague about the steps that might be taken. Some Associated States representatives in discussion clearly had in mind possible use of force. There was also a suggestion that there should be further talks'. Ultimately, he summarised that according to Lloyd the phrase 'confirm territorial integrity' indicated 'no more than refusing to recognise purported [Anguillian] secession'.[73]

Murray's inquiries appear to have been instigated by a request from the British Foreign Secretary, Michael Stewart, of 21 February that they 'explore current thinking of independent Commonwealth Caribbean Governments on St Kitts/Anguilla dispute' following the heads of government conference. Having noted the communique, Stewart wanted 'some elucidation of the attitudes of individual/governments in framing this resolution. Could they enlarge upon what is meant by quote all necessary steps unquote? Would this include use of military force against Anguillans?' Perhaps indicating that the FCO had considered the communique as a potential endorsement of future military action, Stewart then asked 'would the government concerned be likely to either (A) participate in such action and/or (B) support it by public statements, including at the UN if necessary?' He also asked what actions were expected of the UK if military operations were not desired.[74]

How far military intervention was becoming regarded as a possible policy option by Whitehall in late February 1969 is debatable. Following an article in the *Sunday Telegraph* of 16 February which claimed that 'Britain will almost certainly be forced to intervene militarily within the next two weeks in…Anguilla unless there is a marked change in the rapidly deteriorating situation there', Stewart had been at pains to quash speculation of this sort.[75] Clarifying the Wilson government's position for British diplomats in St Lucia, he stated that '[we] do not at present contemplate the use of force to restore either St Kitts or British rule in Anguilla. Nor are we considering negotiating a period of direct British rule…In these circumstances the less said about the use of force or direct intervention the better'.[76] Despite these denials, the interest shown by Stewart in some sort of military operation in his message requesting information about the thinking of independent Commonwealth Caribbean governments, written the same day, shows the undecided nature of British thinking at this time.

Certainly, there was a growing appetite for decisive action of some kind amongst various British policymakers. Tony Lee had expressed frustration that the British had not responded assertively, although perhaps not militarily, within a week of his departure as SBO in January.[77] Having subsequently discussed the situation with Governor Sir Wilfred Jacobs of Antigua-Barbuda around the time of the referendum, Lee also reported that the 'incensed' governor 'considered that HM Government should intervene with force in Anguilla'.[78] Desmond M. Kerr, deputy British representative to St. Kitts-Nevis-Anguilla, also appeared to be an early proponent of military intervention. He wrote on 7 February that 'I am reluctantly being brought to view that we shall repeat shall eventually have to use force to resolve Anguilla situation'. He did, however, believe that many important questions needed answering 'before reaching any final or irrevocable decisions'. These included what action should be brought against the rebel leadership and US citizens; for how long Britain would commit troops; when could they invade and what settlement could be implemented.[79]

There were, nevertheless, still those who clung to hopes of a diplomatic settlement. Lord Caradon, head of the UK Mission to the UN in New York and former Governor of Jamaica, wrote anxiously to the FCO on 14 February 1969 that he was 'disturbed to see that suggestions are being made for the use of force in Anguilla. Anything like this would create serious difficulties for us here [at the UN].'[80] On 20 February Thomas Sewell, based in the FCO's Caribbean Department, also reported that Sir Alan Burns – a former Governor of the Gold Coast and Director of the St Kitts Sugar Company – was planning to meet Bradshaw, explaining that Burns had suggested that he 'try to persuade Mr. Bradshaw (with whom he has certain influence) that he should give up Anguilla'. Sewell and a colleague had responded to this suggestion by stating that 'we thought it most unlikely that Mr. Bradshaw would accept such a suggestion, and that if he did we should still be left with the problem of what to do with Anguilla.' Nevertheless, Sewell conceded that they 'thought that there would be no real harm in Sir Alan Burns trying out his ideas on Mr. Bradshaw, and it might even be helpful to us to know unofficially how he reacts to the suggestion'.[81] Clearly, therefore, the FCO was still interested in pursuing a political settlement in late February despite the increasing calls for decisive action.

On the same day that Sewell reported Burns' plans, Kerr noted to the FCO that '[we] have received news to the effect that Mr. William Whitlock…will be coming to the West Indies to try and work out a solution to the St. Kitts and Anguilla problem'.[82] By the time that Whitlock met with the Commonwealth Parliamentary Association delegation to the Leeward and Windward Islands on 13 February, the Anguilla crisis had worsened considerably since he had hosted Webster and Bradshaw in London the previous October. According to a record of the meeting, Whitlock had told the delegation that he 'sympathised with the Anguillans and believed that they had a genuine grievance in that they had been neglected by the colonial administration from St. Kitts. Their dislike of St. Kitts was inherited and now personified in Bradshaw'.[83] Around this time, Whitlock agreed to visit the Eastern Caribbean to continue Britain's diplomatic efforts. In a meeting of 11 February with Fisher and Chapman – the MPs who had negotiated the Interim Agreement – Whitlock had explained Britain's current policy towards the crisis. Asked by Fisher whether Britain wanted to establish a working arrangement between the two belligerents or simply to impose Bradshaw's sovereignty over Anguilla, Whitlock responded that 'HMGs wish was to get agreement on a looser arrangement with a high degree of autonomy. There was no reason why under such an arrangement the Anguillans should not, bit by bit, sever some of their connections with St. Kitts'. He went on, however, to qualify this answer by stating that 'now after UDI it was a very open question whether Mr. Bradshaw would make any more concessions'.[84] Whitlock would, nevertheless, attempt to pursue diplomatic avenues to solve the Anguilla crisis. Ironically, his efforts provided the final stimulus for British military action.

The Whitlock Affair

Whitlock's first trip was intended to build a settlement acceptable to St Kitts and the wider Commonwealth Caribbean. Bradshaw was persuaded to accept a new proposal on 26 February through the offer of further British aid, Whitlock's deal including an open-ended contract, similar in character to the Interim Agreement, in which Anguilla's council would again work with an SBO in governing the island.[85] The second mission would be more complicated. Opinion was divided amongst some British diplomats about the suitability and value of Whitlock visiting Anguilla and negotiating with Webster directly. Addressing this issue, Kerr in St Lucia complained that Lord Shepherd had declined an invite to Anguilla in 1967 during his stint negotiating a settlement. Subsequently, Kerr argued, '[this] is no doubt why HMG has continually misunderstood the whole situation, which caused the failure of so many talks to bring about a workable solution…It is about time HMG sent in top level officials to see for themselves'.[86]

Sewell of the FCO Caribbean Department, however, raised considerable doubts. He noted that both Lee and Kerr 'are agreed that Mr. Bradshaw would object very strongly to a meeting between Mr. Whitlock and Mr. Webster' and, Sewell further observed, '[for] the Minister to see Mr. Webster (or to go to Anguilla himself) might now be regarded in the Caribbean as consorting with rebels'.[87] Another FCO mandarin, Roland Hunt, concurring with Sewell, writing that '[in] the face of hardening of Caribbean opinion against Anguilla and the advice from our local representatives, I feel that it would not be advisable for a Minister to meet Mr. Webster even if the latter were prepared to risk leaving his own island'.[88]

As Whitlock descended the stairs of his plane onto the hot tarmac of Anguilla's airfield on 11 March 1969, he had no inkling of the traumatic day which lay ahead of him. Accounts differ of the events which unfolded. Certainly, Whitlock was met by enthusiastic crowds and island leaders who had arranged transport and a dinner for the British minister. According to Whitlock's own report, he first 'stressed publicly my intention of touring island to discuss further the proposals' before being driven in Lee's car to a house in Sandy Hill Bay on the south coast. Whilst at the airfield, he further explained, 'Webster appeared disconcerted at the warmth of my reception'.[89] Webster's own account of Whitlock's arrival, written to the Secretary of State for Commonwealth Affairs, described that:

Upon Mr. Whitlock's arrival he proceeded to ignore all semblance of protocol by bluntly reading a statement disclosing that Mr. Tony Lee would be appointed as Commissioner of Anguilla pursuant to the authority of the West Indies Act of 1967. Whereupon he literally threw printed pamphlets at the assembled throng. This was a flagrant insult to members of Government who had come to do him honour. His departure from our Airport, along with his retinue, was without comment, or consideration for the events planned in his behalf.[90]

According to Westlake's account, Whitlock also declined Webster's offer of transport and dinner on the grounds of 'protocol'.[91] Added to these public insults, Webster claimed that Anguillians were incensed by the content of the pamphlet that Whitlock had distributed, comparing it to other British 'propaganda' which Lee had circulated.[92]

Having arrived at the house in Sandy Hill Bay, members of Whitlock's party consulted islanders about a public meeting to be held the following day. Then, at mid-afternoon, the tension rose rapidly. Webster's armed supporters, angered by Whitlock's perceived imperious arrival on the island, turned their attention to the British party. According to Webster, '[the] people were angry and extremely hostile. They clustered around me and demanded that Mr. Whitlock and his party be requested to leave the island immediately. The ground was strewn with shredded copies of the Minister's statement'.[93] Webster's supporters subsequently dismantled the British radio system at South Hill which, Webster later estimated, had been established 'probably to call in military personnel to invade the island, if necessary'.[94]

Whitlock's party was soon prevented from leaving the house at Sandy Hill Bay due to a roadblock erected by armed Anguillians.

According to his recollection, 'I was told to stay put until Webster had come to see me. This he did at 15.50 hrs [and] I protested emphatically about threat of armed force which had already been applied (Webster did not attempt to deny this)'.[95] Having complained about his own treatment at the airport, Webster then produced a counterproposal to the new British document reiterating, according to Whitlock, Anguilla's 'claim to be treated as an independent country'. Webster then stated that he could not guarantee the safety of the British party and advised them to leave the island immediately.[96]

As Webster departed the house, his supporters were assembling with guns on the heights overlooking the building and ultimatums were sent to Whitlock demanding that he leave. As each deadline passed, the British team became increasingly worried about the vulnerability of their position, but reluctant to be chased off the island by a mob. According to Westlake, the American owner of the house in which the team were besieged even carried off a secret note intended for the Senior Naval Officer West Indies in Antigua, pleading that the Royal Navy should reconnoitre Sandy Hill Bay as a show of force.[97] Deteriorating circumstances, however, prevented Whitlock from waiting for naval assistance. After ignoring two ultimatums, the house was visited by an Anguillian policeman. According to Whitlock, when he asked to speak to Webster again:

…the seargant [sic] shouted across to the hill top. The answer was four shots fired in our general direction. It was therefore clear to me that with approach of darkness an attack on the house could well take place and I had to consider the safety not only of members of the party but also of occupants of the house. We left for the airport accompanied by armed jeering supporters of Webster in cars and lorries, egged on by him in person.[98]

Whitlock's team subsequently boarded a charter plane at the airport and flew to Antigua. His sudden ejection from Anguilla on 11 March 1969 through force of arms proved a decisive turning point in the long drawn out saga of the Anguillian revolution. The British had felt justified in sending a Minister of the Crown to Anguilla due to London's surviving responsibility for the external affairs and defence of Anguilla under the West Indies Act 1967. Indeed, during Whitlock's discussion with Fisher and Chapman about his forthcoming trip, it had been argued that Bradshaw would have to tolerate the Whitlock visit to Anguilla on the basis of this jurisdiction.[99] Whitlock's subsequent ejection from the island, therefore, had notable constitutional implications under this legal context. When the Foreign Secretary had stated in mid-February that it seemed 'very unlikely that the forcible solution…will commend itself in present circumstances to ministers', he had added the caveat that '[the] problem might present itself in somewhat different guise if the Anguillans attempted to prevent us discharging our responsibility for external affairs and defence'.[100] Now, on 11 March, an obstruction of this sort had arguably occurred.

The drama of the Whitlock affair predictably dominated media headlines in the following days. The Times featured the headline 'Anguillans 'ruled by fear'' when covering Whitlock's comments to the press in Barbados before his return flight to London. According to the article, when Whitlock was asked about 'Mafia elements' on Anguilla, he responded that 'I have no doubt at all that this type of organization is on the island'.[101] This return to the narrative of Mafia influence was strengthened further the following day when The Times covered Whitlock's comments upon his arrival back in Britain. Under the headline 'Anguillans 'dominated by gangsters'', the article featured Whitlock's new comment that '[the] Anguillan people, who, I believe, are now completely dominated by a gangster element, will not be forgotten.'[102] Similarly covering Whitlock's comments, the *Daily Telegraph* titled their article 'Mafia Gangs 'Rule Island By Fear''.[103] The *Daily Mail*, meanwhile, declared that 'Island gunmen kick out Minister', whilst the *Daily Mirror*, in an article titled 'Why the bullets fly in paradise' declared dramatically that '[four] rifle shots echoed across the tiny West Indian island of Anguilla. They rang out a strong-arm challenge to the British Government.'[104] Furthermore, *The Guardian* described the incident as 'a serious setback to the [British government's] diplomatic initiative for ending the state of rebellion'.[105]

Decision-making in London about how to respond to the Whitlock affair and the Anguilla crisis more broadly now reached the highest levels of government. Michael Palliser – Harold Wilson's foreign affairs private secretary – noted that the Prime Minister had observed, upon hearing about the ejection, that a minister of the Crown had been subjected to 'considerable indignity'.[106] According to Wilson's Secretary of State for Employment, Barbara Castle, when the Labour Cabinet had been informed of Whitlock's ejection on 12 March the PM had been 'petrified that we should become a laughing stock'.[107] Wilson and his Labour Cabinet colleagues now had to decide upon whether to take military action to end Anguilla's rebellion. On 13 February Wilson's Cabinet Secretary, Sir Burke Trend, wrote to the PM that references to 'gangsters' in an FCO memorandum 'are apparently to be taken quite literally' and discussed with him the implications of a military operation. Trend noted that a Royal Navy frigate with marine contingent was available in the area for this purpose but also questioned both the cost of a military occupation and its proposed length.[108] According to Spencer Mawby, Denis Healey also received recommendations on the same day and wrote in his diary about an 'FO [Foreign Office] paper on force to return-clean up Mafia…No political objection whatever'.[109]

The first detailed discussion about a military intervention occurred in a meeting of the Defence and Oversea Policy Committee on 14 March. According to Mawby, the threat of mafia domination in Anguilla – a longstanding rumour which had apparently been confirmed by Whitlock's experience – proved a decisive factor in the eventual consensus favouring invasion.[110] The FCO had been the most decisively in favour of military action, with the Foreign Secretary arguing for it on the basis of removing 'gangster elements'.[111] The Solicitor General further justified invasion on the basis that Britain's legal responsibility for the defence and external policy of the Associated State had been infringed. As mentioned previously, Whitlock's visit was viewed as a manifestation of this legal jurisdiction and, accordingly, his ejection could be interpreted as an obstruction of Britain's purview. Whilst the MoD under Healey were, according to Mawby, 'more sceptical about the intelligence and worried about the practicalities of a military operation' and meeting attendees were 'alert to the potential absurdities' of invading Anguilla, the decision was nonetheless taken to proceed with it.[112]

The Anguilla crisis had therefore moved rather rapidly from the political stagnancy, but relative stability, of the Interim Agreement to the sudden deterioration of political conditions in the first two and a half months of 1969. On the one hand, the speed and nature of this deterioration, to the point whereby London decided to intervene militarily, is perhaps surprising. In January Anguilla had essentially returned to the same political position it had occupied a year previously: a situation of economic sanctions and international non-recognition that it had previously coped with fairly effectively, without the threat of imminent collapse. Meanwhile, British policymakers had remained committed to a diplomatic solution in

Barbara Castle, Britain's Secretary of State for Employment at the time of Operation Sheepskin. (National Archives of Malawi)

early 1969 and Bradshaw seemed no closer to achieving an invasion of Anguilla than he had in late 1967.

On the other hand, certain elements of the Anguilla crisis had indeed changed by 1969 and made the situation more volatile and unpredictable. The most significant was, perhaps, the more noticeable presence of Webster's American colleagues who appeared to the British to be gaining a troubling level of influence over Anguillian politics after Lee's departure. Regardless of these individuals' true backgrounds, intentions and degree of sway over Webster, Whitehall appeared to take the rumour of a gangster takeover increasingly seriously. A second difference was the growing division within the Anguillian leadership between those in favour of pursuing links with Britain and those wanting total independence. With Webster appearing to favour the latter course and holding a referendum that led to a more complete UDI, the British may have felt that events were spiralling out of their control. Certainly, discussions amongst British diplomats about the possibility of invasion increased in February following UDI and simultaneous demands by Commonwealth Caribbean Heads of Government that Britain uphold the Associated State's territorial integrity.

Indeed, the much-discussed communique from the Trinidad conference may have been an additional ingredient that increased the likelihood of British military intervention. London had been reluctant to act militarily throughout the Anguilla crisis without regional Commonwealth cooperation. The earlier failure of the Caribbean peacekeeping team to materialise from the Barbados agreement of 1967 had been a significant blow to British diplomatic initiatives. Now, following the conference communique's release, diplomats pondered British military action seriously for the first time since Barbados. Despite mixed signals about how far the communique constituted an endorsement of invasion, the British would use the phrasing of the document in their subsequent justifications for their intervention.

The final catalyst that led to invasion was the Whitlock affair. The seemingly clumsy or arrogant handling of Webster and his followers by Whitlock's party – depending on which accounts are followed – appeared to make a fragile situation explosive. Regardless of how the provocation occurred, the subsequent ejection of Whitlock again offered new justifications for military action. Firstly, the violent treatment experienced by the British party appeared to confirm British fears and rumours of a gangster takeover in Anguilla which had been increasingly circulating in the weeks prior to 11 March. Secondly, the incident constituted an act of aggression against a

British minister upholding Britain's legal duties. Prior to this point, most Anguillian resistance had been aimed at symbols of Basseterre's authority. Once news of the Whitlock affair reached Whitehall,

discussions about invasion occurred very quickly, suggesting its importance for finally spurring the British government into action.

4
PLANNING A MILITARY INTERVENTION

The Wilson government's decision to intervene militarily in Anguilla in March 1969 was rather at odds with the priorities of British defence policy in the late Sixties. At a time when British forces were withdrawing from their commitments 'East of Suez' following the Healey defence cuts of 1968, thus reorienting Britain's military focus towards Eurocentric NATO defence responsibilities, the Anguillian operation seemed to constitute a return to the recent imperial past of gunboat diplomacy. For over 20 years since the end of the Second World War, successive governments had sustained Britain's ability to launch military interventions across the globe and thus maintain the façade of great power status. This had led to mixed results in the operations launched in Jordan (1958), Kuwait (1961) and East Africa (1964), particularly as the resources allocated to Britain's global power projection became increasingly limited. Hence, Labour's decision to confront Britain's economic reality in 1968 and end its global role should arguably have marked a decisive break with the past. However, alongside its peculiar political situation of seeking to end a postcolonial settlement in favour of a possible return to colonial rule, the Anguilla crisis swam against the tide of history in a military, as well as a political, sense.

British Defence Policy post-1968
The Healey defence reforms of 1968 were not the first occasion upon which Whitehall had attempted to confront Britain's diminished resources and increasingly limited ability to project military power. Defence reforms between 1957 and 1962 under the Macmillan government had attempted to cut expenditure whilst maintaining Britain's global reach. Whitehall would rely increasingly on amphibious warfare capabilities to project British power in the absence of overseas bases and amid shrinking Army manpower, leading Ian Speller to describe this period as a 'renaissance' in the development of amphibious capabilities.[1] Moreover, instead of maintaining large overseas military establishments, a limited number of smaller British garrisons would be retained – including forces in the Caribbean – alongside larger local forces such as the West Indies Regiment which was revived in 1959. A UK-based 'Strategic Reserve' of infantry, airborne forces, artillery and armour would be maintained in readiness to deploy globally when required. The 1962 revisions, moreover, reduced theatre reserves around the world, with Whitehall relying increasingly on a UK-based airmobile central reserve of up to a brigade group to deploy to trouble spots and support forces at the remaining military bases such as Hong Kong.[2] Labour's subsequent Defence Review of February 1966 continued this process of upholding global ambitions whilst cutting costs. It announced that the garrison in British Guiana would be withdrawn, a goal that was completed the same year leaving the British Honduras garrison as the last substantial British infantry force left in the Anglophone Caribbean area. According to the review, '[protection] for island territories in the Atlantic…can readily be provided from our major areas of deployment', perhaps indicating that, depending

on the crisis, troops from British Honduras, amphibious forces or the Strategic Reserve in the UK could be deployed.[3]

The Defence Review of 1968 marked a notable departure from the general policy of dwindling resources combined with continued global military commitments. British forces had withdrawn from the major Middle Eastern base at Aden in November of the previous year amid a Sterling Crisis that damaged the British economy. Harold Wilson announced in January 1968 that British forces would withdraw from most remaining bases East of Suez by the end of 1971.[4] The British Army would be considerably reduced in strength from 211,000 service personnel to 173,000 in 1973 and defence policy would be decisively realigned towards European commitments.[5] Departing from the former Strategic Reserve, a new Army Strategic Command (ASC) came into operation in April 1968 intended to deploy a brigade group in the event of national emergency and another brigade for internal security duties. However, as David French has noted, the Wilson government had abandoned the idea of using this organisation to mount significant overseas military operations outside of Europe.[6] Apart from the Royal Marine detachments of the two frigates under SNOWI's command, amounting to under 50 men in total, and any Royal Navy seamen's detachments available, the only force capable of action in the Caribbean was the British Honduras garrison of 250 troops.

Despite these limited resources and the decisive realignment of British defence priorities, the Wilson government had demonstrated a continued willingness to project limited military power in pursuit of its remaining responsibilities in the Caribbean following the defence review. In March 1968 rioting broke out in St Johns, the capital of the Associated State of Antigua and Barbuda, after a dispute between two unions supported in turn by the Government and Opposition. The Antigua Workers Union called for a general strike and the Governor, Sir Wilfred Jacobs, responded by declaring a state of emergency on 18 March. Subsequently, two days later the police and defence force used tear gas in an attempt to disperse the strikers. However, these demonstrators regrouped and attacked the police with bottles, stones and sticks leading the latter to open fire on the strikers and injure several people.[7] A curfew was subsequently imposed on the capital. British diplomat Desmond Kerr was nevertheless dispatched to Antigua to assess the emergency and reported, according to a colleague, a 'serious deterioration' in the situation following an incendiary public meeting on 21 March after which a shop was burnt down. According to the message received by the Commonwealth Office:

> [Premier Vere Bird] believes further incendiaries and rioting probable and doubts whether police and Defence Force could then any longer control situation. He had accordingly asked for immediate presence of British ship or troops. Kerr agrees with Bird's assessment and supports the request. He believes British

military presence would have essential steadying effect and that without it there may be very serious trouble.[8]

The speed with which the British military acted is confirmed by a message from Air Vice Marshal Peter Le Cheminant to the Prime Minister on the same day stating that '[a] British frigate has been ordered to the area'.[9] Whilst this episode clearly did not constitute a major military intervention and, accordingly, a departure from the new Eurocentric focus of defence policy, it did demonstrate Whitehall's continued willingness to use military strength to uphold Britain's residual security responsibilities in the Caribbean. The military operation planned for Anguilla in March 1969 was, however, on a considerably larger scale to any action in the Anglophone Caribbean since the intervention in British Guiana in 1953, requiring the participation of a Spearhead Battalion from the new ASC and several other British Army units, along with the Royal Navy, RAF and Metropolitan Police.

As the first action to be mounted by the ASC under the 1968 reforms, it remained to be seen whether 'Operation Sheepskin' – as the invasion of Anguilla was to be codenamed – would suffer from similar drawbacks to the interventions mounted through the late 1950s and 1960s under the Strategic Reserve mechanism. As French has noted in relation to Jordan, Kuwait and East Africa, British interventions in the post-Suez era suffered from a range of common problems that hindered the effectiveness of each operation. Firstly, the Strategic Reserve had often been under-resourced, meaning that there were limited troops and equipment available to dispatch to trouble spots at short notice.[10] Secondly, the airlifting of troops and equipment proved complicated and often ineffective due to the limited air routes available to the RAF and its need to refuel.[11] Thirdly, linked to the airlift issue, political constraints had an increasing impact on British military interventions as Whitehall acknowledged the potential international opposition to gunboat diplomacy and, accordingly, placed military operations under intensified political control from London.[12] As shall be demonstrated, Operation Sheepskin underlined that these restraints – resourcing, transport and political repercussions – along with a range of other planning issues, continued to hinder Britain's projection of military power following the landmark policy changes of 1968.

Military planning

After the decision was made in the Defence and Oversea Policy Committee on 14 March to go ahead with a military intervention in Anguilla, the Defence Operations Executive met the same day to discuss initial operational planning. As the report of Assistant Chief of the Defence Staff for Operations Major General Tony Deane-Drummond stated, the Executive were informed that the previous meeting had agreed that 'detailed planning for the operation would have to be carried out in the Caribbean, but that the political aim would have to be clarified in Whitehall'. The Executive then progressed to discuss the size of the military forces required for the operation, including 'whether there should be reinforcement of forces available to SNOWI from the United Kingdom' and the providing of 'a heavy drop capacity for the communications vehicles of the force'. The Assistant Chief of the Air Staff for Operations also raised that he would conduct two studies about whether the airlift should be conducted using a combination of RAF Vickers VC.10s and Hercules C-130s aircraft or just the latter. The timescales for undertaking the operation were also considered, with the meeting being reminded that the Spearhead Battalion was on 24 hours' notice and a 48-hour deployment timeframe. In addition to this,

The RAF Lockheed Hercules C.Mk 1. Alongside the Andover and RAF Vickers VC.10, the Hercules would be used for transportation during Operation Sheepskin. (Albert Grandolini collection)

'[the] timetable for the operation would be influenced by SNOWI's plan, the availability of police and clarification of the legal status of the intervention force.' Indeed, the importance of political considerations in this operation was recognised not only in concerns about its legality, but also in worries about the 'political problem over staging troops through Antigua [en route to Anguilla]. The Prime Minister of Antigua may raise objections, although this is thought to be unlikely.'[13] This meeting of senior military planners, therefore, revealed once again how far a British military intervention in the post-Suez era was influenced by potential political repercussions.

The following day Lt. Colonel Richard W. Dawnay, commanding officer of 2nd Battalion The Parachute Regiment (2PARA), and his Intelligence Officer were summoned to the MoD. His battalion had become the Strategic Command Spearhead Unit on 26 February 1969 responsible for 'Worldwide' Spearhead duties.[14] The Parachute Regiment had been somewhat despondent about recent developments under Labour's defence reforms. As its regimental record noted:

…a Socialist government committed to a British withdrawal from 'east of Suez' decided that even one whole brigade of parachutists was an unnecessary burden on the tax-payer. There were many who wanted to see the 16th Para Bde., and even The Parachute Regiment itself, completely disbanded; but even under that government the movement to kill off Airborne Forces was not strong enough. Instead, it was decided in 1968 that only two battalions should remain in the airborne role at any time, the third being released for overseas garrison duty; Brigade HQ and the Logistics Regt would remain in being – but notice had been served that the paras were expendable.[15]

A fleet of RAF Hawker Siddeley Andover C.Mk 1s of No. 46 Squadron. This aircraft was one of the main workhorses of RAF logistical supply during Operation Sheepskin. (Albert Grandolini collection)

During the 1960s companies of 2PARA had served in the Kuwait intervention, Aden Emergency and Indonesian Confrontation among other tours. With opportunities for theatre deployments like these diminishing considerably by 1969, however, the Paras could have expected relative inactivity for the foreseeable future. As Dawnay recollected about his battalion's assuming spearhead duties, '[from] our intelligence briefings everything seemed quiet'.[16] Described by one soldier as 'a quiet man but…always in the thick of things, never a dull moment on his crew', Dawnay had been commissioned as an officer in 1950 and moved to the Paras in 1958.[17] Having been Officer Commanding D Company 1PARA, he had then assumed overall command of 2PARA in 1968.[18]

After his briefing at the MoD on 15 March, Dawnay had been ordered to proceed to Antigua to liaise with SNOWI, Tony Lee and others in drawing up the military plan for Operation Sheepskin. He flew out from London the same day, along with his Intelligence Officer and one of HM Inspectors of Constabulary representing the Metropolitan Police, who would constitute an important element of the invasion force. SNOWI – now Commodore Martin N. Lucey – had been ordered from his headquarters at Bermuda to Antigua on 14 March where he boarded HMS *Minerva* and met with Lee, Dawnay, the Military Liaison Intelligence Officer, the St Lucia British Government Representative, the HM Inspector of Constabulary and a Foreign Office Legal Advisor.[19] Lucey was an experienced officer, having served in the Royal Navy since 1938 and received the Distinguished Service Cross in 1944. He had recently commanded the 7th Frigate Squadron before becoming SNOWI in 1968, a role through which he assumed overall command of Operation Sheepskin.

The intelligence available to the planners aboard *Minerva* about Anguilla's current political situation, the threat posed by its defence force and the extent of their armaments was very limited. As Lt. Colonel Dawnay recalled, 'it was clear that due to the hiatus of the previous 18 months there was little known on the intelligence side. Such information as we were given was, as we discovered later, highly subjective and the events of the previous Tuesday were much in

people's minds'.[20] Dawnay was referring here to the Whitlock incident of Tuesday 11 March, thus suggesting that intelligence discussions about the level of resistance to be anticipated from the Anguillians was influenced by the Minister's treatment. The lack of available intelligence was also partly symptomatic of wider British security weaknesses in the Associated States. Intelligence gathering was poor in regions such as the Leeward Islands, with island police forces under-resourced and British aid procedures restricting London from remedying this policing issue.[21] SNOWI noted in his post-operation analysis that an opportunity was missed to insert a Special Branch Officer into Anguilla in the days leading up to the military operation.[22] As Lucey elaborated:

The island was swarming with newsmen and photographers who would have provided excellent cover for him. Had this been done, we would have known in advance of the non-hostile attitude which was taken to the arrival of troops, and some early information might have been available on the disposal of weapons. Thus our arrival might have been made in an entirely different way and our search for weapons made easier.[23]

This intelligence weakness therefore had a major bearing on Operation Sheepskin. This was particularly the case regarding the armed opposition that the British military had to plan to overcome. Dawnay recalled that '[such] was the lack of intelligence that a tactical appreciation became worthless and we finally had to plan on a worse case of being opposed in our landing by up to 200 men armed with an assortment of weapons, including an anti-tank gun (later found to be a Boyes Gun in perfect condition)'.[24] The boasts of Webster in the media about the firepower available to his Defence Force and his willingness to resist an invasion may also have played a part in military calculations. In an interview with the *Daily Telegraph* published on 14 March, he threatened Britain with 'a little Vietnam' if it invaded to remove his government.[25] Webster was also reported elsewhere to have claimed that if Britain intervened militarily, it would be 'the beginning of the First West Indies War', boasting that his Defence Force had 'plenty of modern stuff' in its arsenal.[26] Once again using exaggerated claims about his military resources, as he had done previously in an effort to deter the earlier threat of invasion, Webster may have unintentionally increased the disproportionate response made by Britain.

The scale of potential Anguillian hostility to the invasion force was therefore difficult for the British to predict. A draft operational plan of 16 March highlighted that local intelligence reports 'while broadly confirming earlier appreciations, indicate that feeling in Anguilla has in fact hardened against Britain, because Webster has effectively represented our "package proposals" as a sell-out to

St. Kitts'. Consequently, the plan continued, '[it] is expected that a landing will be resisted by those previously regarded as holding neutral views as well as by the extremists'.[27] Hindsight would, of course, prove that the Anguillians would not contest the British landings and that Webster's Defence Force was not as sizeable or well-equipped as feared. As mentioned previously, a report of July 1969 by Detective Inspector Williams assessed that a maximum of 46 people was all that ever mustered in the Defence Force and 'volunteers' across 1967 to 1969 and that Webster could only have called upon around 25 Defence Force members to defend Anguilla at any one time. Moreover, Williams noted that Defence Force members patrolled 'in the main with worn out, unserviceable weapons' and concluded that this force was 'poorly led, ill-equipped and could provide nothing more than political support for Webster and a basis for propaganda'.[28] As Lt. Colonel Dawnay stated, however, limited British intelligence about Anguilla's defences meant that operational planners had to factor in a potentially well-armed force of up to 200 people.

Limited intelligence availability also affected British planning for Psychological Operations (Psyops) in Anguilla. As one of Operation Sheepskin's primary goals was to install a civil administration on the island, the invasion force needed the ability to communicate effectively its intentions to civilians and to counter hostile propaganda coming from opponents. A report of July 1969 noted that '[the] effectiveness of a psyops plan is largely dependent on up to date and comprehensive intelligence'.[29] However, as Lt. Colonel B.R. Johnston – responsible for psyops support in the operation – stated, 'For [Anguilla], information in the United Kingdom was lacking on broadcasting and listening habits, printing press facilities and on printed matter generally. Knowledge of all of these would have helped to formulate the outline of a psyops plan in advance'.[30] Ultimately, therefore, the lack of intelligence meant that the invasion force went in without knowledge of how to communicate with Anguillians effectively.

Moreover, the psyops effort would be notably under-resourced. It was recognised that the services of an entire psyops team was required for Operation Sheepskin and yet Johnston was the only resource available. This meant that, according to SNOWI, '[one] Lieutenant Colonel only was sent, who tried his best to do the work of six, but nevertheless the lack of this Team seriously affected the prosecution of the operation'.[31] Indeed, the only fully constituted team of this nature was stationed in Hong Kong at the time of the intervention. The 'accepted policy' on raising psyops teams prior to Sheepskin, as outlined in Johnston's post-operation report, seemed inappropriate for a military intervention like Anguilla, which was planned and implemented quickly and relied on winning the hearts and minds of the population:

...the psyops staff officer should first make an "on-the-spot" assessment of the psyops situation and then make his recommendations for psyops support to the Ministry of Defence...The psyops unit is "shadow posted" and has to be called up, organised and equipped. It is not trained in psyops techniques and equipment and the personnel are changed every six months.[32]

Even these limited resources were, therefore, unavailable to Johnston. Furthermore, his efforts were further constrained by a lack of contact with FCO personnel which would have ensured that military psyops in Anguilla mirrored Britain's political messaging in the outside world. A report later examined by the Chiefs of Staff stated the need for:

... detailed psyops planning between the political and military sides, both in the preparation and execution of psychological operations. We consider that there is a need for a carefully prepared propaganda effort conducted by the FCO in consultation with MOD directed at outside opinion to back up the psyops effort directed at the territory concerned.[33]

However, it was reported that 'the political officers involved in [Sheepskin] were unable for various reasons to provide the assistance required'.[34] Ultimately, therefore, intelligence availability had a significant impact on the planning of psyops in Anguilla, but subsequent implementation of these efforts was also hampered by significant under-resourcing. Nevertheless, British psyops plans needed to meet three objectives. Firstly, they needed to counter the hostile propaganda disseminated by Webster's government since the Whitlock affair. Secondly, they needed to justify the military intervention and explain Britain's intentions for Anguilla. Finally, they needed to anticipate Webster's public response to the invasion and implement a counterpropaganda operation.[35]

Strategic planning for the insertion of troops on to the island was notably complicated by political calculations, somewhat mirroring the growing importance of this factor in British interventions across the 1960s as a whole. The task force would fly via RAF Hercules and VC.10 transport planes to Antigua, where troops would board HMS *Minerva* and *Rothesay*, the latter having arrived at Antigua from Trinidad on 16 March. According to Peter Harclerode, a historian of the Parachute Regiment, it was decided that the force would attack from the sea, rather than from the air, due to the British government's political need to keep the operation as low-key as possible.[36] A.C. Watson of the FCO Caribbean Department observed that Operation Sheepskin could be 'described as an interesting example of what needs to be done in the very difficult half-way house between normal military assault, and the introduction of military force with the agreement and assistance of the local authorities'. One implication of this politically sensitive dynamic was, accordingly, that the British had 'the task of introducing a small force in circumstances where it would be politically unacceptable to provide covering fire'.[37] Indeed, political caution was such that the landings would be made from Royal Navy frigates to the Anguillian beaches using boats and dinghies without covering fire or air support. SNOWI subsequently highlighted the 'danger to which the troops were exposed landing in unprotected boats against a threat of small arms opposition' as a chief problem in planning and executing Operation Sheepskin's amphibious assault.[38]

Regarding the size of force allocated to Sheepskin, SNOWI later stated that an operation of this nature possessed 'two clearly sensible military courses'. The first option consisted of a 'surprise landing by a small force able to respond quickly', whilst the second option involved a 'more effective, if slower, response by a balanced military force, prepared to meet and deal with resistance'. SNOWI conceded that the first solution was less likely to have occurred 'because of delays built in by political considerations'.[39] These considerations may, perhaps, have included establishing a legal justification for the operation, consulting with allied nations as to Britain's intentions, preparing Britain's response to international and media criticism and, furthermore, the planning required to ensure a swift transfer of control over Anguilla to civilian administration. The second solution, according to SNOWI, 'needed assault craft or helicopters, with fire support from HM Ships'. However, as covering fire was deemed politically unacceptable and neither a Landing Platform Helicopter (LPH) or Landing Platform Docks (LPD)

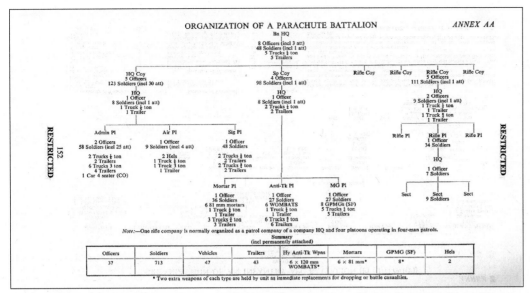

The official war establishment of an 'in role' parachute battalion according to the 1968 edition of *Notes on the British Army*. The heavier weapons in the Support Company would not have been appropriate for an operation such as Sheepskin, however the personnel would have been available to the commanding officer for other roles as needed. As noted, one of the rifle companies would usually be task organised to form a patrols company, a change that would later be formalised. (Private collection)

Navy and Royal Army Medical Corps (RAMC) and members of 14 Regiment Royal Signals Detachment.

Most importantly, however, the task force was accompanied by a Metropolitan Police contingent of 40 members of Scotland Yard's Special Patrol Group (SPG) under the command of Assistant Commissioner Andrew Way. Way, an experienced police officer with 35-years' service, was an imposing figure who, according to Westlake, 'had originally been an officer in the mounted police, but as his weight had risen above three hundred pounds it was thought best he not ride horses anymore'.[42] In 1961 he had been seconded to the Montreal Police to assist with their reorganisation and, according to the *Daily Mirror*, had helped to tackle a white slave gang in Canada during the same year before going on to become responsible for London traffic until 1968.[43] Now he would command the new Anguilla Police Unit (APU), initially composed of men from the SPG, who would become the main instrument for establishing and upholding British rule once the military had initially secured the island. The RAF would also play a significant role in Sheepskin, responsible for the vital job of transporting personnel and supplies to Anguilla following the initial invasion using RAF Hawker Siddeley Andover C.Mk 1s and Hercules transport planes. However, according to a report later examined by the Chiefs of Staff, 'In [Sheepskin] the RAF member [Air Support Liaison Officer] asked for arrived after the rest of the reconnaissance team and became the Airhead Commander. He remained in Antigua and was not available to act as air advisor to SNOWI who was in Anguilla.'[44]

were available to accommodate the necessary vehicles, this second and larger response was also not possible. Ultimately, therefore, SNOWI concluded that the solution adopted by military planners fell 'between the two ideal solutions'.[40]

The initial amphibious assault would be carried out by a rifle company, patrol company and tactical HQ of 2PARA, amounting to a strength of 150 troops. They would be followed later by a second rifle company and an assortment of support personnel.[41] The Paras would be accompanied in their initial landings by a platoon of Royal Marines and the seamen's platoon of HMS *Minerva*, whilst the seamen's platoon of HMS *Rothesay* would remain on ship as a reserve. Apart from these teeth units intended for the initial assault, the British force would also consist of several tail units who would support the infantry and assist in winning hearts and minds once the island was secured. These included the Field Surgical Team of 23 Parachute Field Ambulance (RAMC), medical officers of the Royal

SNOWI and his planning team in Antigua sent draft proposals to the Chiefs of Staff for approval on 16 March, which were then submitted to Defence Secretary Healey and Foreign Secretary Stewart that evening. To prepare him for an executive decision the following day, an "under the counter' copy' was also smuggled to Prime Minister Harold Wilson that evening.[45] The document identified that the immediate British objective was to establish Her Majesty's Commissioner, Tony Lee, as the source of renewed law and order on Anguilla and, correspondingly, there was a need to 'disarm and displace the small group of armed men

The RAF Hawker Siddeley Andover C.Mk 1. As this photo demonstrates, this aircraft had a kneeling landing gear for easing loading and unloading. (Albert Grandolini collection)

who are now intimidating the island'. The longer-term objective was 'to facilitate a lasting solution of the Anguillan problem on lines acceptable to its inhabitants'.[46] Recognising the need for Britain to also retain the support of Basseterre, however, the document noted that 'as long as the present arrangements governing Associated Statehood exist it will be necessary for any lasting solution to be acceptable to the State Government'.[47]

The military strategy for occupying the island involved the deployment of a Para company and Royal Marine platoon from the two frigates using Gemini dinghies, ships' boats and Royal Navy Westland Wasp helicopters at first light on 19 March. Geographically and infrastructurally, Anguilla may have presented a relatively simple target for planners assessing how to occupy the island most effectively. A generally flat and low-lying platform of limestone, Anguilla's landmass covers only 35 square miles and, in the 1960s, possessed little vegetation other than low bush and scrub.[48] The number of key landmarks which the British needed to seize was also limited. In roughly the centre of the island lay Anguilla's largest settlement, The Valley, in which most administrative buildings were located and from where British military and police operations would be directed after the initial occupation. More strategically important upon first arrival were the island's crossroads in the middle of the island, their priority being reflected in the allocation of two Wasp helicopters to land a Para platoon to seize them. As these Wasps, according to a post-operation report, 'required some light for landing troops in safety, dawn nautical twilight was established as the best time for the assault'.[49] These Paras would have to hold the crossroads – important sites for communication and transport – until another platoon, landing by sea at Crocus Bay to the west, was able to link up with them.

The main military landings would take place at Crocus Bay on the north-central coast and at Road Bay situated slightly further down the coastline. As the troops would be landing in unprotected boats and therefore exposed to potential small arms fire, it was decided to reduce risks by launching the amphibious assault in darkness. This darkness, in turn, affected the landing sites available to the military planners as 'risks could not be taken with landing places, however attractive, that had unmarked coral reefs off them'. The choice of landing site was additionally impacted by the need, until Anguilla's airfield was seized and troops and supplies landed by air, to secure a jetty through which this support could be initially funnelled. Road Bay possessed 'the only possible landing place with a jetty…[but] was three miles from the important crossroads' in the centre of the island.[50] This made the site less useful in a plan depending upon rapid reinforcement from the coast of the heliborne troops who had seized the crossroads inland. Consequently, a Para platoon would attack Crocus Bay and advance towards the more closely situated crossroads. Meanwhile, a platoon of Royal Marines would attack Road Bay and secure the jetty before another Para platoon passed through their position to seize the airfield to the south of The Valley. Once secured, the airfield could then be used by RAF Andover planes to reinforce and supply the occupation force.

Once the British military had seized these strategic points and secured the island, Her Majesty's new Commissioner – who would be sworn in with special powers prior to the military assault – would 'land as soon as practicable'.[51] This Commissioner, Tony Lee, would be tasked by a government directive with establishing 'effective control over the whole Island as quickly as possible' and to govern according to 'the existing laws of the Associated State'. In order to do this, Lee was 'authorised by the Order in Council (except as otherwise specifically provided) to discharge in Anguilla the functions vested

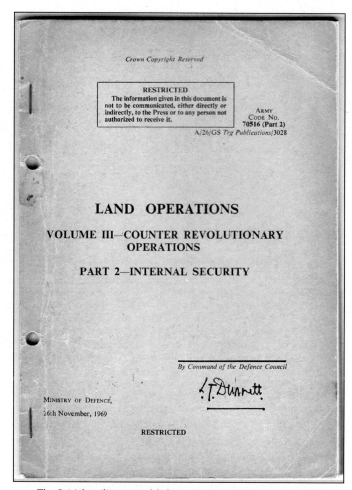

The British military establishment maintained an extensive body of manuals detailing procedures for dealing with a wide range of circumstances. Published shortly after the events of Operation Sheepskin, this particular volume of *Land Operations* deals with internal security matters, the focus was firmly upon more hostile environments such as had been encountered in Cyprus, Borneo or Aden but included action in support of the civil power. (Private collection)

in the Governor, the Cabinet and Ministers of the Associated State'.[52] If Lee encountered Anguillian resistance to his administration, he was assured that 'such assistance as may be required will be provided to you by the Force Commander in accordance with the orders issued to him by the Chiefs of the Defence Staff'.[53]

Force Anguilla – as the British military occupation force became known – would be 'operating in aid of the civil powers' and their ability to respond to provocation would be restricted by the need to operate under English Common Law by which, according to a draft plan, 'a member of the armed forces is, like any other citizen, under a duty to come to the aid of the civil power where the civil power requires his assistance to enforce law and order'.[54] Accordingly, SNOWI was instructed by the Chiefs of the Defence Staff that, in the British soldier's interaction with the Anguillian population, 'Minimum force should be used at all times'.[55] Restrictions upon soldiers would include reliance upon CS Riot Control Gas to disperse opponents, rather than reliance on the 7.62mm rounds of the British infantry L1A1 Self-Loading Rifle. Alongside contributing to riot control, Force Anguilla would support the civil power by assisting 'in the collection of any illegal arms and ammunition', such as the weapons seized from the Kittitian police in 1967 and also, operational planning noted, 'it may be necessary for the [British] forces…to apprehend certain persons and to search certain premises'.[56] Force Anguilla would, therefore, be involved in the interrogation of individuals about the location of weapons and in the detaining of those US citizens and Anguillians considered militant troublemakers.[57]

Ultimately, however, following the initial assault planned for 19 March, the British military would assume a secondary supporting role to the APU under Assistant Commissioner Way. As instructions to Lee stated, '[the] Commander of the police contingent will be responsible to you for the maintenance of public security in the island and he will look to you for general guidance in this regard. The operational control of the contingent will, however, be in his hands.'[58] The APU would accordingly be at the forefront of public relations, riot control and investigations on the island. Whilst the armoury of their military colleagues was to be somewhat restricted, the degree to which the APU would be responsible for undertaking the main security role was perhaps reflected in their being issued with semi-automatic pistols taken from Special Branch and SPG arsenals.[59]

Members of the MoD's Defence Operations Executive reviewed and endorsed the military plan drawn up by SNOWI's planning team on the afternoon of Sunday 16 March and it was presented to Prime Minister Wilson and relevant Cabinet colleagues the following morning. With the plan therefore given executive approval on 17 March, the Defence Operations Executive were then informed of the decisions made at the ministerial meeting. As summarised by the Assistant Chief of the Defence Staff for Operations, it was decided that Operation Sheepskin would take place on the morning of Wednesday 19 March and aim to achieve 'Tactical surprise' against opponents. Nevertheless, it was made clear that 'Mr Webster was not to be harmed' and that Anguillians needed to be reassured that 'our intentions are entirely friendly'.[60] The Executive then discussed outstanding planning issues, confirming that a second company of 2PARA would be flown into Anguilla one day after the initial landings and that two RAF Hercules would be rigged to drop communications vehicles on the island.[61]

Political and legal planning

The Defence Operations Executive's attention was also inevitably drawn to the political considerations of an operation which was proving distinctly political in nature. Regarding the need to ensure that Anguillians were made aware of Britain's peaceful intentions, the Executive were informed that the FCO would be hosting a meeting in the afternoon of 17 March to discuss public relations and political problems. The Executive also noted that Operation Sheepskin was already making a public impact in Britain as '[the] operation had already leaked to the press and the arguments between keeping silent and making a public announcement were finely balanced.' Despite the temptation for the British government to begin justifying its plans to the public, however, the meeting acknowledged that it was 'essential to preserve tactical security, to avoid unnecessary casualties' during the initial military operation.[62]

Whitehall did, however, need to plan its legal and political justifications for Operation Sheepskin in order to defend against potential media or international criticism. An FCO message to certain British Missions around the world stated that '[our] intervention [in Anguilla] follows from our responsibilities, under Section 7 (2) of the West Indies Act 1967, for the external affairs and defence of the Associated State whose interests and territorial integrity have been violated by illegal acts and the intrusion of foreign elements.'[63] An Order in Council was made under the Act on 18 March to invest the British Commissioner with his powers to govern Anguilla. Nevertheless, British planners could not disregard the possibility that the legality of this Order would be contested, a draft plan noting that:

> The question whether the Order would be a valid exercise of the power contained in S. 7(2) has been considered by the Law Officers. They do not advise against making the Order, but say that the possibility of its being successfully challenged in the courts cannot be ruled out.[64]

The Law Officers also considered whether British actions would contravene the UK's responsibilities under the United Nations Charter and a consensus emerged amongst the planners that it would not.[65] This did not mean, however, that the UK would escape criticism for its actions from the UN and, accordingly, planners had to consider Britain's potential response. Whilst it was acknowledged in the draft plan that there 'has so far been no Anguilla lobby at the U.N.', it nevertheless acknowledged that 'it is possible that our more vociferous critics would not resist the temptation to seize this opportunity to castigate us for a "colonialist" act'.[66] Indeed, it was predicted that comparison might be made between Britain's willingness to use military force in Anguilla but reluctance to do so in Rhodesia. This referred to an illegal UDI against Britain made by the white settler regime of Prime Minister Ian Smith in November 1965. Despite calls for the Wilson government to suppress the rebellion militarily, after some deliberation London opted to instead implement rather ineffectual sanctions. Now, a few years later, Wilson's government appeared willing to quickly suppress black Anguillians who had illegally declared independence, whilst allowing the rebellion of Britain's white Rhodesian 'kith and kin' to go unchecked.[67]

The level of UN resistance to Operation Sheepskin was predicted largely to 'depend on the amount of force we may have to use in the operation'. Accordingly, a bloodless restoration of law and order 'would be unlikely to attract more than transient interest', whilst a bloody confrontation was considered more likely to gain the criticism of the Committee of 24. Depending on the outcome of the military operation, therefore, the draft plan stated that British diplomats should be prepared 'to explain our position both in the corridors and in a brief statement in the Committee of 24, but refuse to participate in any discussion of the matter'. Ultimately, the plan concluded, Britain's defence of its actions at the UN should focus on its responsibility to uphold the territorial integrity of the Associated State 'which has been violated by illegal acts and by the intrusion of foreign elements'.[68]

Alongside preparing a legal and political defence for Operation Sheepskin, the British needed to ensure that allies with a stake in the region were informed of London's intentions. Indeed, the wider objectives of the draft plan asserted the need 'to restore confidence among Caribbean Governments in our willingness and ability to carry out our responsibilities in relation to the Associated States' and to 'reassure the United States who are greatly concerned that there should be stability in the Caribbean and regard us as primarily responsible for ensuring this as regards the Associated States'.[69] Accordingly, on 17 March the Foreign Secretary messaged the British Embassy in Washington DC requesting that they explain Britain's justifications for the military action to the US State Department 'in strict secrecy'. He wanted it emphasised to the Americans that the British 'are convinced the action contemplated will be an important and necessary contribution to stability in the Caribbean, which is increasingly prejudiced by the present illegal situation in Anguilla'.[70] Stewart then concluded that the British 'hoped the Americans will sympathise with this aim and will give us public and diplomatic support in the United Nations and elsewhere'.[71]

Whilst the Canadians were also informed of Operation Sheepskin on 17 March alongside the Americans, the timetable for alerting other allies and regional states perhaps revealed their level of importance in British planning or, alternatively, London's possible desire to keep certain governments in the dark until the last minute. The Governors and Administrators of Bermuda, Bahamas, St Vincent and the British Virgin Islands would be informed 24 hours before the intervention, although they would have to wait until one hour before the operation to inform their elected governments. The Netherlands government, who held colonial responsibility for the nearby islands of Saba and St Eustatius alongside half of St Maarten (the closest island neighbour to Anguilla), would be told 12 hours prior to the operation, along with the Bradshaw government on St Kitts and the Antiguan government. Curiously, the French government – who governed the other half of nearby St Maarten and also St Barts – would be informed only one hour before the intervention, alongside Anglophone governments such as Jamaica, Trinidad-Tobago and Guyana.[72]

Collectively, by Monday 17 March most detailed planning was complete, the executive decision to proceed with Operation Sheepskin had been taken and elements of the task force were on the move. Faith in the military intervention had not always been unanimous and unwavering during the planning phase. In what may have been a notable crisis in confidence about the use of military force under current circumstances, Tony Lee – soon to be Her Majesty's Commissioner in Anguilla responsible for the island's governance – wrote to the FCO on 16 March expressing doubts about the operation before then making a quick about-turn. In his concise first message he wrote that the intervention:

> … will be resisted with force and casualties inevitable. In my view absurd to contemplate this certainty (with all its other attendant evil results) especially when seen against background of vindictive policy on the part of St. Kitts Government with regard to Anguilla over recent years. Our objective is to achieve some sort of long term stability in Anguilla and effects of use of force now may be to postpone this indefinitely.[73]

Lee, therefore, seemed to argue that bloodshed was certain if the currently scheduled military intervention occurred and that British policymakers needed to view Operation Sheepskin within the wider historical timeline of injustice towards Anguilla, perhaps suggesting that islanders would view British forces as part of the same long-term oppressive threat. He consequently advised that the 'dire results' of the military intervention currently planned should be avoided by pursuing a diplomatic solution whereby Bradshaw's government would relinquish control of Anguilla for a period of five years with a possibility of a further extension to this agreement.[74] The same day as he sent this assessment, however, Lee again messaged the FCO with a revised analysis that suggested that he had reflected further upon his previous advice:

> I agree that we should go ahead. In any event the operation is required. If the line expressed in my telegram No. 50 had been feasible it would have minimized difficulties in Anguilla during operation and reduced requirement for special measures, (especially security), after it, but I accept that Bradshaw could not be brought to agree.[75]

In this second message, therefore, Lee endorsed the current version of Operation Sheepskin and acknowledged that Bradshaw would not agree to his proposed diplomatic solution. However, he appeared to claim that such a solution would have made the British military occupation more acceptable to Anguillians, who may have viewed it as part of the process of relinquishing Basseterre's control and, accordingly, were less likely to resist the occupation.

Regardless of the merits of his advice, the fact that Lee – a senior and key member of the planned British administration of Anguilla – had doubts about Operation Sheepskin was significant. Indeed, it raised concern in Whitehall. According to an FCO official, P.T. Hayman, who telephoned Lee seeking clarity about his views, the latter had begun to develop doubts about the military intervention having considered the propaganda produced by Webster and his allies and had become 'greatly concerned about the policy and the St. Kitts Government with regard to Anguilla'. This perhaps indicates that Lee feared that Operation Sheepskin would be used as a method through which London would hand control of Anguilla back to the Bradshaw government against Anguillian wishes. Hayman went on to state, however, that Lee 'was reassured when I reminded him that the whole basis of our operation was to let the Anguillans live apart from Bradshaw and co. for a number of years'. Having consulted Whitlock about Lee's thinking, Hayman reported that Whitlock 'told me that the whole episode was completely in keeping with Mr. Lee's personality. He was extremely volatile, and it would be quite like him to have last-minute cold feet. Mr. Hunt [another FCO official] fully confirms this.' Ultimately, Lee's doubts led, in turn, to doubts in Whitehall about his suitability for assuming his leadership role on a long-term basis. Hayman concluded that 'this incident shows that he [Lee] does not have the right personality to hold the post of H.M. Commissioner in Anguilla for long (Mr. Whitlock confirms this)'.[76]

The media leak
The nature of state-media relations during the initial stages of Operation Sheepskin was likely to be complex, with Whitehall having to balance the conflicting priorities of maintaining military secrecy to preserve the element of surprise – thus hopefully reducing casualties – and justifying its decision to intervene to a potentially sceptical domestic and international audience. Attention was therefore paid during operational planning to the timescales in which information about the intervention would be released, factoring in security considerations. According to a draft plan, Whitehall spokesmen would answer questions from journalists that might arise 'from possible leaks due to troop movements or from any other cause, by saying that they represent journalistic speculation only…Whitehall spokesmen will not be drawn further.' Accordingly, a 'Parliamentary statement would break the news of a landing. It would be most helpful from the News point of view if the statement could be as full as possible…This would be timed to coincide as nearly as possible with the time of the landing'. The British government, therefore, planned to keep Operation Sheepskin as secret as possible until the military landings. In contingency planning for a situation in which news of the landings surfaced prior to this Parliamentary statement, the document went on to state that 'if we know that the landing has, indeed, taken place, Whitehall spokesmen will confirm it. They will go on to say that the landing was to secure the entry and establishment of a Commissioner appointed by Her Majesty's Government, and that a Parliamentary statement will be made within hours. They will refuse to be drawn further.'[77]

Despite the initial secrecy intended, the British also planned their public relations responses once the invasion story gained traction in the media. MoD Public Relations Officers would supply journalists with the British viewpoint on military operations once ashore in Anguilla. Once the military phase was over, a British Information Officer (BIO) attached to the High Commission in Trinidad could travel to Anguilla to advise any remaining journalists. This BIO would also support Britain's diplomatic messaging in the region and could be assisted, if necessary, by other BIOs based in the United States, Jamaica, Barbados and Guyana.[78] How far Whitehall wanted to facilitate a significant media presence during Operation Sheepskin was, nevertheless, uncertain. This was evident in a telephone conversation between Prime Minister Harold Wilson and Defence Secretary Denis Healey on the evening of 17 March. Wilson informed Healey that press sources had told him that the MoD was arranging for some journalists to accompany the task force to Anguilla. Healey responded that, as reporters could independently charter their own transport, it would be impossible to stop them reaching the island. Nevertheless, he was unaware of the MoD arrangements mentioned by the Prime Minister and was also under the impression that there would be no room on the RAF transports for journalists. Healey accordingly agreed to check what plans had been made by his department to support the media.[79]

Wilson's concern about the media presence during Operation Sheepskin had stemmed from what had occurred earlier in the day of 17 March. At 10.10am on that morning a reporter from the *Evening Standard*, Robert Carvel, had telephoned the FCO and indicated that he had gained information about the operation and the number of police involved. According to a government report, when Carvel was asked how he had got the story he had laughed and responded that 'it sounded like a good tip from the barracks at Devizes', thus suggesting that someone at that military base had leaked the planning information.[80] As Carvel intended to publish his article alerting the British public about the deployment that day, he asked the FCO whether a D-Notice was in force for the operation and, according to a Cabinet Office Note of a subsequent meeting about the incident, had been 'allowed to infer that it was not'.[81] A D-Notice – or Defence Notice – was an official government request that the media avoid covering certain issues in the interests of national security. The *Evening Standard* subsequently published Carvel's revelations on its front page under the title 'Rebel Isle – Skymen Alert' on the same day as the phone call. Announcing that '[it] is thought that Mr. Wilson and other top Cabinet Ministers have decided on this dramatic move [to intervene militarily] as the only way to reassert constitutional authority in the territory', it estimated that the military and police taskforce could depart the UK for Antigua that night and then sail to Anguilla.[82] The article also named Assistant Commissioner Way as the commander of the police contingent and identified the size of this group from the SPG.

Wilson was horrified by the apparent leak of operational details prior to a military deployment in which lives were at stake. Furthermore, it may have fed his longstanding obsession about control of government secrets and media relations following the highly damaging D-Notice Affair of 1967 that Christopher Moran claims 'has a genuine claim to be considered the British Watergate'.[83] This crisis developed when Wilson threatened legal action against the *Daily Express* for publishing Henry Chapman Pincher's controversial article about the British state's routine surveillance of certain private correspondence, allegedly in defiance of D-Notices, and subsequently rejected the findings of a committee which he himself had called for to investigate the incident. Lady Falkender, Wilson's former private secretary, recollected that '[we] all became obsessed with the matter…The whole lamentable affair had hung

like a heavy cloud over us for many months'.[84] Now, in March 1969, Wilson was again faced with media disclosure of government secrets, made worse this time by its potential to ruin Operation Sheepskin's tactical element of surprise and potentially put lives at risk.

Wilson was informed of Carvel's article at a meeting on 17 March and the prospect of using a D-Notice had been both discussed and rejected. According to the Cabinet Office notes of a subsequent meeting of 20 March, 'The Evening Standard story as published had given certain circumstantial details, in particular the name of the senior police officer taking part in the operation, which afforded strong prima facie evidence of a leakage of information'.[85] The extent of Wilson's horror and outrage at the suspected leak was confirmed in the notes of a meeting held in 10 Downing Street on the night of 17 March whereby he reportedly told the Attorney General and Lord Chancellor that he 'took an extremely serious view of the apparent leakage of official information…[and that] The Robert Carvel article contained detailed information, some of which he had not himself been personally aware of. He referred in particular to the name of a police officer who, the article said, was going to command a force of policemen'.[86] Ultimately, according to the meeting notes, Wilson claimed that 'this incident was one of the most monstrous leaks he had known. It would be a particularly serious matter if the force which was being dispatched to Anguilla was met by organised resistance and lives were imperilled.' He also complained that the incident had the potential to give the opposition Conservative Party material through which to strongly criticise his Labour government.[87]

The Prime Minister therefore acted quickly and decisively to identify the source of the leak. He instructed the Permanent Secretary at the MoD, Sir James Dunnett, to initiate an inter-departmental leak procedure involving his department and also the FCO and HO. He also consulted the Lord Chancellor, Lord Gardiner, about the possibility of referring the incident to the Security Commission – a non-departmental public body established to investigate security breaches – or holding an inquiry under the Tribunals of Enquiry (Evidence) Act 1921. The Lord Chancellor subsequently noted that, if an independent inquiry were conducted, then the fact that a D-Notice had not been issued for information relating to Operation Sheepskin when Carvel had made his phone call on 17 March would factor into the inquiry's considerations. Indeed, according to a summary of the discussion with Wilson, Gardiner argued that 'if Carvel had raised this point specifically, he thought that the Government would be in a weak position'.[88]

Wilson then stated that it was his understanding that the D-Notice had not been issued as ministers were concerned that this issuance would be reported in the media which, Wilson reportedly stated, 'would have made the situation worse rather than better'.[89] With the trauma of the damaging D-Notice Affair of 1967 still fresh in Whitehall, perhaps a desire to prevent any further public attention being drawn to D-Notices played a part in the decision not to pursue this option in responding to Carvel. As Moran observes of the 1967 scandal, 'although the D-Notice system survived by the skin of its teeth, confidence in its utility as a protector of genuine national security concerns was severely dented', which perhaps resonates with the climate of decision-making over Operation Sheepskin in March 1969.[90] Moreover, Wilson also observed that a D-Notice could not have prevented Operation Sheepskin from being reported outside of the UK media, further explaining the decision not to use this option.[91]

Ultimately, both the Attorney General and Lord Chancellor were doubtful about the use of a general inquiry into the leak when considering the current situation on the night of 17 March. Perhaps indicating that he believed that the leak had a simple origin not warranting a large independent inquiry, Gardiner reportedly argued that 'information about an operation of this sort could easily become available as a result of troop movements or gossip by wives'. He did, nevertheless, believe that 'detailed inquiries by the police, together with the leak inquiry that had been instituted, could serve a useful purpose'.[92] Ultimately, therefore, the MoD inter-departmental leak procedure was pursued, whilst the Attorney General ordered the Director of Public Prosecutions to launch an investigation into whether a security breach had occurred sufficient to warrant prosecution under the Official Secrets Act. Whilst the leak continued to be regarded with all seriousness in the weeks following the incident, a meeting held on 20 March – possessing a small degree of hindsight – acknowledged that the Carvel article had not been as damaging to Operation Sheepskin as originally thought. A Cabinet Office Note of the meeting stated that, regardless of Carvel's revelation, the deployment 'could anyway hardly have failed to become public knowledge at any time from midday on 17th March, when the troops moved to the United Kingdom airfields at which they emplaned for Antigua'. Consequently, the meeting note continued, 'The Evening Standard disclosure had probably made only a few hours' difference'.[93]

As to whom the identity of the leaker was remained a matter of debate for some time. Regarding the possibility of the source coming from outside the MoD, in their phone conversation of 17 March Healey had reportedly said 'that he thought this [leak] had come from the Home Office or the Police. The Prime Minister said that he was inclined to the same view'.[94] Moreover, Walter Terry – political editor of the *Daily Mail* – wrote on the newspaper's front page of 18 March that '[the] finger of suspicion pointed at Scotland Yard. Apparently the idea of a military excursion to the West Indies proved overmuch for the normally calm temperaments of the Yard'.[95] The possibility of it being a member of the military was, as demonstrated by Gardiner's remarks, also considered. Indeed, this prospect had been raised originally by Carvel's comment about 'a good tip from the barracks at Devizes'.[96] According to the findings of the MoD's inter-departmental leak procedure reported in April 1969, this military site could be fairly easily discounted as the source of the leak on the following grounds:

> The barracks at Devizes were not used by the troops earmarked for Anguilla. However the transit camp there was alerted to prepare for a contingent of troops in transit though no indication of the destination of the troops was given. The first troops did not arrive at Devizes until 6 p.m. on Monday, 17th March. It seems most unlikely that Robert Carvel obtained his information from this source.[97]

According to this inquiry, 466 questionnaires were completed within the MoD and more gathered from the task force. The report's conclusion was that '[none] of these replies, nor of the answers to the questionnaires, nor of the reports from other Departments gives any clear indication of the source of the leak'.[98] With the investigation ultimately unable to blame any department decisively for the leak, the Head of the Home Civil Service wrote in May 1969 that the 'enquiries have been comprehensive and I do not think that we could usefully take them further'.[99] The investigation therefore fizzled out inconclusively. This episode had, nevertheless, underlined Wilson's continuing preoccupation with the connected themes of state-media relations and the safety of government secrets.

Anguilla braces for invasion

Whilst it may have been evident to Ronald Webster and his colleagues in Anguilla that the stakes in their island drama had been raised notably following Whitlock's expulsion of 11 March, the prospect of a British military intervention may have become a more serious concern for the rebels on Friday 14 March. According to Ian Ball in the *Sunday Telegraph* '[the] rebel regime learned in broadcasts from the neighbouring island of St. Kitts that the joint chiefs of staff had conferred with the Cabinet in London on Friday on the Anguilla situation'.[100] Consequently, Webster's government embarked on a multipronged effort aimed at deterring London from adopting this military action. Soon after hearing the news of possible intervention, Webster opted to pursue his old deterrence technique of sabre rattling before the media. Ball's article of 16 March, titled 'Anguilla Tests Its Defences', reported that Webster was planning 'field manoeuvres' which, Ball stated, 'would seem to suggest that Mr. Webster now seriously believes that Britain might be considering taking military action'. On the question of whether Webster's force would stand and fight, Ball gave the assessment that '[the] rebels left me with the impression of a band of quietly determined men. My guess is that they would probably offer resistance. "We hope to survive somehow," said Mr. Webster. He made the remark to me almost in a whisper, but his black eyes flashed with fire'.[101] The Webster regime, therefore, presented an image of resolute defiance and courage which perhaps, as had happened in Anguillian sabre rattling against Bradshaw in the past, was intended to deter the British invaders with the prospect of casualties. Webster also ordered the four remaining Britons on the island – a Anglican canon, a teacher and two nurses – to leave. In a letter of 15 March to the Anglican Canon, Guy Carleton, Webster justified the recipient's ejection 'to prevent the British from inventing the excuse of rescue as justification for the armed invasion of our island'.[102] Alongside sabre rattling, therefore, Webster aimed to deter the British by allowing them no excuse to intervene militarily to protect UK citizens.

His government also pursued one last avenue of support in the form of rallying international opinion. Jerry Gumbs, who had campaigned for Anguilla at the UN periodically over many months, first presented a message from Webster to Secretary General U Thant on 14 March inviting the UN to investigate Whitlock's claim that the island was now dominated by thugs. Gumbs instead alleged that Whitlock had aimed to wrestle control of Anguilla in what was essentially 'a coup that failed' and invited the UN to send a fact-finding mission to the island to ascertain the truth about conditions there.[103] With British troops landing in Antigua on 18 March, Gumbs was granted the opportunity to present a petition to the Committee of 24, prompting a walk-out by the British delegation.[104] The petition emphasised that 'the urgency of a visiting mission has been greatly increased' by British troop movements and requested that the UN mission be sent 'at once to Anguilla to get a first-hand understanding of the situation…Only prompt action by this distinguished Committee can prevent a human tragedy'.[105]

Despite British indignation at the attention given to Gumbs, the fact that the UN did not respond more vigorously to the Anguillian overtures perhaps bore out the assessment of the UK Mission that 'as yet there is little sympathy here for Anguillan secessionism'.[106] This tendency may arguably be attributed to the fact that, according to a British planning document, 'the majority of [UN] members, and especially the Africans, are opposed to secessionist movements', a circumstance perhaps encouraged by the recent bloodshed generated by Katangese secession from the Congo (1960–63) and Biafran secession from Nigeria (1967–70).[107] Gumbs efforts at the

UN did, nevertheless, draw attention to the Anguilla crisis at a pivotal moment. A letter of 18 March from Lawrence and Dolores Landry, prominent Chicago civil rights leaders, to U Thant demanding '[on] behalf of the black people of the United States' that the UN 'stop the English from invading Anguilla' demonstrated sympathy with the island which would be replicated on a larger scale in UN correspondence once Operation Sheepskin had been undertaken. Viewing Britain's actions as an act of renewed colonialist aggression, the Landry letter went on to ask '[how] long will white imperialists continue to steal black land. Failure to act will render the United Nations a useless body.'[108]

Whilst Anguilla braced for invasion, the British military

The Leander-class frigate HMS *Minerva* (F45). Commissioned in 1966, *Minerva* would enjoy a long career with the Royal Navy, including combat operations in the Falklands War of 1982. (Albert Grandolini collection)

units earmarked for the task force were on the move. The process of transporting men and supplies was, like other aspects of operational planning, not without controversy. Denis Healey told the Prime Minister that he believed that press attention about Operation Sheepskin on the afternoon of 17 March had stemmed from Robert Carvel's *Evening Standard* article published that day.[109] This spotlight occurred just hours before troops and police reached military bases in the UK ready to depart for the Caribbean. According to regimental records, 2PARA were given the order to move at 1pm on 17 March and two hours later the battalion's Leading Element – consisting of the Tactical HQ, a mortar platoon, D (Rifle) Company and elements of C (Patrol) Company – left their barracks at Aldershot for the British Army's air transit camp at Devizes, Wiltshire.[110] The *Daily Telegraph* stated that journalists were turned away from the gates of Devizes camp when the paratroopers arrived there in combat kit during the night.[111] It was whilst the Paras were at Devizes that, according to Lt. Colonel Dawnay, 'ITV "News at Ten" gave virtually the outline plan for the operation due to take place 36 hours later'. Addressing concerns that he claimed to have had at the time of Operation Sheepskin about the launching of a deployment from military bases in the UK, Dawnay later acknowledged that '[security] is impossible to achieve in an open barracks such as we occupy in Aldershot. The Press sit outside and are able to see a great deal of what goes on.' He then went on to hint at his own conclusions about the source of the leak to the media, claiming that 'I am entirely satisfied that there was no hint of a security leak from within the Army but once the Home Office had to inform individual members of the Metropolitan Police that they were to move in 48 hours, then security in the military sense was bound to suffer.'[112]

The *Daily Mail* noted that paratroops began arriving at RAF Lyneham, around 15 miles from Devizes, 'soon after midnight amid strict security precautions' and the article identified transport planes on the tarmac into which soldiers and airmen loaded supplies 'by flood-light'.[113] These RAF Hercules and Vickers VC.10 transports took off from Lyneham in the early hours of 18 March. Meanwhile,

the police contingent under Assistant Commissioner Way flew from RAF Brize Norton in Oxfordshire during the night. The Paras landed at Coolidge International Airport, Antigua, around midday on 18 March where they were met by Lt. Colonel Dawnay who had been sent to the Caribbean three days previously to assist with planning Operation Sheepskin. Dawnay noted that the subsequent transfer of troops and supplies from Coolidge to the Deep Water Harbour of St Johns, where they would embark HMS *Minerva* and *Rothesay*, 'was not entirely straightforward from a soldier's point of view'.[114] 2PARA, according to Dawnay:

…had to change from a strategic trooping posture with kit "all crated up", move to the docks in an ad hoc collection of transport found by the local PWD [Public Works Department] and embark in two frigates which were to sail to separate assault beaches; all in four hours. All our briefings and the issue of equipment and ammunition had to be completed within this time to enable the frigates to sail before last light. In the event we met the naval deadline by eight minutes.[115]

Added to this logistical challenge was the reception encountered by the task force during their time in Antigua. According to Westlake, '[most] ordinary Antiguan citizens had taken the Anguillan side in the dispute' and, accordingly, the British troops travelling in hired buses and PWD trucks from the airport to the harbour 'passed unfriendly natives who shouted 'Shame!' and political slogans'.[116] Moreover, a British report written after Operation Sheepskin also noted 'the presence of black-power agitators and American tourists' in the vicinity of the harbour where British troops were being issued with their supplies.[117] Whilst the hostility of onlookers in Antigua did nothing to disrupt the British timetable, it may have underlined to those taking part in Sheepskin the controversial nature of London's decision to intervene militarily. Westlake notes that the Premier of Antigua, Vere Bird, incurred criticism from the electorate for allowing the British to stage their intervention through the island

The RAF Hawker Siddeley Andover C.Mk 1. This aircraft would transport personnel in and out of Anguilla. (Albert Grandolini collection)

Sharp, threatened on 18 March to halt the airlift through Gander at what, according to the High Commission, 'could have been a critical stage'.[123] Early the following morning Sharp was telephoned by Foreign Secretary Michael Stewart in an effort to placate him and justify Britain's actions. According to his subsequent account of the conversation, Stewart claimed that the British government 'regarded these flights as covered by the normal arrangements which had been in force for over ten years', by which he referred to an Order in Council of 1957 allowing for Anglo-Canadian reciprocal use of airfields. This arrangement had been used previously for British transportation to military commitments in Malaysia.

and argues that this partly contributed to Bird's electoral defeat in 1971.[118] According to Webster, however, Bird's political opponent George Walter messaged the Anguillian leader 'to say that British troops had arrived and were about to invade Anguilla' meaning that, as Webster explained, '[we] knew they were coming.'[119] Indeed, HMS *Minerva* and *Rothesay* proceeded north from Antigua at 4pm on 18 March with the intention of arriving off the Anguillian coast early the following morning.

When implementing the airlift of personnel and supplies from the UK to Antigua, military planners may not have anticipated the political obstacles previously encountered over flights during controversial military interventions in the 'East of Suez' era.[120] Nevertheless, a failure to consult the Canadian government over the use of Gander airport in Newfoundland – through which certain transports passed on their way to support Operation Sheepskin – would cause a significant diplomatic headache in London and Ottawa. This development once again highlights the increasingly political and controversial nature of British military intervention in the post-colonial world, even when involving the cooperation of a close Commonwealth ally. According to the British High Commissioner in Ottawa, Sir Colin Crowe, on the morning of 18 March his Defence Advisor received 'a signal giving details of the air movement plan for operations in Caribbean covering movements through Gander'. The rather out-of-the-loop Crowe instructed his advisor to seek MoD 'confirmation that appropriate clearances had been obtained from Canadian authorities' to use the airport and admitted that '[the] first we heard that Gander was to be used was from the signal'.[121] The British failure to consult the Canadians was clear in a subsequent message from the High Commission later that day, with Crowe predicting that '[serious] fence-mending over our failure to consult seems likely to lie ahead.'[122]

Britain's diplomatic blunder was highly embarrassing for the Canadian government. Canadian territory had been used, without consultation, for a British military intervention in the Caribbean at a time when Ottawa's relationship with the West Indies was already poor. The Canadian Secretary of State for External Affairs, Mitchell

However, according to Stewart's account, Sharp had responded that 'the assumption underlying the Order in Council was that there would be consultation about the purpose of any military operation using these facilities'. Stewart noted that he had then countered that 'there had been little opportunity to consult anybody: indeed the British Parliament had not yet been informed about the proposed operation'. In a subsequent phone call later in the day also outlined by Stewart, Sharp stated that 'the Canadian Government would prefer the flights scheduled for later today not to pass through Gander. But if this were impossible from the point of view of our operation, or if we wanted to stand on the Order in Council then we could send the flights through Gander.'[124]

The fact that Ottawa had requested that their facilities be used no further to support Operation Sheepskin demonstrates what a difficult and embarrassing situation they had been placed in through London's lack of consultation. Having liaised with the MoD, Stewart responded later on 19 March that it would be 'impracticable' for currently airborne British aircraft en route to Gander to be recalled; however, he reassured the Canadians that '[we] are endeavouring to make alternative arrangements for all remaining aircraft as well as for aircraft originally due to stage at Gander on return flights'.[125] The precise cause of Britain's failure to consult its Canadian allies is difficult to pinpoint. If the timetable for alerting Washington and Ottawa of Operation Sheepskin was followed correctly, then the Canadians would have known about the military intervention 48 hours prior to the landings. Their surprise about the use of Gander, therefore, suggests that detailed military plans were omitted from the diplomatic alert. The consultative oversight may perhaps have been due to the hurried pace of operational planning. Alternatively, the rather blasé approach of the British to the Order in Council of 1957 may have meant that planners did not consider the use of Gander to be controversial. At a time when London needed diplomatic support for Operation Sheepskin from allies in the face of international criticism, however, this episode proved a significant blunder and could, if the Canadians had blocked use of Gander earlier in the airlift, have affected the military operation more seriously.

5
OPERATION SHEEPSKIN AND ITS IMMEDIATE AFTERMATH

HMS *Minerva* and *Rothesay* arrived off Anguilla two hours before first light on 19 March 1969. According to SNOWI's post-operation report, the two frigates had 'set course 300° at 18 kts, passing South of St. Maarten, and approaching Anguilla from the West. Ships were darkened at 2100 but kept navigation lights burning until the run-in at 0400'.[1] *Minerva* finally anchored near Road Bay whilst *Rothesay* did the same at Crocus Bay, ready to dispatch their respective infantry to the allotted beaches. The troops had been scheduled to conduct their landings at first light to achieve the element of surprise against Webster's Defence Force. However, the scale of attention that the task force had received in Antigua meant that those in command feared that word of British military movement might have reached Anguilla which, as Webster claimed, it had.[2] Therefore, according to Lt. Colonel Dawnay, 'it was decided to bring forward the timing of the landing to half an hour before first light in order to achieve some measure of local surprise'.[3]

19 March 1969

The Paratroopers and Royal Marines thus clambered into their Gemini dinghies or ships' boats whilst other squaddies prepared to board the Wasp helicopter of each frigate. Boarding the seaborne troops could have proven unexpectedly complex due to the revised earlier time schedule. Dawnay recalled that 'we had been unable to rehearse embarking into Gemini assault boats down the landing nets of the frigates, in the dark and fully kitted'.[4] Nevertheless, the troops departed *Minerva* and *Rothesay* without much difficulty and hit the Anguillian beaches a short distance away around 5.15am.[5] As Westlake describes the military landing, '[the] troops, ducking and weaving, dashed from the open boats across bare stretches of white beach, their automatic rifles held at the ready. They ducked behind bushes and upturned boats before moving again, cautiously, into the interior.'[6] Webster, having been alerted that troops were on their way, was observing the amphibious arrival. He wrote that '[when] the British boats arrived off Sandy Ground, I was there on Shannon Hill [situated inland to the west of Road Bay], sitting behind a large black rock with a news reporter…He took pictures of the boats ferrying the troops and of all the activities.'[7] The marines experienced no opposition as they reached Road Bay and proceeded to secure the high ground beyond the beach. This allowed the 2PARA mortar platoon commanded by Captain J.R. Bonner to move through the marine positions on the way to their inland objective of the airfield.[8]

The first wave of paratroopers to hit the beaches further up the coast at Crocus Bay, commanded by Lieutenant Fieldhouse, had a more eventful time. There had been concern about weather conditions with, according to SNOWI's report, 'a possibility of heavy swell in Crocus Bay. In the event the coast was approached in perfect conditions, no wind, no swell, and low clouds shielding the first light of dawn.'[9] Mick Cotton, who had joined the Paras in 1965 and seen action in the Aden Emergency, received a bloody nose from a fellow squaddie in the competition to see which soldier would be first to reach the Anguillian shore. He recalled what happened next:

… as soon as we got ashore in the darkness we came up to this little road and all these headlights come towards us. So we thought, oh God, they're here already. They're on to us. And we lay there and somebody shouted 'hey Sarge, can we put a round up the spout' and they said 'yeah' so we all cocked our weapons like mad and he said 'for God's sake don't do anything till I give the word' and these vehicles pulled up and there was slam, slam as the doors shut.[10]

Westlake notes how the Royal Navy gunnery control officers aboard the frigates 'tensed as they saw sudden white lights streaming across the island in the darkness – automobile headlights moving toward the beachheads and the landing parties. The automobiles stopped. The

On deck aboard HMS *Minerva* and HMS *Rothesay* alongside one another. A Para checks his L1A1 Self-Loading Rifle. Note also the Sterling submachine gun in the bottom-right corner of the photo. Whilst such weapons were carried in Anguilla, it was anticipated that CS Riot Control Gas would be relied upon for pursuing a minimum force strategy. (Airborne Assault Museum)

gunners waited, hands gripping their gun mounts.'[11] Dawnay and Commodore Lucey were nervously watching these fast-moving developments through their binoculars on the bridge of *Minerva*. Observing a sudden volley of flashes develop across the coast, Dawnay said 'This is it!' to Lucey but added that 'we'll wait for a report and request for Naval gunfire from the assault company'.[12] The two senior officers waited, according to Dawnay's recollection, 'somewhat tensely for the sound of firing and the contact report on the radio – but none came'. Fortunately for the British, concerns that the flashes had come from the weapons of Webster's Defence Force descending on the beachheads were mistaken. As Dawnay continued:

A Royal Navy seamen's platoon being directed off a ship's boat. This may have been HMS *Minerva*'s seamen's platoon landing at the Road Bay jetty to take over positions occupied by the Royal Marines during the initial amphibious assault. (Albert Grandolini collection)

In fact it was the Press who had rightly appreciated that we would land there on that morning. The flashes were from their cameras. Thank goodness the fire control was good, as the leading waves of Gemini also thought that they were being fired on but couldn't hear shots due to the noise of their outboard motors.[13]

Back on the beach at Crocus Bay, Mick Cotton witnessed the surreal media encounter first hand. He recalled that 'there must have been about five news crews from America, you know, whatever they were at that time: CBS, the ABS…whatever. They're going like 'Hi guys'…you know… 'You're a bit earlier than we expected… we expected you at 6 oclock'. So that was a bit of an anti-climax.'[14] Webster, watching the troops' arrival from Shannon Hill, also identified the possibility for misinterpretation caused by the media camera flashes, recalling that:

The thing that worried me was the flashes of the photographers' camera bulbs. I was afraid the troops would think it was shots being fired. Because of those flashes I was glad to move from there. Before morning broke, I walked from Shannon Hill to Stoney Ground and picked up my Peugot [sic] and drove back home.[15]

This farcical encounter with the flashbulbs has become a regular staple of accounts about Operation Sheepskin since 1969, seeming to be emblematic of a farcical military intervention generated by misunderstanding and overreaction. Curiously, the precise timing of this event is not entirely clear. Whilst the vast majority of accounts – including Dawnay's, who monitored his men's progress through binoculars – appear to suggest that the journalists arrived as the first wave hit the beaches of Crocus Bay, SNOWI's post-operation report may suggest otherwise. Discussing the decision to move Operation Sheepskin's timetable earlier to increase the element of surprise, he argued that 'this decision probably saved the lives of several

pressmen in Anguilla who arrived on the landing beaches at 0530, and met the second wave. Had they met the first assault, using flash bulbs in the darkness, they might well have been shot.'[16] Whether the notorious bulb-flashes occurred during the first or second wave of beach landings or, alternatively, they occurred in separate incidents, it is testament to the fire control of the British troops that shots were not fired.

The helicopter-borne paratroopers, commanded by Lieutenant Brian Martin, flew from HMS *Minerva* and *Rothesay* when enough light permitted the journey. They were dropped off 'in the dim light of dawn' at the main secondary school near Mahogany crossroads in the centre of the island, which they had been ordered to hold until platoons from the coast could reinforce them.[17] According to the *Washington Post*, many Anguillians were 'awakened by the whir of helicopters overhead'.[18] Nevertheless, the troops were able to easily establish their positions at the crossroads, meaning that they were able to control key approaches to the strategically important airfield. At around the same time, *Minerva*'s seamen's platoon under Lt. Commander Graham Price had taken over British positions at Road Bay and its valuable jetty, thus freeing up the Royal Marines. The second wave of 2PARA had also reached Crocus Bay and, passing through their own comrades' positions, proceeded inland in three four-man patrols under the command of Lieutenant R.J.S. Penny. Their objective was to seize the airfield to facilitate the first heavy drop of vehicles scheduled for 6.45am.[19] Much like the crossroads platoon, Penny's force reached their objective and secured it unopposed, thus allowing four Landrovers to be dropped at the airfield just prior to the arrival of the 2PARA mortar platoon that had advanced from Road Bay.[20] According to 2PARA regimental records, the mortar platoon then remained at the airfield whilst 'the rest of the force was consolidated at a school near the crossroads', presumably having reinforced Lieutenant Martin's men.[21] Ultimately,

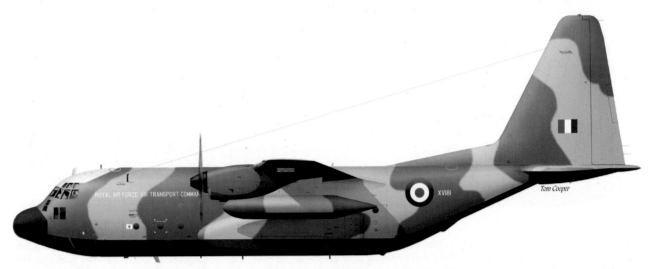

The export variant of the C-130H developed for the RAF received the designation C-130K: in British service, this received the designation Hercules C.Mk 1. Having entered service in 1966, this was still a relatively new appearance at the time of Operation Sheepskin. Nevertheless, five units were operational with the Hercules, including No. 242 Operational Conversion Unit, and Nos. 24, 30, 36 and 47 Squadrons. Initially, the aircraft wore the livery depicted here, comprising a standardised camouflage pattern in light stone (BS381C/361) and dark brown (BS381C/450) on upper surfaces and sides, and night (BS381C/642) on undersurfaces, with the cockpit roof in white. The full service title of the Royal Air Force Air Transport Command was applied on the upper side of the forward fuselage. (Artwork by Tom Cooper)

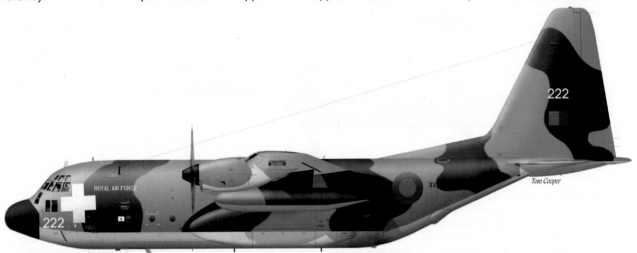

By the time of Operation Sheepskin some C.Mk 1s had received this standardised camouflage pattern in dark sea grey (BS381C/638) and dark green (BS381C/641) on upper sides, with undersurfaces in light aircraft grey (BS381C/627). Several – including XV222 (depicted here), and XV302 – had a large white cross on the cockpit side where they usually wore squadron crests. Aircraft involved in Operation Sheepskin were drawn from No. 242 Operational Conversion Unit, and Nos. 30 and 47 Squadron: both of the latter had a rich history of service around the world before and after, and their participation further highlighted their expertise in this type of mission. (Artwork by Tom Cooper)

At least two Hawker Siddeley HS.780 Andover C.Mk 1s were deployed in support of Operation Sheepskin. Drawn from RAF Abingdon-based No. 46 Squadron – which converted to this type in 1966 – they were used to carry troops and equipment to and from Anguilla. Both wore this standardised camouflage pattern in light stone (BS381C/361) and dark brown (BS381C/450) on upper surfaces and sides (with hard edges), and night (BS381C/642) on undersurfaces, and had their cockpit roofs painted in white. Unit insignia was applied high on the fin, and the full service title was worn down the upper portion of the centre fuselage. (Artwork by Tom Cooper)

Another RAF-operated transport to become involved in Operation Sheepskin was the Vickers VC.10. Two examples from No. 10 Squadron were used to transport VIPs, both wearing the standard white over grey scheme with large blue lightning flash down the fuselage. The artwork here shows serial number XV103 after conversion to the C.Mk 1K tanker/transport configuration. At the time of Operation Sheepskin, it wore the same livery, but had no in-flight refuelling probe nor underwing refuelling pod. (Artwork by Rolando Ugolini)

To soften the political profile of the intervention, the first of 315 troops of 2nd Battalion The Parachute Regiment (2PARA) to reach Anguilla during Operation Sheepskin did so on board two Westland Wasp HAS.Mk 1 helicopters of Naval Air Squadron 847. The Wasp was a small helicopter equipped with a unique four-wheeled caster undercarriage allowing it to land on small, pitching flight decks. It was designed as an anti-submarine helicopter, and all the examples were painted in extra dark sea grey overall (BS381C/640). The two Wasps involved in Operation Sheepskin were from frigates HMS *Minverva* (hull number F45; Leander-class) and HMS *Rothesay* (F107; Rothesay-class). Additional Paras followed and landed on the beaches in Gemini assault craft. (Artwork by Tom Cooper)

The principal ground vehicle of 2PARA during Operation Sheepskin was the Short Wheel Base version of the Series II Land Rover. Powered by the 72hp (54kW) 2.25-litre petrol engine, the lightweight paratrooper version usually lacked a cab. Painted in dark green overall, none of the examples deployed in Anguilla are known to have had any kind of armament. (Artwork by David Bocquelet)

This soldier of 2PARA wears the iconic Para red beret (the colour being officially described as 'maroon'), although squaddies would also use jungle hats in Anguilla. His jungle green shirt is made from lightweight Aertex cellular cotton, ideal for Anguilla's hot climate. His jungle green trousers are also made of lightweight cotton. The soldier is equipped with 1944 pattern webbing, which supports a haversack, rolled poncho and other pouches. He is armed with a L1A1 Self-Loading Rifle with wooden furniture, a British derivative of the Beligian FN FAL, chambered for the powerful 7.62mm NATO round. The SLR, as it was almost universally known, had been introduced in 1958 to replace the venerable Lee-Enfield rifle that had served in various marks since the late nineteenth century, and fortunately was only used to fire the occasional warning shot during Operation Sheepskin. (Artwork by Renato Dalmaso)

An officer of the Anguilla Police Unit (APU). When the contingent from the Metropolitan Police arrived in Anguilla, they did so wearing standard blue serge tunics unsuitable for local conditions. Adapting to the climate, however, they soon wore military-issued khaki lightweight cotton trousers whilst retaining their police shirts and caps. The APU were also issued with Walther semi-automatic pistols from the arsenals of Special Branch and Scotland Yard's Special Patrol Group, although – in the best traditions of the British 'Bobby' – it was stated that they would only carry these weapons under exceptional circumstances. (Artwork by Renato Dalmaso)

A member of a Royal Navy seamen's platoon involved in Operation Sheepskin's initial military landings. He wears a Marine Pattern Steel Helmet and the Royal Navy's standard No. 8 Action Working Dress of cotton shirt and trousers. The shell of the helmet, a Second World War-era design, was the same as that used by the Paras and the Royal Armoured Corps and differed primarily in terms of the straps and internal webbing depending upon role. The seaman is also equipped with Mark III ammunition pouches and 1937 pattern webbing. He is armed with an L1A1 Self-Loading Rifle with wooden furniture. (Artwork by Renato Dalmaso)

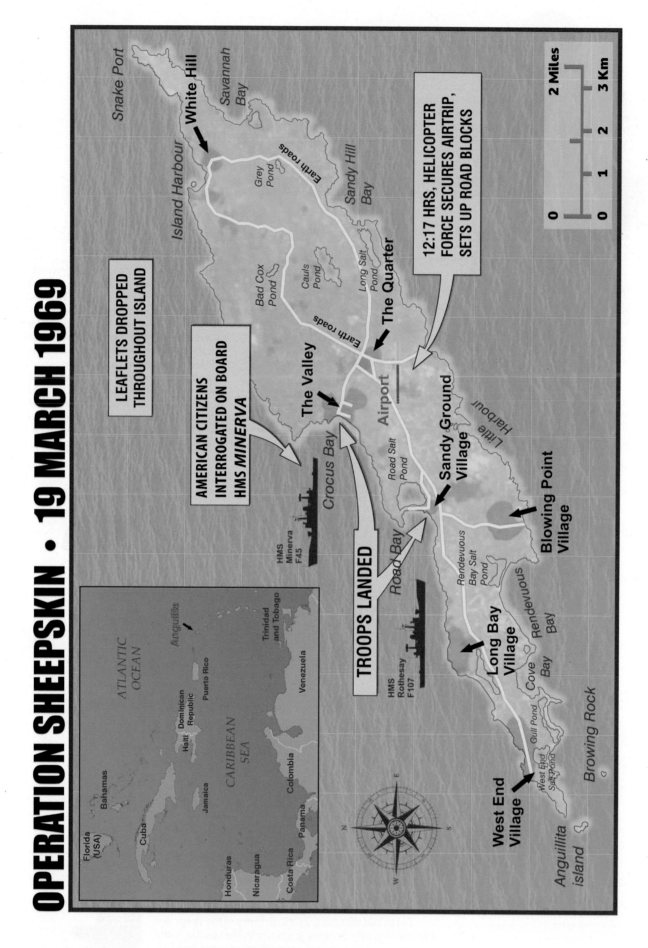

OPERATION SHEEPSKIN · 19 MARCH 1969

LEAFLETS DROPPED THROUGHOUT ISLAND

AMERICAN CITIZENS INTERROGATED ON BOARD HMS MINERVA

12:17 HRS, HELICOPTER FORCE SECURES AIRTRIP, SETS UP ROAD BLOCKS

TROOPS LANDED

White Hill

Snake Port

Savannah Bay

Island Harbour

Earth roads

Grey Pond

Sandy Hill Bay

Bad Cox Pond

Cauls Pond

Long Salt Pond

The Quarter

Earth roads

The Valley

Crocus Bay

Airport

HMS Minerva F45

Road Salt Pond

Sandy Ground Village

Little Harbour

Blowing Point Village

Road Bay

HMS Rothesay F107

Rendevuous Bay Salt Pond

Long Bay Village

Cove Bay

Rendevuous Bay

West End Village

Gull Pond

West End Salt Pond

Browing Rock

Anguillita island

ATLANTIC OCEAN

Anguilla

Bahamas

Florida (USA)

Cuba

Jamaica

Haiti

Dominican Republic

Puerto Rico

Trinidad and Tobago

Venezuela

Colombia

CARIBBEAN SEA

Honduras

Nicaragua

Costa Rica

Panama

2 Miles

3 Km

A map of Anguilla with major scenes of the British military intervention during Operation Sheepskin, on 19 March 1969. (Map by Anderson Subtil)

Two members of a Royal Navy seamen's platoon share cigarettes with a Royal Marine. Note the variety of headgear, including a steel helmet, bush hat and the Marine's beret. The helmet is the Marine Pattern Steel Helmet and shared the shell with a number of other helmets in British service, differing primarily in the arrangement of the straps and internal webbing. The seaman on the left carries an L1A1 SLR with wooden furniture while the man on the right carries a Sterling 9mm sub machine gun. (Albert Grandolini collection)

therefore, by 7.15am – two hours after the initial amphibious assault – all military objectives had been achieved.[22]

A Para talks with Anguillians whilst covered by a comrade. Note that both of the Paras appear to be wearing a late version of the Denison Smock and Olive Green trousers, items that became as iconic as their red beret. Although orders had been issued in 1961 to replace the Denison Smock these were largely ignored even after the adoption of DPM, and the Denison Smock was retained until the late 1970s. (Albert Grandolini collection)

An RAF Hercules manoeuvres on Anguilla's runway. (Albert Grandolini collection)

Contrary to the estimates of several decisionmakers involved in planning Operation Sheepskin, the military landings had been made without any resistance. As SNOWI summarised in his post-operation report, 'it soon became clear that Webster had ordered no opposition to the landings. Weapons had been hidden, or possibly taken off the island, and no troublemakers were encountered.'[23] Westlake claimed that the Anguillians had buried their guns in nearby St Maartin.[24] The reason why Webster's government ordered no resistance to British forces, despite the previous sabre-rattling rhetoric, is difficult to pin down. Perhaps the scale of the British response – sending its elite Spearhead Battalion from 2PARA rather than relying solely on a small marine party from a frigate – underlined to the Anguillians the challenge they faced and the likelihood of military defeat. Alternatively, or additionally, the decision may have been in line with Webster's previous tactic of using military capability primarily as a weapon of deterrence. Once the British had called his bluff through deployment of formidable force, Webster may perhaps have recognised that armed resistance no longer served any useful purpose. The Anguillian leader instead understood the value of media coverage during the invasion. As he recalled, 'many reporters descended on Anguilla, and we welcomed them, since we felt they would give us a measure of protection. We wanted whatever happened to be seen as it happened.'[25]

The journalists accompanying the task force were allowed ashore from HMS *Minerva* at 7.30am, whilst Commissioner Tony Lee and the first party of the new Anguilla Police Unit arrived at Road Bay around 8am.[26] With no apparent initial opposition to the military landings, the British task force's priorities changed. As Dawnay recalled, '[having] arrived on the island without opposition, the first problem was to tell the islanders why we were here. This was only a week after the Whitlock debacle and the extremists were still both smarting from the alleged insults of that day, and also cocky with having seen off the island he who had insulted them.'[27] The British Army therefore turned its attention to communicating with the Anguillians, explaining their presence on the island and countering Webster's own political messaging.

Members of A Coy with local women. One Para uses his radio set, a form of communication that sometimes caused the British difficulties during the early stage of the military occupation. (Airborne Assault Museum)

Unfortunately for the British, the under-resourcing of psyops during both the planning and implementation of Operation Sheepskin hindered these initial public relations efforts. The Wasp helicopters spent part of 19 March dropping quantities of the 10,500 leaflets produced both in the UK and aboard *Minerva* to the islanders that explained Britain's intentions. The leaflet drawn up in the UK reassured Anguillians that:

IT IS NOT OUR PURPOSE TO FORCE YOU TO RETURN TO AN ADMINISTRATION YOU DO NOT WANT … Our purpose is to end intimidation so that you can live in peace and express your opinions without fear…Her Majesty's Government have therefore taken the necessary measures to appoint Mr. Lee as Her Majesty's Commissioner so that there can be peace, stability and progress in the Island. He comes as your friend … Please cooperate with him and with the Police and Armed Forces who have come to assist him…The quicker law and order is restored, the sooner you can resume a normal and peaceful life.[28]

Webster's supporters were able to discredit this leaflet and a subsequent one bearing a personal message from Lee. According to a post-operation report by Lt. Colonel B.R. Johnston – the Army officer responsible for psyops – 'The first [leaflet] was discredited because it was impersonal and had no authenticating mark, either a crest or a signature, and the second because it was so obviously locally produced.'[29] Moreover, according to SNOWI's report, Anguillians were also not keen on the military's method of distributing these leaflets by helicopter, noting that the 'method was resented by the islanders who regarded it as an ill-mannered method of delivering a letter'.[30] Printed communication therefore proved a public relations difficulty for the task force from early on in the military occupation, with the inability to produce high

quality leaflets at short notice being a particular issue. Indeed, it was estimated that there would be a delay of at least three days between a request for printed material to the UK and its arrival in Anguilla, by which time the public relations situation may have changed and opportunities to influence Anguillian opinion may have been missed.[31] Consequently, commentators analysing Operation Sheepskin's lessons recommended that a mobile printing press be made available for situations like this in future and, additionally, considered the possibility of a portable printing press being made available to British frigates in the Caribbean.[32]

The British military also experienced other technological difficulties in their public relations campaign. Although Anguilla had no local radio station, islanders could tune into radio broadcasts from St Kitts that, according to a British report, 'inflamed them with its provocative repetition of Bradshaw's statements'.[33] Initially, however, the task force had limited means of countering Basseterre's narrative. Fortunately, HMS *Minerva* had the equipment necessary to broadcast on civilian frequencies meaning that a makeshift radio station could be established on the frigate that could project Britain's messages from offshore. Even this fall-back solution would, nevertheless, prove problematic for the military. Johnston noted that '[the] programming of a radio station is both time-consuming and difficult if amateurism is to be avoided. More than once… broadcasting seriously interfered with other, and more important, communications of the ships and on one occasion broadcasting had to be cut off in the middle of a programme.'[34] The psyops officer, therefore, discouraged reliance on frigates as radio stations of this kind in future operations, observing that the United States Army had five-ton trucks that operated in pairs as mobile radio stations and suggesting that the British Army could adopt similar equipment.[35] Adding even further communication difficulties to the task force's burden, the Wasp helicopters used as the main workhorse of aerial operations around the island on 19 March, were not fitted with loudspeakers which could have been used to explain the rather bland leaflets being thrown to the Anguillians below.

Considering that the British armed forces had recently engaged in almost 25 years of almost constant counterinsurgency and military intervention East of Suez, in which public relations campaigns were often crucial for winning hearts and minds, these communications problems encountered in Operation Sheepskin are perhaps shocking. Kumar Ramakrishna, for instance, has underlined the pivotal importance of propaganda for achieving British success in the Malayan Emergency (1948–1960).[36] However, Operation Sheepskin was fairly distinct in the speed with which the military intervention was planned and implemented, centring on an island which was underdeveloped in terms of communications outlets such as radio and printing facilities.[37] Consequently, at a time when its psyops units were already under-resourced, the British military were forced to rely on their own equipment to conduct public relations campaigns for which this technology was not especially well suited. However, the conditions of Anguilla cannot, perhaps, alone explain these psyops difficulties. Interestingly, David Charters acknowledged that psyops remained similarly under-resourced in the opening phase of Operation Banner in Northern Ireland, to which the British Army deployed in 1969 only months after Operation Sheepskin. He wrote that '[despite] several decades of experience in fighting against "propaganda wars backed by force", both the British Government and the Army appear to have been unprepared to fight that kind of war in Ulster. The Army's psyops resources were insignificant at the outbreak of the war, so its efforts tended to be *ad hoc*.'[38] Whilst the context of Northern Ireland was considerably different to Anguilla, it is evident that psyops posed a significant weakness of British military capability in the late 1960s.

Alongside the difficulties it encountered in communicating with the Anguillian public, the British task force also faced notable problems in its own signals and cypher communications between its component services and partners. Whilst SNOWI concluded that, despite notable challenges, the communication plans were 'in general terms…most successful', the FCO's Communications Department took a more critical view, judging that 'from the communications point of view this operation was both poorly planned and executed'.[39] Summarising some of SNOWI's findings, the Communications Department noted the 'routeing of Secret signals via non-U.K. channels' and the use of 'unserviceable equipment' such as Royal Signals 119 radios and Navy KL-7 cypher machines, the department assessing the extent of such equipment to be 'frightening'.[40] SNOWI observed many of the communications pressures first-hand as his flagship, HMS *Minerva*, received all military, police and diplomatic signals traffic during the initial phase of Sheepskin, the frigate's equipment and personnel encountering particular strain. Diplomatic signals, in particular, were a source of complaint for SNOWI, who later criticised:

> …the total disregard by the diplomatic service of anything approaching message writing discipline. The verbosity of the diplomatic traffic passed in this operation was enough to horrify any Naval Communications Officer…this sort of traffic pouring into a Frigate's Comcen [Communications Centre] can easily swamp the whole machine and bring the military operational traffic to a halt at a time when it is most urgently required.[41]

The Communications Department were, nevertheless, fairly unsympathetic to SNOWI's plight, responding that 'we feel that

A Para strides around one of Anguilla's many beaches whilst another operates a radio. (Albert Grandolini collection)

SNOWI and his staff have quite failed to realise that in operations of this sort in the present day world, the need for meticulous care in legality and presentation is bound to cause a large volume of diplomatic telegraphing' and, consequently, the military 'must find means of dealing with such telegrams'.[42]

Other communication problems also arose between various services. Although Para and Royal Signals radio operators were posted to the RAF Airhead in Antigua to coordinate air management with *Minerva*, SNOWI noted that 'neither of these managed to achieve proper radio contact'. This could have impacted the schedule for airdropping supplies and equipment at Anguilla's airfield but, SNOWI highlighted, '[luckily] the RAF responded to a previously arranged timetable and the Aircraft arrived overhead contacting MINERVA on UHF [ultrahigh frequency]'.[43] The FCO Communications Department also complained about SNOWI's decision to hold back a Diplomatic Wireless Service (DWS) operator from accompanying the military landings which, they asserted, 'was contrary to our specific instructions'.[44] This individual would be responsible for establishing HM Commissioner's permanent link with London but, as *Minerva* was initially handling Lee's traffic and the British Government Representative on St Lucia needed assistance with communications to the UK, SNOWI held the DWS operator back accordingly. This was later branded a 'most annoying decision' and, indeed, the FCO vetoed it, sending the DWS to Anguilla. The Communications Team underlined how fortunate

Two Paras sit by the roadside. In the initial days of the military occupation, British troops manned roadblocks as a show of force and to search Anguillians in vehicles and on foot. (Albert Grandolini collection)

this about-turn was, noting that 'within a very short period the situation arose when the DWS operator formed the only means of [FCO] communication with the Services and Police on Anguilla as well as with H.M. Commissioner'.[45]

Finally, different armed services varied in their success at maintaining communications with the UK, SNOWI highlighting that the DWS operator maintained 'direct contact with U.K. without any apparent difficulty and handling a vast amount of diplomatic traffic, while we in the ship, and the Royal Signals ashore with our huge hunks of machinery were only able to work Nassau'. Coincidingly, however, the RAF successfully maintained contact with the UK 'using equipment which fitted into two small suitcases'.[46] Ultimately, therefore, from an signals and cypher perspective, Operation Sheepskin highlighted a range of planning, technological and operational shortcomings. Indeed, it was fortunate for the British that these shortcomings did not impact operational effectiveness more than they did. Had the invasion been resisted, the results of communications failure could perhaps have been more severe. SNOWI concluded that:

This was a most interesting operation from every angle and as always it hinged on good communications. That on the whole this was achieved owes much to the co-operation and forebearance [sic] of JRS Nassau and the Authorities in U.K. There are bound to be shortcomings however when a politico-military operation of this nature is mounted and controlled from a frigate…[47]

Once the main military objectives had been seized on the morning of 19 March, the task force set about securing the island and establishing their presence. According to Webster, '[the] invading forces quickly dug in, mounted machine guns, established control points along the roads, stopped, searched, and questioned everyone'.[48] The Paras also began fanning out across the island. Lt. Colonel Dawnay made a reconnaissance flight around Anguilla in one of the Wasps and his men, according to Westlake, commandeered civilian vehicles to dominate the island quickly.[49] The limited number of military vehicles airlifted to the island by this point perhaps explains this decision by the Army.

Whilst the British military had been fortunate not to experience opposition during their exposed amphibious landings earlier in the morning, this did not mean that they were out of potential danger nor that the soldiers lost their alertness. In one incident, a 'sharp

report sent the parachute troops leaping into defensive positions – until they found that it came from a backfiring motor cycle being ridden by a young islander'.[50] The *Daily Telegraph's* correspondent, Ian Ball, observed that:

The greatest danger to the invasion force would appear to lie in guerrilla warfare and sniping attacks once they have landed and set about trying to "secure" the island. Arms, including carbines, are hidden throughout the scrublands and maize plots. Although there is no jungle vegetation on Anguilla, there are plenty of places – rocky outcrops, ravines and coves – where guerrillas could operate. It would, however, be suicidal resistance.[51]

If the Anguilla Defence Force had chosen to engage in guerrilla warfare – ambushing patrols in quick contacts before dashing back into the scrub – then they could have posed a notable challenge. This may only, however, have constituted a short-term threat due to the small size of the island and, consequently, the limited freedom of movement available to these hypothetical insurgents. Fortunately for the British the Anguillians did not choose this strategic option. Nevertheless, the formidability of the Anguillian landscape was underlined in an article from *Pegasus*, 2PARA's regimental journal, which noted that:

Apart from occasional patches of cultivated land, most of Anguilla is covered in thick scrub above six feet high. It looks harmless enough, and to those veteran warriors who had traversed the jungles of Malaya and Borneo it was not expected to present any difficulty in navigation. However on one exercise certain members of "B" Coy entered it at night to re-emerge two days and 800 metres later with a terrible tale to tell of the impenetrable undergrowth.[52]

In the afternoon of 19 March, Commissioner Way and members of his APU landed at the airfield along with more units of 2PARA. According to *The Sunday Times*, 'the army's emergency stores contained no tropical drill uniform large enough to fit the massive figure of Assistant Commissioner Andrew Way…which has left him sweltering in his regulation blue serge'.[53] Way would, however, explain his attire differently. According to Westlake, he complained that 'I blame the Navy for this. They dropped my case with my light clothes in it out of one of their helicopters'.[54] His policemen would soon be dressed in a mixed uniform of khaki summer trousers, pale blue police shirts with black ties and police caps. The APU and military would soon establish a joint headquarters at The Valley Secondary School, near the strategic Mahogany crossroads. The School would also provide accommodation for 2PARA Battalion HQ, C and D companies over the next couple of weeks, whilst A Company were stationed at Sandy Bay around three miles to the north-east.

The general reception from islanders received by task force personnel in these first few hours of military occupation was mixed. SNOWI's report claimed that '[the] reception of the troops by the islanders was friendly, and many seemed pleased they were there and said so'.[55] The *Daily Telegraph* similarly noted that Anguillians greeted the helicopter-borne leaflet drop with 'friendly waves'.[56] Indeed, their correspondent Ian Ball assessed that '[many], perhaps a majority of the 6,000 Anguillans, welcomed the invaders'. He added, however, that 'there were many hundreds of Anguillans seething with anger' and noted that some islanders shouted protests at paratroopers and marines.[57] Indeed, Ball noted that Anguillians who had recently been pro-British were now staunchly opposed to the military intervention which they viewed, according to the article, 'as an act of betrayal and deception'.[58]

Interviewing several angered islanders, Ball recorded one, who had previously opposed Webster's government, complaining about the excessive nature of London's military response, stating that '[we] wanted British negotiations, not the British… We did not need this invasion. Maybe a show of force offshore while sensible negotiations went on, but not military occupation'.[59] Another islander, protesting against troops at the airfield, drew the predictable comparison between Britain's willingness to use military force in Anguilla and hesitancy

Officers from the Metropolitan Police arrive in Anguilla. Note their standard blue serge tunics in the Caribbean sun. Soon their uniform would adapt to tropical conditions. (Albert Grandolini collection)

to do so to end illegal Rhodesian independence. The protester explained that '[we] are standing here to show Britain we are not afraid of her…You come here with troops but not in Rhodesia. Yet there is fighting and bloodshed in Rhodesia but none here'.[60] Ball claimed that around one thousand Anguillians, some waving rebel flags, shouted protests such as '[shame] on you British' at the troops stationed at the airfield unloading military supplies.[61] One islander, Olive Rogers, recalled taking part in this protest at the airfield and at subsequent locations, stating that:

> We hear that the paratroopers were comin to raid Anguilla we step up, and some of us said we goin to the airport. We went down in a pick up, […] and the paratroopers they were all on top Albert Lake's shop. I see them and shout, "You come to raid we, but we come to raid all you." And we took rocks and started letting go of the rock at the paratroopers by the old courthouse […] They look more afraid of we than we afraid of them![62]

Numerous Anguillians may have had curiously mixed feelings – including anger, bemusement, uncertainty and surprise – about the arrival of British troops, which was reflected in the reception they gave the soldiers in the first days of the military occupation. The *Chicago Tribune* noted that disgruntled islanders 'stood in small groups watching impassively as the Britons set up roadblocks and posted guards at the crude airstrip and other strategic points'.[63] Indeed, clusters of spectators were reported to have gathered to watch military activity at various locations, including at The Valley Secondary School where the Army and police were establishing their headquarters. As onlookers moved closer to see the military at work in one instance, Lieutenant Jeff Robinson of the Royal Marines told one of his men to 'not be so threatening with those weapons', perhaps aware that some islanders were yet to pass judgement on British troops and their intentions.[64] *The Guardian* recorded the ambiguous atmosphere of an incident whereby 'a crowd of Anguillans shouted to some Paratroops leaning against a wall, "Give us our freedom," they retorted: "Give us some bleeding

rum." Whereupon four bottles were promptly produced'.[65] The curious mixture of opposition and friendliness was similarly evident on the afternoon of the day following the invasion, when some Anguillians held a demonstration, the *Navy News* reporting that '[the] colourfully-dressed crowd were orderly…There were more smiles than scowls'.[66] Taxi driver Charlie Gumbs also told the *Washington Post* that 'I have nothing against Mr. Lee…but if he is going to push Mr. (Ronald) Webster out as our president and let Bradshaw in, he will have to take over an empty island. Anguillans are not afraid to die'.[67] The British administration and its forces, navigating this uncertain atmosphere where Anguillians were yet to trust British troops, needed to vigorously police their own actions. Indeed, Walicek notes that two soldiers were prosecuted for rape.[68]

Alongside attempting to establish a trustful relationship with islanders, British forces and police also set about rounding up key targets for questioning on the first day of the occupation. According to Ball, the task force had arrived in Anguilla with a 'black list' of 20 names.[69] Paratroopers had soon located US citizens Jack Holcomb, Pastor Freeman Goodge and Lewis Haskins. Each of them was taken away for questioning by police.[70] Goodge told the *Washington Post* that soldiers had thoroughly searched his house for guns, complaining that Paras 'swept through everything, even my wife's underwear…They tore the beds down and went through a new Bible leaf by leaf'.[71] He also claimed that the police had interviewed him to obtain any information about weapons and the Mafia.[72] Deportation of some foreign citizens on the target list may have been considered. Only one, however, actually occurred on 19 March. Following Jack Holcomb's questioning by the British authorities, it was decided to deport him from Anguilla that same day. Ball recorded the haste with which the British tried to eject the American, claiming that the authorities attempted to commandeer a plane that had been chartered at the airfield by British journalists and that an 'armed line of paras spread across the runway to stop the pilot from taking off while an official asked that Holcomb be placed aboard and flown to San Juan in Puerto Rico'. When the pilot resisted the request claiming, as Ball summarised, 'that deportation was not his business',

Ronald Webster, accompanied by an APU officer. (Albert Grandolini collection)

the British had to wait for another charter plane which agreed to undertake the flight.[73] Assistant Commissioner Way explained this sudden deportation as having been implemented because Holcomb 'was a dangerous element in a civil situation'.[74]

Webster, the main face of the Anguillian rebellion, recollected that when he heard about the police questioning of individuals in the morning, he drove to The Valley and was stopped at a roadblock by British troops. According to Webster, 'they asked me to go to the Secondary School…They followed me down there but did not touch me at all.' Upon meeting with the police, Webster stated that:

… they asked me some questions and I gave them my answers. I did not try to hide things from them, except that which had nothing to do with them. I was very frank. I answered most of what was asked, but there were certain things I refused…Seeing how influential I was, I believe they had been warned not to try to intimidate me.[75]

The British may indeed have chosen to avoid pursuing Webster due to his political prominence and the potential for this course to enflame Anguillian public opinion. Webster was therefore able to hold a demonstration on the afternoon of 20 March, which SNOWI described as 'noisy but well behaved', in which he demanded the withdrawal of the military occupation force and Lee as HM Commissioner.[76] On the evening of the following day Webster then took a fishing boat to St Maarten, from where he would make the journey to the UN in New York 'to protest the British invasion'.[77]

Despite the targeting of specific individuals for questioning by police in the hours after the initial military takeover, it was noted in *The Times* that many of the people originally rounded up by the Army were reporters and press photographers sent to cover Operation Sheepskin.[78] Indeed, military-media relations became strained in the peculiar atmosphere of anticipation and anti-climax of 19 March. As Westlake noted, reporters were 'heartily disliked by both sides [military and Anguillian]' and were 'strolling around in shirts open at the neck, taking pictures, interviewing soldiers who were trying to keep their minds on the war, and generally making the troops self-conscious, which the troops didn't much care for'.[79] In these circumstances, therefore, it was perhaps unsurprising that the only shot fired by a paratrooper across the entire day was one discharged in warning at a charter plane landing journalists at the airfield which was flying close to where an RAF Hercules was dropping equipment.[80]

As the momentous first day of the military occupation – 19 March – drew to a close, Force Anguilla had reason to be both relieved and slightly uncomfortable. The island had been seized easily without bloodshed and the reception provided by islanders was generally

one of tolerance. However, the military operation had underlined major weaknesses in public relations and many Anguillians appeared uncertain about British motives whilst also influenced by Webster's messaging. The British Army was also yet to encounter the firepower or mafia influence that they had been led to anticipate. That night, whilst army units maintained positions inland, the Royal Marines camped on the beach and the naval party returned to HMS *Minerva*. Two sailors and a marine were left in charge of guarding Tony Lee, who had established his residence in a white villa situated above Road Bay. One member of this bodyguard, Chief Petty Officer Stuart Bowen, remarked that 'I don't know why sailors were chosen, but the captain said I was the biggest and ugliest man for the job… That night I slept on a settee outside Mr. Lee's bedroom with one ear open and one hand on my revolver, not knowing quite what to expect'.[81]

Political and media responses

On the afternoon of 19 March, Foreign Secretary Michael Stewart stood up in the House of Commons to announce the successful completion of the military's landings and to justify the Labour government's decision to launch Operation Sheepskin. Stewart reassured the Commons that 'it is not our purpose to see the Anguillans living under an administration that they do not want'.[82] Then, as decided in Sheepskin's legal planning phase, Stewart explained that the UK had 'a responsibility under the West Indies Act. We took action because conditions in Anguilla were such that it was impossible for us to discharge our constitutional responsibilities for defence and external affairs.'[83] He further highlighted that the Caribbean region was 'particularly susceptible to exploitation' and that 'fragmentation' was a threat amongst small islands. Additionally, he highlighted the call to action over Anguilla made to London by the Caribbean Heads of Government Meeting in February. Finally, he confirmed that HM Commissioner would remain in Anguilla 'until a lasting settlement can be negotiated which will pay full regard to the wishes and interests of all concerned, in particular to those of the inhabitants of the island'.[84]

Whilst there were some voices of support for the government's actions, various responses to Stewart's announcement demonstrated scepticism. Reginald Maudling, Shadow Defence Secretary, questioned whether the government could:

…really maintain that their action has been part of defending Anguilla against external aggression? Secondly, how can they [the British] remain there for the long time envisaged by the Foreign Secretary on that basis unless they have the request and consent of the St. Kitts Government? In those circumstances, can they expect the people of Anguilla to be confident that their wishes will be regarded as paramount?[85]

Similarly, George Brown – Labour's own Deputy Leader – also questioned the extent to which the British could address Anguillian grievances considering London's relationship with the Bradshaw government.[86] He also raised the predictable comparison with non-intervention in Rhodesia, indicating that a stronger justification needed to be made for intervention in Anguilla following the previous Rhodesian decision. He asked how 'having defended ourselves for not using force there [in Rhodesia] on moral principles, how we could now defend ourselves [about Anguilla], when all we are arguing now is that the opposition to overcome was small, whereas in the other case it was big'.[87] Leader of the Opposition Edward Heath similarly questioned the legal foundations of the military intervention, assessing that 'the Government have imposed direct rule on this island by force. The grounds on which the Government justify this action are that it was necessary for the external defence of the island. This will, I think, to say the least, require careful consideration'.[88]

The coverage of Operation Sheepskin in the British press ranged from mild support to blistering criticism and ridicule. Positive analysis came, to an extent, from the *Daily Telegraph* who judged the Foreign Secretary's speech in the Commons to be 'a modest triumph'.[89] A letter to the editor of this newspaper also appeared to defend Sheepskin from one particular criticism, stating that '[surely] it is quite absurd to draw a parallel between the decision to send troops to Anguilla but not to do so in the case of Rhodesia' and concluding '[let] us therefore not be bombarded by a lot of nonsense from any quarter, especially the United Nations, in dealing with two totally different matters in our own way'.[90] *The Times* also noted that the tactical plan of Operation Sheepskin 'appeared to work as planned'.[91] However, the said newspaper also stated in another article that there 'was an almost audible sigh of relief from all sides of the Commons that this episode, rapidly taking on all the elements of a tragicomedy, had been concluded without bloodshed'.[92]

Criticism was, however, more direct in other British newspapers. Following the leakage of military planning details, *Daily Mail* political editor Walter Terry claimed that an MP had told him that it was 'becoming Wilson's Bay of Piglets. The affair has become a joke, but it also is a disgrace'.[93] In another article, the newspaper also criticised the Wilson government's poor communication about the invasion and questioned the scale of the threat existing in Anguilla which had led to Operation Sheepskin. It complained that '[there] has never been anything like the Anguilla incident since Don Quixote set out to tilt at windmills. Farcical? – lord, yes. But an unfunny farce, at that. Indeed, this ridiculous episode is as serious as it could be'. The article went on to conclude that '[if] Anguilla does not prove to be the Government's Waterloo, it could easily be Mr Harold Wilson's Suez'.[94] Similarly, *The Guardian* stated mockingly that 'we can all glory once again at the splendid sight of the British sledgehammer, coming down unerringly on a colonial nut'.[95] Letters to the newspaper's editor were similarly critical. One of them complained of how he had 'viewed with growing alarm the mishandling of the Anguilla situation over the last 18 months', also regarding the use of troops as a 'tragedy' and assessing that concern about mafia influence seemed 'extremely far fetched' and intended to cover Britain's diplomatic failure.[96] Another letter viewed the Anguilla crisis as 'the all-time low point in British diplomatic ineptitude' and compared Britain's military actions with the Soviet Union's recent invasion of Czechoslovakia, arguing that, allowing 'for the differences in scale, import, and setting, and there is still an arresting, shaming parallel with Czechoslovakia. There it was protection against revisionist, subversive elements; here it is protection against lawlessness and trumped-up Mafia. The evidence is equally suspect'.[97]

Non-British newspapers also ridiculed Operation Sheepskin. The *New York Times* emphasised the anachronistic gunboat diplomacy of Britain's actions, noting that 'memories of grandeur and the days of Lord Palmerston die hard. And they were all revived again by what some people call "the six-minute war"'.[98] The *Chicago Tribune*, ridiculing the lack of opposition to the British Army, mockingly described how '[whelks] and winkles on the beach gazed up in awe as the queen's finest, supported by a backup contingent of London bobbies flown to the scene, showed that the British lion can still muster something between a mew and a roar'.[99] Similarly, the *Los Angeles Times* announced that the 'British lion, subduing a mouse that roared, took control of Anguilla', whilst the *Washington Post* observed more seriously that 'London looks silly. What is left to it now is to do something substantial to upgrade the welfare and status of Anguilla, so as to level off the discrepancies which made Anguilla fearful of federation with St. Kitts'.[100]

The British Foreign Secretary had hoped that the United States government would provide 'public and diplomatic support in the United Nations and elsewhere' for the UK's military intervention.[101] However, whilst solidarity was shown in Washington's response, it was perhaps somewhat lacklustre. On the day of the military landings, the *Daily Telegraph* predicted the detached nature of US policy, observing that the 'official attitude of the American Government to the situation in Anguilla is that it is a problem for Britain to solve. Washington is not likely to give public support for British military intervention'.[102] A couple of days later the same newspaper noted that '[officially] and in public, the American position is one of "sympathy" with Britain's long-range goals in the Caribbean; nothing stronger than that. But privately, senior Washington officials feel Britain over-reacted to a ludicrous degree'.[103] The British may have expected more American support considering Washington's security and political concerns in the Caribbean region. A memorandum by the Foreign Secretary in July 1969 noted that the 'last U.S. administration [under President Lyndon Johnson] made it clear to us on many occasions that they expected us to play our traditional part in maintaining the security of the area. We have no reason to suppose that the present U.S. administration [of President Richard Nixon] would think differently'.[104] However, the seemingly excessive use of military force against an island that had shown no resistance – relying on unilateral gunboat diplomacy rather than a peacekeeping coalition such as that envisaged in the Barbados agreement of 1967 – may have dampened American enthusiasm for Britain's solution to the Anguilla crisis.

Condemnation of Britain's military intervention was widespread across the international community. This was evident at the UN, where Secretary General U Thant received letters from diverse writers angered by Britain's perceived return to colonialism. Tim Hector, Chairman of the Antigua Opposition Party, demanded that the 'United Nations must protest Britains [sic] invasion and occupation of tiny defenceless Anguilla' and claimed that 'Britain has today established old style colonial regime in Anguilla'.[105] Charles Kindle of the United Negro Protest Committee similarly asked the UN to condemn London's actions and that the UN supervise elections on the island, whilst the President of the Students Guild at the University of the West Indies also stated that their St Augustine Campus 'condemns British invasion' and demanded a UN investigation.[106] Even an Englishman, Dr F.W. Boon, wrote to the UN disassociating himself from 'the repressive action' of the British government and complaining that an 'England led by a megalomaniac like Harold Wilson with self-interest as the determinant consideration is not in the interests of world affairs'.[107] The Committee of 24, long a thorn in Britain's diplomatic side over Anguilla, also expressed that they were 'gravely concerned by the landing of British troops…[and] deem it necessary to send urgently a visiting group of the Special Committee to the Territory'.[108]

International condemnation was also evident in media coverage around the world, which was reviewed by *The Times*. Charles Hargrove wrote that whilst the French press had been 'on the whole restrained', a 'common feature of its comment had been surprise that the proverbial British common sense – not to mention sense of ridicule – should have been so conspicuously lacking in

Whitehall's handling of the affair.'[109] Soviet news agency, *TASS*, correspondent Eduard Baskakov claimed that the British government 'having discredited itself by a new crime against the 6,000-strong people of Anguilla, is trying in every way to justify its actions in public eyes.'[110] Furthermore, *The Times* article summarised the *New China* news agency's view as being that 'the armed threat against independent Anguilla once again laid bare the ugly features of the rapidly declining British imperialism which was still putting up a last-ditch struggle'.[111]

Not all foreign media coverage was, however, negative. As *The Times* noted, Dutch newspaper *Algemeen Dagblad* assessed that Operation

Patrol Company, 2PARA, Operation Sheepskin, Anguilla 1969. Para patrols were vital for establishing trust with Anguillians and projecting Britain's political messages. (Airborne Assault Museum)

Sheepskin 'was not without seriousness. The British Government knew well what it was doing.'[112] Similarly, Croatian military scholar Andro Galbelić, identified more coherent and strategic motives in Britain's actions. Referring to the Defence White Paper of 1968, Galbelić noted that, despite the planned withdrawal of troops from East of Suez, the British had retained the capacity to deploy forces overseas when needed. Accordingly, Operation Sheepskin had been a manifestation of Britain's continued commitment to a global role offering security to many former colonial territories even after the retreat from East of Suez.[113] Whitehall noted this more detailed investigation of its defence policy, with the British Ambassador to Yugoslavia commenting that '[this] is, so far, an isolated voice' in the Yugoslav public sphere, although Operation Sheepskin had received a surprisingly 'easy ride' in the country overall.[114] Ultimately, however, despite these less satirical assessments, international media coverage was largely dominated by ridicule and criticism of London's actions.

Harold Wilson was able to personally assess the response of Trinidadian Prime Minister Dr Eric Williams to Sheepskin when the latter visited him in Parliament on the evening of 19 March. According to Wilson's foreign affairs private secretary, 'the Prime Minister said that he understood that Dr. Williams was not happy with the action which the British Government had had to take in Anguilla. Dr. Williams confirmed this.'[115] The Foreign Secretary, however, reportedly identified a more complex response from the Trinidadian Prime Minister, having met him for lunch earlier in the day. A minute to Wilson noted that 'Stewart gained the impression that there was in fact a difference between Williams' public and private view'. Although Stewart assessed that Williams could not endorse the invasion due to his position on Rhodesian non-intervention, the Foreign Secretary believed that over Anguilla 'Williams probably accepts privately that we were right to do what we did'. It was added to the meeting summary, however, that these assessments were 'an impression and not based on anything firm said to Mr. Stewart by Dr. Williams'.[116]

The evolution of military strategy

As Force Anguilla entered its first full day of military occupation, their momentum and focus in fulfilling their strategic objectives began to slip. SNOWI later wrote to the Chief of the Defence Staff, MRAF Sir Charles Elworthy, that '[things] started to go wrong on the morning of 20th March, when, because of the lack of opposition to the landings and generally friendly reception, it became politically unacceptable to proceed with deportations and the search of private property for arms.' Consequently, SNOWI concluded that, facing these issues combined with other public relations problems, '[it] was at this moment that we began to lose the political initiative'.[117] The aim of deporting foreign citizens from Anguilla who were deemed troublesome quickly encountered problems. Whilst Holcomb had been hurriedly deported on 19 March and the Anguillian homes of several US citizens searched, insufficient evidence had been found to support detaining Haskins and Goodge family members. Moreover, although it was subsequently decided to deport the Goodge family on 24 March, growing public hostility meant that, according to a British report, 'the deportation was cancelled in case it aroused feelings still further'.[118]

Weapons searches also yielded few results. Several military and police patrols were sent to the East End to investigate the whereabouts of these weapons on 20 March, but it was concluded at a British command meeting that evening, according to SNOWI, that '[little] information on the whereabouts of arms was forthcoming'.[119] Webster later stated that these arms were placed in 'vaults' prior to the invasion.[120] He recalled that the British 'had a couple of metal detectors, but they did not seem to work very well. We had a lot of iron and scrap around, so signals came up everywhere. Each time they made an approach and dug up something, it was of no consequence'.[121] A British report noted that there had been many 'rumours' about where the guns were hidden. However, none were 'sufficiently precise for action to be taken', apart from one report that the arms were on Scrub Island – off the north-east tip of the main island – causing the Royal Marines to search this location unsuccessfully on 23 March.[122] Westlake appeared confident that the weapons were instead buried on Franco-Dutch St Maarten, where he claimed they still remained at his time of writing in the early 1970s.[123] By the end of 20 March only one rifle, one shotgun and one pistol had been voluntarily surrendered and the British opened an amnesty the following week to encourage more submissions.[124] A report from July 1969 by Detective Inspector Williams suggested that the amnesty had been fairly successful, yielding a Boyes anti-tank rifle, seven pistols, 27 shotguns, 11 rifles and, famously, a Napoleonic-era cannon.[125]

Whether the British did eventually obtain a significant proportion of the Anguillian arsenal or whether arms caches remained out of their reach, Force Anguilla were concerned in the first days of the occupation that they had not succeeded in achieving a key objective by disarming the island. Weapons searches by the Army would thus continue into April. SNOWI, complaining about the political unacceptability of mounting arms searches in private property, among other challenges, assessed that:

> At the beginning of the operation, opinion seemed to be that we were using a sledgehammer to crack a nut. As I signalled at the time, I would have liked one blow with the sledgehammer, and then a quick withdrawal of troops. I fear we failed to deliver the blow immediately after landing, when it would have been most effective, and have been trying to crack the nut ever since.[126]

The prospect of a lingering threat perhaps posed by potential undiscovered weapons was highlighted by the MoD. At a Chiefs of Staff meeting on 21 March it was raised that there was 'a risk that weapons not found could later be used against the Police'.[127] Brigadier Peter Martin of the Army Strategic Command, who visited Anguilla in late April, also reported that moderate Anguillians 'said they were not prepared to stick their necks out too far, because Webster still had all the weapons and they would be killed if the British withdrew from the island'.[128] Ultimately, the lack of results achieved in weapons searches proved a notable strategic problem until, perhaps, Williams' report of July 1969 stated that a significant number of guns had been surrendered, some destroyed and many assessed as unserviceable.[129] From this report, HM Commissioner was able to conclude that 'the threat to security posed by unrecovered weapons is negligible'.[130]

With the British unable to find evidence of weapons caches or gangster activity in the first few days of the occupation, ministers in the Wilson government soon began to lose patience. Mawby describes a 'fractious Cabinet meeting on 20 March…followed by a full-scale row on 25 March'.[131] Richard Crossman, Secretary of State for Social Services, recorded around this time that 'Whitlock gave us a lot of information about the mafia and that Anguilla might be turned into a gambling hell. Now it appears that British correspondents are saying all this is sheer gossip. The island is a perfectly peaceful, religious, primitive place…and the mafia talk is all invention'.[132] Anger, particularly aimed at the FCO, erupted on 25 March and resulted, according to Mawby, in a policy transition facilitating a more conciliatory British approach towards Webster.[133] Barbara Castle, describing the meeting, recorded that 'the dam of our patience burst. We really do feel we have been made fools of – by somebody. Denis [Healey] weighed in first. He complained that a lot of our information had been wrong.'[134]

Healey himself would later conclude, reflecting on the lessons of the military intervention, that '[no] government should ever carry out such an operation unless it has good intelligence of the local situation, has first consulted all governments which may feel themselves concerned, has clear political objectives, and has made careful psychological preparations.'[135] Wilson similarly

A Para, armed with an L7A1 7.62mm General Purpose Machine Gun, sits near an Anguillian woman. (Albert Grandolini collection)

admitted a degree of regret for undertaking the operation, stating in his memoirs that '[we] were advised by our man on the spot that Anguilla was under the control of a group of men in close touch with property developers, indeed Mafia-type gangsters, though what we learnt later threw great doubt on this.' Although Wilson claimed that the Whitlock affair, combined with Anguilla's rejection of both Kittitian and British governance, 'made it necessary for us to act', he also admitted that 'I have, on subsequent occasions, been very doubtful whether the decision we took – to which course I was a fully consenting party – was right.' Ultimately, however, at his time of writing in 1971 he concluded that 'all that has happened since has, on the whole, convinced me that it was [right]'.[136]

At the command meeting held on the evening of 20 March involving HM Commissioner Lee, SNOWI, Assistant Commissioner Way and their various staffs, the leaders of the military occupation took stock of the situation on the island. The meeting assessed that the British administration's ability to communicate with Anguillians and counter the messaging of the highly influential Webster was poor, whilst information about weapons was unforthcoming and, whilst there was no hostility to British troops and policemen, 'there was a strong element in the island calling for their removal'.[137] It was therefore decided to adjust the British military strategy by launching a 'Hearts and Minds' campaign. British troops patrolling the island would accordingly be thoroughly briefed on Britain's political messaging so that they could spread this to islanders by word of mouth. Other communication outlets, including loudspeakers, leaflets and radio would be mobilised, whilst *The Beacon* would be encouraged to restart publication. Entertainment would be laid on in the forms of sporting events, a cinema using Royal Navy equipment, children's entertainment and the establishment of a makeshift radio station broadcasting from *Minerva*.[138]

This face-to-face public relations campaign implemented by Force Anguilla and the APU was relatively successful. According to a report by psyops officer Lt. Colonel Johnston, he issued political guidance to 2PARA and police officers who, in turn, 'briefed their troops and constables on what could and could not be said to the civil population'. Johnston even stated that both the Paratrooper and London bobby were particularly effective in this public relations role, claiming that the 'above average selection grading and the intelligence of troops of the Parachute Regiment and the experience and quality of the police constables of the Metropolitan Police made both particularly suitable for this work'. Whilst Johnston acknowledged that these public relations activities were 'unusual and not always popular', he concluded that 'most officers and troops conducted the work with enthusiasm and the results were most effective', confirming that the 'British soldier, correctly briefed, can be a natural propagandist'.[139] The effectiveness of these face-to-face interactions was evident in the *Pegasus* journal, which claimed that '[refreshment] was pressed liberally on to hot and tired soldiers and these regular patrols developed into social welfare visits at which advice or help in a multitude of problems was asked for and often given'.[140] 'A' Company of 2PARA was initially responsible for patrolling the north-east area of Anguilla, C Company the south-west, and D Company was held in reserve at the Secondary School.

Men of 2PARA with locals in Anguilla, 1969. Whilst Anguillians often mistrusted Britain's political intentions during Operation Sheepskin, by the time of 2PARA's departure in September 1969 they had conducted a fairly successful Hearts and Minds campaign. (Airborne Assault Museum)

From mid-April onwards, these patrols also assumed another objective that would assist in intelligence-gathering, measuring public opinion and conducting local government. From a headquarters nicknamed the Parapit or Paramount, an island-wide census was directed under the codename 'Grass Roots', the first to be conducted in almost 10 years. As 2PARA's regimental history outlined, Grassroots Patrols, 'by carefully plotting each house and chatting idly to the occupants, were able to discover the number of dependants and their opinions on sensitive issues'[141]. This information was then fed back to headquarters, where Captain Michael Jackson transferred it to a 'master map and built up a card index system of the population'.[142] Information about the 'political mood' of each area of Anguilla was then sent to HM Commissioner's office for analysis of the public reception of government policies.[143] By the time the operation was completed in mid-June, almost 100 percent of the island's population had been included in the census.[144]

An unanticipated long-term legacy of the Grassroot patrols was the 'Toys for Anguilla' scheme, which would constitute a considerable public relations success for the British Army later in the year. According to an article by Colour Sergeant Major Knowles in *Pegasus*, a Para corporal had noticed whilst patrolling that Anguillian children did not appear to possess many toys and spent 'most of their playing time with such fascinating things as an empty coke tin filled with stones or a piece of wood being dragged along with a string collar'.[145] Consequently, B Company 2PARA considered whether the regiment could obtain a supply of toys for the 2,000 children on Anguilla and also generate good PR benefits from such a scheme. It was accordingly decided to attempt the launching of a media campaign and the *Daily Express* was contacted in late June outlining the Grassroots Patrols and requesting the appeal for toys. According to Knowles, the *Express* circulated this appeal at the British Toy Manufacturer's Fair in late October and

Father Christmas. The donations of the 'Toys for Anguilla' scheme were distributed to children at a series of Christmas parties. (Airborne Assault Museum)

consequently '[the] response was magnificent and toys and books of the latest design flowed into the [Daily Express] Action Line Office in Fleet Street'.[146] RAF Support Command then transported the toys to Anguilla, where they were organised by the Royal Engineers and distributed by this regiment to children at a series of Christmas parties arranged by HM Commissioner's office.[147]

Whilst the Toys for Anguilla idea had originated from B Company 2PARA and the regiment had put significant energy into its implementation, the scheme's results emerged after the regiment had left the island and hence, according to Knowles, the Paras 'did not receive much direct publicity from this exercise'.[148] Nevertheless, Knowles, the only Para who was attached to the scheme until its completion, acknowledged that Toys for Anguilla did constitute a major PR success for the British Army as a whole, involving amongst its media publicity a 'four-minute news feature showing the distribution of the toys…shown at peak [television] viewing time on Christmas Eve'.[149] The scheme ultimately demonstrates that the British military occupation, rather than being the footnote to an embarrassing and miscalculated invasion, involved some creative hearts and minds and PR initiatives from a regiment often more at home with the sharp end of war.

Good relations with islanders were also assisted by the medical treatment provided by the Royal Army Medical Corps, Royal Navy medical officers and the Field Surgical Team of 23 Parachute Field Ambulance. Medical services in Anguilla had been very limited prior to the military intervention. According to the report of Major F.B. Mayes of the RAMC, upon the British arrival 'there was an acute shortage of drugs of all kinds, the situation being complicated by the state of the main dispensary which for some time had been re-supplied almost entirely by boxes of 'professional samples' from America.' Moreover, Mayes continued, 'there was a pool of untreated sick, owing to poor clinic attendances, and in part to failure to open the peripheral clinics regularly, both factors resulting from the local political situation'.[150]

In addressing the resources issue, the dispensary was reorganised and a purchase of drugs was authorised by HM Commissioner. To deal with the backlog of untreated Anguillians, both static and mobile clinics were staffed and arrangements put in place for the longer term sustaining of these clinics. In the first weeks of the occupation, the clinics at South Hill and West End were run by Captain Michael Harley, Regimental Medical Officer of 23 Parachute Field Ambulance, and also by the surgeon lieutenant of HMS *Minerva*. Meanwhile, Major Mayes and Major Nick Burbridge, also of 23 Para Field Ambulance, worked with the mobile clinic focusing on the Island Harbour area.[151] A Field Surgical Team established at the main hospital also cleared the backlog of those islanders awaiting elective surgery and dealt with emergency cases, performing operations that included amputations, burns, fractures and dentistry, although on two occasions the surgical programme was hindered by the failure of the hospital's power generator. The Royal Navy also provided specialist teams to help partly renovate the hospital, dealing with plumbing, electrics, cleaning and redecoration. Following his departure from Anguilla in late April, Mayes was able report an improvement in the medical facilities on the island, listing 'the Cottage Hospital with a capacity of 25 beds, a central clinic with well equipped dental surgery, three peripheral clinics, and a fully equipped mobile clinic. There are adequate numbers of well trained nurses staffing these establishments, including district midwives and a health visitor'.[152]

Adding to the face-to-face conversations with islanders and the improvement in medical services, Force Anguilla also provided entertainment. The frigates offshore broadcast makeshift radio shows and music. 2PARA also ran cinema screenings using navy equipment and formed a team to run these evening shows in villages across the island. The latter projected British light entertainment and documentaries, proving, according to British reports, to be 'very popular' and providing 'a valuable means of winning confidence'.[153] However, on an island with very poor infrastructure, a key method of winning hearts and minds would be British investment in building projects. Such plans had produced limited results in the Interim Agreement period and there were still many infrastructural improvements that could be made. SNOWI had accordingly signalled to London soon after the initial invasion indicating the value of sending Royal Engineers (REs) to undertake this building work. This deployment was discussed at a Chiefs of Staff meeting on 21 March in which it was acknowledged that, regarding building projects, '[in] order to show good will it was desirable for positive results to be seen in the near future.' Furthermore, it was recognised that the REs could perform a useful security role in Anguilla after the inevitable and impending withdrawal of the Paras. It was therefore decided to send immediately a reconnaissance party of six REs to Anguilla to 'provide an estimate of the total liability', who could then be followed by a main RE party of around 70 men.[154] The reconnaissance party reached Anguilla on 24 March, led by the commander of 33 Field Squadron RE, Major R.L. Plummer.

Whilst the main force of REs was indeed subsequently dispatched by London and arrived in Anguilla on 28 March, their immediate public relations impact was limited. At a debriefing meeting held at the MoD following the return of a senior army officer from visiting Anguilla in mid-April, it was reportedly assessed that Anguillians 'respect the Paratroops and the Police but they are not so impressed with the Sappers so far'. This may have been due to the limited progress on building projects up to that point, a summary of the MoD meeting recording the assessment made that '[to] date the Royal Engineers have not be[en] able to make enough progress on the "Hearts and Minds" front. They have not really launched their two major projects (a) Road building (b) Building of a school. There are other tasks to be undertaken and as equipment is being got together progress is expected.'[155]

Continued unrest and the Caradon agreement

Whilst relations between troops and islanders remained generally amiable and perhaps grew notably warmer as a result of the long-term Hearts and Minds campaign, Anguilla still remained ripe for unrest whilst the political situation continued to be uncertain. Indeed, the internal security situation appeared to worsen for the British in the days after the initially peaceful occupation of the island. On the morning of 22 March, Tony Lee was confronted by a group of around 150 demonstrators on his way to his office in the Administrative Building located near the airfield. The crowd, bearing signs demanding that HM Commissioner leave Anguilla, had already prevented a British magistrate from entering his office and had attempted to access the balcony of the building.[156] Lee, who had been warned of the demonstration, nevertheless arrived in a green Volkswagen which was soon surrounded by demonstrators who could not be contained by the roughly half-dozen APU at the scene. According to *The New York Times*, Lee subsequently 'received some roughing up, but was uninjured. His car, however, was dented on the hood and roof'.[157]

The confrontation was described by *The Sunday Times* as 'the first expression of violence by the Anguillans since Britain invaded', with some demonstrators carrying pointed sticks wrapped in

Mr Tony Lee. Her Majesty's Commissioner, seated next to the army driver, in discussion. Note the Union Jack on the vehicle's bonnet. Lee is, perhaps, showing the flag as part of the vital public relations campaign. (Airborne Assault Museum)

personification of this British administration, attracted particular anger from those islanders suspicious of the UK's political motives. This opposition to Lee was evident amongst the crowd, with voices reportedly heard screaming 'Kill him, kill him' and another man, echoing signs held by protesters, shouting that '[we] don't want Mr. Lee here!'[164] Meanwhile, whilst the demonstration was ongoing, Lt. Colonel Johnston – head of psyops – was driving around the island with a policeman broadcasting a message from Lee emphasising that Anguilla would not be returned to St Kitts and that the REs would soon be undertaking building projects. Moreover, he reassured Anguillians that 'policemen and the soldiers and sailors are your friends' and that the 'London policemen will themselves go as soon as a local police force can take over'.[165]

the Anguillian flag. According to the newspaper's account, one policeman was knocked down and almost trampled upon and another, calling for calm through a loudspeaker, was also hit.[158] This latter officer may have been the one reported in another newspaper as having been wounded in the hand by a woman wielding a bicycle pump.[159] The handful of overwhelmed APU soon called for reinforcements and around 40 policemen descended on the demonstration. The Paras were also reportedly called to the area but stayed out of the confrontation.[160] This stance was in line with the military's allocated role of acting in support of the civil power, using minimum force and handing the primary security role to the APU. Tempers in the crowd flared further when Assistant Commissioner Way arrived and moved through the crowd to reach the police cordon. It ultimately took around an hour overall to establish a sense of calm. Sergeant Edward Cook, who had been injured in the hand, told the media that '[we] are playing it cool' when discussing the APU attitude towards the demonstrators and, indeed, no arrests were made during the confrontation.[161] Instead, the police showed considerable restraint and handled the situation, according to the *Daily Telegraph*, 'with sunburnt hands and low-keyed banter. The relaxed approach worked in the end'.[162] Tony Lee, meanwhile, had abandoned his commute to the office and returned to his residence.

Once the tension had subsided, the police were able to spread out into the crowd to discuss the political situation in a less confrontational manner asserting, according to *The Observer*, that 'Mr Lee must stay here to help you. We want time to get a few things done. Mr Lee won't force Anguilla back under the control of St Kitts.'[163] Indeed, events on 22 March had somewhat represented a physical manifestation of the larger ideological battle for control of Anguillian loyalties that was being waged between the British administration and the revolutionaries. Tony Lee, as the

Despite reassurances that the UK would not return Anguilla to the Associated State, the lack of concrete political proposals for initiating a resolution to the Anguilla crisis undermined trust in the British administration amongst many islanders in the early days of the occupation. Webster had demanded that the British hold a referendum to again assess whether Anguillians wished to remain part of the St Kitts-Nevis union or gain independence. However, Lee had refused to pursue this option until his new administration had had time to establish itself properly. *The Guardian* stated on 24 March that 'British policy may be clear to Westminster and Whitehall but it is not understood by Anguillans. The refusal to allow a referendum for an indefinite period or to permit the election of an advisory council to the Commissioner has created grave suspicion that Britain intends one day to force Anguilla back into the hated St Kitts-Nevis federation.'[166] Moreover, what was regarded by many islanders as an unnecessary military intervention by Britain had arguably further intensified Anguillian feelings of vulnerability.

The growing Anguillian mistrust of the British administration, in turn, increased the prospect of further instability and Lee admitted to journalists after his ordeal of 22 March that '[the] situation has deteriorated since we got here'.[167] Reports from military patrols in subsequent days highlighted, according to SNOWI's later summary, 'that the campaign against Mr. Lee was spreading, and that there was evidence of intimidation and threats being made against the moderate and friendly element'.[168] The first Paras had originally been scheduled to leave the island on 25 March but the growing instability, combined with the likelihood of more demonstrations to come after Webster's return to Anguilla, persuaded Lee, Lt. Colonel Dawnay and Assistant Commissioner Way to recommend postponing this military withdrawal.[169]

Having left Anguilla on 21 March, Webster had sailed to St Maarten and then took a flight from St Croix to New York where he intended to protest Britain's invasion at the UN. Whilst in New York he had two meetings with Lord Caradon, head of the UK Mission, and the latter had agreed to travel to the island in the capacity of a British government special envoy and attempt to negotiate a settlement. Lord Caradon was particularly well suited to undertake this task due to his considerable political experience of decolonisation, having served in a range of administrative posts in Palestine, Libya, Cyprus, Jamaica and Nigeria. His obituary in *The Times* underlined Caradon's, and those of his Colonial Service generation's, 'great diplomatic skill in bringing together disparate and sometimes hostile

Ronald Webster walks with Lord Caradon. (Airborne Assault Museum)

ethnic communities to form a nation state. Towards the end, they were more counsellors to local cabinets than governors.'[170] Caradon was able to bring this considerable diplomatic skill to the UN upon his arrival in 1961, rising to the post of Permanent Representative from the United Kingdom to the United Nations in 1964. According to his obituary he was 'well respected by delegates from all regions and he carried out public debates with much eloquence and dignity', handling questions with 'courtesy and firmness'.[171] Now, in late March 1969 Caradon was wading into the quagmire of Anguillian politics, a territory already traversed by Shepherd, Chapman, Fisher, Whitlock and Lee.

Lord Caradon arrived at Anguilla's airfield to large crowds on the morning of 28 March. With the risk of violence breaking out between Anguillians of different political persuasions, police reinforcements were called up to separate the factions whilst troops were, according to SNOWI, 'kept well in the background'.[172] Indeed, the British Army's visible presence around the island would be noticeably reduced during Caradon's three-day visit, with all day-time patrols by troops withdrawn and the army confined to their bases at the Secondary School and Sandy Bay, and restricted to only patrolling jointly with the APU at night. A brigadier who later visited the island believed that soldiers had thus been 'virtually confined to camp in order not to annoy Mr Webster', an approach which this senior officer judged to be 'a mistake, and it certainly distressed the soldiers who began to feel there was not much point in their presence on the island'.[173] Nevertheless, Caradon was able negotiate a seven-point agreement, signed with Webster, Harrigan and others on 30 March.

Recognising that Anguilla needed 'a period of constructive co-operation' achieved through 'working together in agreement and friendship', the signatories agreed that government would be carried out by HM Commissioner 'in full consultation and co-operation with representatives of the people of Anguilla'. Through

Lt. Colonel Richard Dawnay talks with Lord Caradon. (Airborne Assault Museum)

this latter provision, Webster essentially recognised the authority of Lee. However, the agreement also recognised the Island Council of 1968, which included Webster, 'as elected representatives of the people' who would now form the council to cooperate with HM

Commissioner. Acknowledging Anguillian grievances with the military occupation, the Caradon agreement also stated a hope that 'this initial period can start at once to enable a very early return to normality and withdrawal of the Parachute Regiment'. Perhaps to demonstrate good faith about this withdrawal, A Company 2PARA left the island on 1 April, the day after Caradon's own departure. Additionally, looking to the longer-term political future of Anguilla, the agreement stated that there would be 'further consultations, including consultations with Caribbean Governments', whilst again reassuring islanders that Britain did not intend for Anguilla to be forced under a government that it did not want.[174]

According to SNOWI, Caradon left Anguilla 'amid general acclamation and euphoria' on 31 March.[175] The special envoy had indeed achieved a notable diplomatic breakthrough. Whereas the security situation had been worsening in the days leading up to his visit and Webster had been protesting Britain's invasion on the international stage, by the end of Caradon's stay an agreement had brought the various parties in Anguilla towards a spirit of cooperation, whilst securing Webster's recognition of the British administration and reassuring islanders about Britain's political intentions. Webster himself later recollected that he was 'very happy with the declaration because it had recognized the 1968 elected Council and had provided hope for the island's future. The visit from the British diplomat was good for us because it had helped to ease some of the tension which had escalated since the invasion.'[176] Indeed, SNOWI observed that the island 'remained relaxed' following Caradon's departure, with military operations scaled back and focusing on the hunt for weapons caches. SNOWI himself also left Anguilla for Bermuda and handed the post of Commander Force Anguilla to Lt. Colonel Dawnay on 3 April.[177] This transfer of military command was perhaps an indication of how far the security situation was regarded as having improved.

The spirit of optimism was not, however, shared by the Bradshaw government, which Lord Caradon visited in St Kitts following the Anguilla agreement. The Premier of the Associated State refused to recognise the recently signed declaration. When asked for his thoughts about it by journalists the day after his two-hour meeting with Caradon, Bradshaw replied '[what] agreement? Constitutionally Anguilla is part of the associated state of St. Kitts-Nevis-Anguilla and cannot be separated any more than Scotland can from the United Kingdom.'[178] Moreover, whilst recognising Caradon's considerable diplomatic success in generating a spirit of cooperation, newspapers also acknowledged the limitations of the declaration. It was noted in The Times that 'Anguilla's national revolution appeared to have petered out today in a web of peaceable vagueness spun by Lord Caradon' and that '[nothing] has been settled except that Mr. Anthony Lee…will now be able to work with a council of islanders to keep the place running while more decisions are made.'[179] The Daily Mail, meanwhile, assessed the declaration as 'an astonishing feat of diplomacy. He [Caradon] made almost no promises to the islanders. He conceded virtually nothing.' The article also went on to state that 'no one on Anguilla is certain that the detente will last'.[180]

Collectively, the period between the initial occupation of Anguilla on 19 March and Caradon's departure on 31 March had been a military and political rollercoaster for many of those involved. The events of the Anguillian crisis, starting in 1967, had often been characterised by their unanticipated, sometimes farcical and weird nature. Operation Sheepskin and the early military occupation were no different. An amphibious landing that was predicted to encounter armed resistance proved uneventful and Anguilla was secured quickly, only for the security situation to notably deteriorate days later. The anticipated gangsters had proven to be illusions and the weapons searches had produced limited initial results. The British taskforce – lacking sufficient intelligence and psyops resources – had needed to adapt strategically to the circumstances found on the island, a challenge they overcame fairly effectively. Indeed, their Hearts and Minds campaign would prove over time to be a notable success. The political situation had, in one sense, also moved quickly across late March, transitioning from violent demonstrations and Webster's UN protest to a diplomatic agreement encouraging a new spirit of cooperation. Some things, however, had not changed. Bradshaw continued to challenge Anguillian secession, whilst little concrete progress had been made towards resolving the long-term issues at the heart of the dispute. Whilst the events of 19–31 March had thus been an important milestone in changing the political course of the Anguilla crisis, much remained yet to be resolved.

6

RESOLVING THE ANGUILLA CRISIS

Despite the initial optimism over the Caradon Declaration, it did not take long for dispute and confrontation to return to Anguillian politics. One contributing factor was somewhat due to unlucky timing. The Beacon had finally resumed publication, following an earlier breaking of its print roller, with an edition on 31 March. Whilst the newspaper was thus able to publicise the new agreement, this edition was also the first occasion upon which it could cover the regulations with which HM Commissioner had been able, if needed, to govern Anguilla since his arrival on 19 March. The regulations included giving the police and military the power to search buildings and make arrests without warrants and also allowed these security forces to search people. The regulations also covered, among other issues, the requisitioning of property, deportations and the powers of the new APU.[1] According to Westlake, '[when] the Anguillans saw the notice in the same issue of The Beacon as the agreement signed with Lord Caradon, they thought these regulations were about to start now'.[2] In fact, the regulations had applied since the new British administration had started. However, Webster would soon interpret The Beacon announcement as evidence that Lee had declared martial law after the Caradon Declaration had been signed, thus violating the agreement.[3]

A second source of political dispute derived from the nature of HM Commissioner's collaboration with the Island Council under the Caradon Declaration. In early April, Lee held a meeting with this council at which he assumed chairmanship. As Webster had held this position since UDI and the members of the council remained the same under the new administration, he believed that the chairmanship should remain his. Furthermore, Lee would reconstitute the Island Council – which, according to the Wooding Report, Britain had not previously recognised as a legal entity –

into an Advisory Council without the post of a chairman, which Webster interpreted as a dissolution of the council. Consequently, Webster again left Anguilla to protest the perceived violation of the declaration to Caradon in New York.

The fall of Tony Lee

Lee had been the focus of anti-British feeling in Anguilla prior to the Caradon Declaration and, with the new deterioration of the political situation in early April, Anguillian anger towards him grew once again. Whilst the FCO issued a statement defending Lee by asserting that '[nothing] has been done in Anguilla by Her Majesty's Commissioner which was not strictly in accordance with the terms of the agreement with Lord Caradon', Lee's continued tenure as Commissioner was increasingly in doubt.[4] The *Daily Telegraph* of 10 April concluded that Lee 'could find himself the sacrificial lamb of the Anguillan crisis' and that 'though it is unreasoned and unjustified it seems that his continued presence will be used by the hard-core rebels to generate more unrest'.[5] Lee himself, speaking to a *Telegraph* reporter, judged that there was a '50-50' chance that London would remove him from office.[6] When Caradon subsequently returned to Anguilla for a two-day visit on 11 April, Lee's unpopularity was a dominant issue. On the first day of the visit, a crowd of around 200 chanted 'We want Lee' outside the Commissioner's residence, where Caradon was staying.[7] When demonstrators attempted to enter the building, violent clashes broke out with police. One constable, Jack Gooday, was badly wounded by a blow to the head and received numerous bite marks. As the situation deteriorated, Assistant Commissioner Way requested help from the military. A Royal Marine platoon from HMS *Rhyl* – the frigate that had replaced *Minerva* on 2 April as the vessel supporting the British administration from offshore – arrived with 2PARA and barbed wire barricades were established around the residence.[8] The infantry then guarded the building with bayonets fixed throughout the night.[9]

Caradon left the island on 13 April without making any political progress. He had met briefly with Webster soon after his arrival but, according to the *Daily Telegraph*, another meeting was rejected by the Anguillian leader as Caradon would not include Lee in the discussions, Caradon not wanting HM Commissioner at the forefront of talks whilst also the focus of angry demonstrations.[10] Moreover, the Wooding Report noted that Webster had laid down various conditions for engaging in talks with Caradon, including the immediate withdrawal of troops and, furthermore, the report had noted that hostile crowds had prevented Caradon from meeting Webster or other councillors.[11] Caradon, exasperated by the political deadlock he was faced with, stated before he left Anguilla that he would come back to the island when there was 'a return to good sense and a period of co-operation and friendship'.[12]

The trip did, however, yield one somewhat predictable result. Caradon announced on 12 April that Tony Lee would be going on indefinite leave from his post, to be replaced by John Cumber. Whilst the Foreign Secretary would initially deny in Parliament two days later that Lee had been dismissed, it was soon clear that he would not return to Anguilla.[13] Lee had worked hard to help resolve the Anguilla crisis since 1967 and had faced some very challenging circumstances, including becoming the focus of anti-British feeling on the small island. His dismissal was primarily due to the problem that, in the words of the *Daily Telegraph,* 'unjustly he became the victim of a "go home" campaign by militant supporters of... Webster'.[14] Lee had also needed to work with Webster to generate the spirit of cooperation which could assist political progress, but their relationship had seriously deteriorated. The Commissioner's ability to help resolve the Anguilla crisis was therefore hampered. Whether earlier British doubts about Lee's suitability for undertaking his post for the long-term, expressed prior to Operation Sheepskin, had also influenced the decision to replace him is difficult to assess. He was flown out of Anguilla on an RAF Andover on 20 April.

A new HM Commissioner would perhaps be able to forge new relationships with new energy, whilst approaching the challenges of the Anguilla crisis through fresh eyes. John Cumber had considerable experience within the Colonial Service upon which to draw in his new role, having previously served in Kenya (1947–63) and then as Administrator of the Cayman Islands (1964–68). According to his *Times* obituary, Cumber 'built his work on the foundations of carefully-drawn structures and the clean-lined presentation of plans and proposals. His sense of fairness and his continual wish to preserve and raise standards gave others confidence in his judgements'. Moreover, Cumber's 'controlled personal style overlayed a deeply-compassionate and warm nature which was very rarely expressed other than in his deeds'.[15] Cumber soon made his mark on the island, restoring regular and visible military patrols after they were wound down during Caradon's first visit and also personally getting out amongst the Anguillian people. Cumber's relationship with Webster, however, fluctuated. As Westlake described it, '[some] days Webster felt like getting along with the new Commissioner... and some days he didn't'.[16] Nevertheless, Lord Caradon would later state how 'tremendously impressed' he was with Cumber, especially when the latter had had to explain to the Council a recent, possibly unpopular, development from London. Cumber reportedly did not attempt 'to disguise the difficult or awkward or unpleasant features of the arrangements...but obviously gaining their [the Council's] confidence by speaking straight to them. He has won confidence and established his authority in a remarkable manner'.[17]

Evaluating the military situation

Whilst the political situation continued to show mixed signs of cooperation and stalemate between Webster and the British throughout the remainder of April 1969, the military situation in Anguilla was also under review. On 19 April Brigadier Peter L. de C.

An RAF Andover at Anguilla's airfield. An APU officer looks on. (Albert Grandolini collection)

Major Lorimer, Corporal Bell and PC 605. (Airborne Assault Museum)

a sledgehammer to crack a nut. As I signalled at the time, I would have liked one blow with the sledgehammer, and then a quick withdrawal of troops.'[18] However, by mid-April few soldiers had been withdrawn – only A Company 2PARA soon after the arrival of the REs – and recent unrest had seen both the Paras and Royal Marines called upon to support the hard-pressed APU.

The *Pegasus* journal described the view that greeted British military personnel as they reached Anguilla on RAF Andover aircraft sent from the Antigua airhead. The island 'first appears spread like a prayer mat at the foot of the mountainous St Martin, criss-crossed with white tracks and scattered with little box-like houses'. Upon landing on the dirt runway, the soldier may have seen 'the RAF control tower, built from old packing cases' which, according to the article, 'typifies the Caribbean attitude as it climbs crazily skyward to be topped by a proudly fluttering Union Jack'.[19] It is this scene that may have greeted Brigadier Martin at the beginning of his visit. His subsequent report to London was wide-ranging, covering his views on Anguillian society and politics, combined with the security situation. Perhaps reflecting the colonial lens through which Britons could continue to view Anguillians, he claimed that the island's 'men are indolent and the women do all the work, are very talkative, bossy and volatile. 2 PARA soldiers told me they could think of no worse fate than being married to an Anguillan woman'. Older islanders and children were seen as generally friendly, although adolescents could be 'sullen'. Martin also stated that 'the people are very volatile and I was told by Government police and Army officers that crowds would gather very quickly and that trouble can erupt at the drop of a hat'. As for the political composition of Anguillian society by mid-April, Martin noted that the intelligence assessment was that 10 percent were 'hard core anti-British trouble makers', 20 percent were influenced by these militants, 40 percent were moderates and 30 percent were 'sitting on the fence'.[20]

Martin of HQ Army Strategic Command arrived on the island for a three-day visit to assess the security situation and the appropriate future troop levels. SNOWI recollected that '[at] the beginning of the operation [Sheepskin], opinion seemed to be that we were using

Sergeant Millar of D Coy 2PARA and a Bobby. Paras would sometimes undertake joint patrolling with the APU, demonstrating good cross-unit cohesion. (Airborne Assault Museum)

Despite the 'excellent' working relationship between the British Army and the APU – Paras claiming that Anguilla was 'the first time they have ever been popular with the police' – the professional background of the London bobbies was regarded as making the continued troop presence on the island necessary. Martin explained that:

If the police in Anguilla were equipped and trained as a colonial police force, I would recommend the immediate removal of 2 PARA from Anguilla. However the police are neither equipped, trained, nor mentally attuned to riot work, are reluctant even to carry side arms and are determined to go on operating as they do in this country. This means that at the first hint of major trouble

Riot training, Anguilla 1969. The reluctance of the APU to embrace riot drill meant that 2PARA was relied upon to undertake these duties in particularly challenging situations. (Airborne Assault Museum)

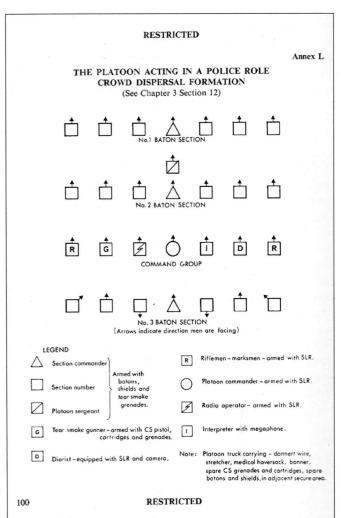

This image is taken from the volume of the British Army's *Land Operations* dealing with internal security matters. It is one of a number detailing the formations to be adopted by Army personnel acting in a police role to disperse rioters. (Private collection)

they immediately call on 2 PARA to stand by. The company of 2 PARA is in effect a riot police unit.[21]

Policing historian Georgina Sinclair has stated that the APU was expected to operate according to the policing techniques followed in the British metropole.[22] These differed from the methods used by traditional paramilitary colonial police forces, used to dealing with large crowds through heavy-handed tactics. Accordingly, Sinclair notes that the Police Federation of England and Wales had become concerned by the regulations under which the APU were free to operate, 'for they gave rise to questions as to the SPG's legal status'. For instance, the potential routine carrying of the Walther semi-automatic pistols with which the police had been issued in London caused concern, leading to reassurances that the guns would only be carried in exceptional situations.[23] Clearly, the APU remained hesitant to engage in colonial policing methods and thus relied on the army for suppressing especially violent unrest. Accordingly, Martin noted that the APU chief had assessed that 'the danger of riots or worse will continue until a political solution satisfactory to all the people has been achieved, and that the soldiers must be retained in Anguilla until then'.[24]

Martin also reported on the work of the Royal Engineers who were intended to conduct a long-term Hearts and Minds campaign on the island in the form of infrastructure projects. The REs had three main projects planned: building a school, surfacing three miles of road and constructing a deep water jetty. Progress had so far been limited, the sappers waiting for civilian contractors to lay the school's first foundations before working alongside them.[25] In the meantime, the REs had worked alongside 2PARA since early

April in constructing a permanent military camp on the site of the old Government House that had burnt down in 1967, roughly half a mile north of Force Anguilla's original HQ at the Secondary School near Mahogany crossroads and a mile away from the airfield. Indeed, *Pegasus* journal described the military camp as featuring the same 'unique style of architecture' – using oddly assembled packing cases – found at the airfield.[26] The journal described fondly that:

With amazing ingenuity the blackened ruins have been burrowed out and shored up to house the nerve centre for Operation Sheepskin. Nearby, the tents of "B" Coy lines lay clustered around a lone turpentine tree, the site of the canteen and hence a focal point for the whole camp. "Nasty's Friendly Bar" as it was called initially, gained a reputation for fiery entertainment which ranged far throughout the Caribbean. In the eastern end of the island platoons in rotation occupied a similar but smaller camp above a beautiful beach at Sandy Bay.[27]

The construction of the main camp had both political as well as functional uses, with Martin noting that its presence 'shows our intention of staying on the island for some time'.[28] The REs had furthermore, according to Martin's report, repaired generators in the island's hospital and in several pumping stations. Perhaps calculating that any building projects undertaken by the REs had political implications and also had to meet Force Anguilla's Hearts and Minds objectives, Martin noted that Cumber had withdrawn a task set by his predecessor of renovating the island's jail. Instead, this building project would be undertaken by local contractors and, indeed, the REs would be working closely with local contractors on the school and with local labour on road improvement. Perhaps reflecting some recent complaints, Martin therefore stated that he was 'satisfied that full use is being made of local labour and it is quite untrue to suggest that the sappers are taking away work from the local contractors'.[29]

Ultimately, Martin's report to London concluded that a company of regular infantry needed to remain in Anguilla 'until a satisfactory political solution has been reached in order to assist the police with Internal Security'. He recommended that the British government plan for this military presence to be in place for 'at least six months' and, moreover, suggested that further building projects be undertaken once the initial RE tasks had been completed.[30] These conclusions reflected the consensus reached amongst senior British personnel in Anguilla during Martin's visit about the necessity of retaining a sizeable military presence into the future. This necessity was subsequently also accepted in Whitehall on the basis that the current Para companies be replaced by another one from the same regiment. B Company 2PARA, which flew from the UK on 23 May under the command of Major J. Porter-Wright, thus took over from C and D companies and was informed that it would be committed to a posting of around four months.

It may have been disconcerting, however, for Whitehall decisionmakers now having to envisage a continued military deployment in Anguilla with no clear endpoint. One draft message to Defence Secretary Healey concluded that 'I cannot see when it will be possible to dispense with such a [military] force altogether' before outlining the factors considered by Martin and British personnel in Anguilla to justify this continued military commitment.[31] These included the inability of the APU to cope with particularly violent unrest, the undesirability of distracting the REs from their development projects to carry out an additional internal security role and, finally, the possibility of further disturbances on the island until Anguillians were assured that they would not be returned to the Associated State.[32] Until such challenges were resolved, therefore, the presence of regular infantry was regarded as necessary.

The rotation of Para companies in May also saw a transition in military command, as Lt. Colonel Richard Dawnay – who had previously assumed leadership of Force Anguilla from SNOWI – handed the reigns to 2PARA's second-in-command, Major J.E.N. Giles, who was promoted to local Lt. Colonel for the duration of the tour. Dawnay left Anguilla as a respected and reliable commanding officer of Force Anguilla, Martin noting in his report that the colonel had been 'a tower of strength to the successive Commissioners and I have heard nothing but praise for his efforts'.[33] Dawnay had faced the diverse challenges of planning a quick military intervention in which casualties had been anticipated, followed by implementing a Hearts and Minds campaign of a very different and unanticipated tone, with considerable strategic adaptability. Moreover, Dawnay's time in command had seen his regiment – a teeth-arm fighting force – working closely and effectively with the APU. With 2PARA's Battalion Tactical HQ leaving Anguilla around the same time as C and D companies, Lt. Colonel 'Norrie' Giles now commanded a force of 150 troops. Lord Caradon, discussing in late June the prospect of Anguilla experiencing only limited outbursts of unrest in future, noted that Giles had informed him that 'the company recently

A Para plays football with an Anguillian. Sports were an important part of military life in Anguilla, whilst these events could also contribute to the Hearts and Minds campaign. (Albert Grandolini collection)

arrived is mainly composed of young soldiers who can benefit from a month or two of such experience'.[34]

Indeed, B Company 2PARA did have a relatively smooth tour of duty between May and September 1969. These troops, nevertheless, did make a notable contribution to Force Anguilla's long-term Hearts and Minds campaign, successfully implementing the Grassroots Patrol programme – resulting in the Anguillian census – and initiating the 'Toys for Anguilla' scheme which brought the British Army's role on the island renewed and positive media attention. Military life was filled with physical exercise during these months of mid-1969, no doubt intended to stave off boredom as well as to maintain a state of preparedness amongst the Paras. According to *Pegasus*, the company's daily schedule began with a run at 5:30am and every afternoon was devoted to sports. The latter perhaps also contributed to Force Anguilla's public relations campaign, the journal stating that:

> Football topped the bill, and "B" Coy's star team was sure to draw a large crowd of enthusiastic local supporters. Cries of "Stovey"! and "Mac"! echoed from Anguillan throats, and the results were always broadcast on Radio Anguilla that evening. If you did not play soccer there was always rugby, cricket, volleyball and, of course, swimming.[35]

Indeed, cricket would serve a useful political purpose for a later Acting Commissioner, Richard Posnett. Upon hearing that Webster was a keen cricketer, Posnett – himself eager to settle into the island – challenged the revolutionary leader to a match. According to Posnett's memoirs, Webster 'entered into the spirit of things and selected a local team. My team included locals, paratroopers and policemen'.[36] Posnett went on to emphasise the political benefits of the match, noting that:

> In the event a good time was had by all: I hit a six, Ronald made two catches, and his side won by two runs – a perfect result for my purposes. For days afterwards, the match was the talk of the island and I was welcomed everywhere. 'You de man hit de sixer!' After that administration was easy.[37]

Although military exercises and training were restricted 'by lack of space and uncertainty of local reaction to unexpected bangs', these activities were nevertheless still accommodated on

A soldier of the Army Catering Corps prepares food. (Albert Grandolini collection)

the island.[38] Weekly anti-riot exercises were held in Webster Park, involving baton charges and deploying in square formation, aimed at deterring potential troublemakers.[39] A firing range was also established at a beach on the north coast, allowing both troops and police to practice their marksmanship. According to *Pegasus*, '[shooting] was especially popular amongst the Metropolitan Police who understandably get little chance to practise with their pistols'.[40]

There was also plenty of time for the Paras to enjoy relaxation time in the Caribbean sun, although this privilege could quickly wear thin for a regiment used to the sharp end of war. There was sunbathing on Anguilla's many beaches and opportunities for swimming. As a 'local boy' article in the *Aberdeen Evening Express* highlighted about Private Martin Cowie of D Company, however, whilst he was a keen swimmer the sea was '[not] only for pleasure but out of necessity – in an island where water is scarce the sea serves as bath and laundry as well as for swimming'.[41] Troops also had the opportunity to stay in Antigua through an exchange programme with the RAF or to enjoy a 'Randall's Weekend', staying at the Anguillian hotel of an American couple who, according to *Pegasus*, 'provided superb food and hospitality away from all the tribulations of camp life. "Randall's Weekend" became a byword for the Caribbean ideal – sea, sun, good food and no worries'.[42] Rather predictably, 'Nasty's Friendly Bar' in the main camp was also at the centre of military life. Evenings spent drinking evidently produced vivid memories, the Para journal recollecting fondly the colourful personality of '"Big Joss", the policeman who could crush beer cans against his brow' and the 'potent punch' recipe for which the APU became famous.[43]

Establishing the Wooding Commission

Premier Bradshaw arrived in London for talks with Foreign Secretary Stewart on 7 May. According to *The Telegraph*, the Kittitian 'showed clearly that he was not going to be party to the break-up of the island grouping over which he presided'.[44] Indeed, the messages emanating from Bradshaw's long UK visit demonstrated how far his position on the Anguilla crisis had remained consistent despite the seismic events that had occurred since March. Moreover, these messages also perhaps reflected the political situation generated by the twin, arguably contradictory, dialogues that the British had maintained with both Bradshaw and Webster throughout these months. Arriving

at Heathrow Airport, Bradshaw defended the UK government's decision to conduct Operation Sheepskin and stated that British action had been undertaken at his own request and, subsequently, 'the situation had been stabilised and should eventually return to normal'.[45] Furthermore, according to the article, Bradshaw wanted the Anguilla crisis 'first to be settled between himself and Britain, and consultation with the Caribbean governments', rather than allowing these regional neighbours the primary role in deciding Anguilla's future.[46] The British had, however, highlighted in the Caradon Declaration that it was 'no part of our purpose to put them (the Anguillans) under an Administration under which they do not want to live'.[47] It remained to be seen, therefore, whether the British would disappoint Bradshaw or Webster.

The main outcome of the visit – an announcement on 21 May of a commission to investigate the Anguilla problem – kicked the negotiating of a settlement into the long grass. The commission's terms of reference, however, appeared to favour Bradshaw, including '[recognising] the fact that the island of Anguilla is part of the unitary State of St. Kitts-Nevis-Anguilla in accordance with the Constitution of that Associated State'.[48] This announcement caused inevitable concern in Anguilla. An anonymous article in *The Beacon* described the situation as 'a case of Hot British approbation and reprobation – blowing hot and cold at the same time', before questioning how the Foreign Secretary could reconcile the controversial terms of reference with the assurances previously made to Anguilla.[49] Indeed, the opinions expressed in the article were serious enough for HM Commissioner Cumber to respond in a subsequent edition, reassuring islanders that 'I have received written confirmation from London since the talks with the State Premier, that these talks have in no way modified the repeated assurance that it is no part of our intention to place Anguillans under an administration which they do not want'.[50] Webster would also accuse the terms of reference of infringing the Caradon Declaration, but was eventually reassured that Britain's promises to the island still stood.[51] In late November the former Chief Justice of Trinidad and Tobago, Sir Hugh Wooding, was announced as the chairman of the new Wooding Commission due to report its recommendations in 1970.

Despite the political uneasiness caused by Bradshaw's London visit and the commission announcement, Anguilla had entered a phase of relative stability and peace, with Webster and his colleagues cooperating with the British administration. Lord Caradon evidently detected this calm when he returned to Anguilla for his third trip between 27–28 June 1969. He summarised that 'I found the situation greatly improved and relations between the troops and the police on the one hand and the Anguillans on the other better than one could have dreamed possible.' Furthermore, the British diplomat was assured by Webster 'when I saw him alone that he would meet my request for "six months of calm water".[52] It was clear by mid-July that this relatively stable situation was enduring. A report from Cumber stated that '[apart] from minor political manoeuvres by Ronald Webster and his supporters on the Anguilla Council, the general situation has remained quiet in the last three months. The attitude of the public is, for the most part, friendly and co-operative, but a large majority take their cue from Webster'.[53]

The reason for this quiet is difficult to pinpoint. Certainly, the continued assurances to the Anguillian leadership that Britain would never hand the island to an administration that islanders did not want proved a stabilising factor. Secondly, the various activities of Force Anguilla's Hearts and Minds campaign – from sporting events and Grassroots Patrols to medical assistance and building projects – continued to improve British relations with the Anguillians. Whilst

Lord Caradon addresses forces in Anguilla, July 1969. The reduction of Force Anguilla's visibility on the island during Caradon's first visit had caused soldiers to begin questioning the importance of their role in Anguilla. The troops, nevertheless, always held Caradon in high esteem. (Airborne Assault Museum)

The APU commander underlined the benefits of the new approach in his report:

Whilst the general pattern of policing is foot patrols... each Division has adequate motor transport and radio communications. Thus the public relations aspect of police duties in Anguilla is combined with mobility and flexibility in that substantial reinforcements can be moved to any trouble spot in the island with maximum speed. Meanwhile, dispersal and direct contact with the public provides the necessary intelligence to anticipate trouble and ensure early deployment to deal with it.[55]

Despite this reorganisation, however, there was still considerable reluctance on the part of the APU commander, Chief Superintendent J.H.

the British had initially struggled to communicate with the islanders and build trust, the longer-term initiatives may have helped to strengthen Anguillian confidence in the British administration. Furthermore, this campaign would soon be complemented by a new radio station established on the island and supervised by a FCO specialist, broadcasting high quality programmes for 45 hours a week and taking the responsibility away from the makeshift broadcasts produced from Royal Navy frigates. Finally, the generally good working relationship established between John Cumber and the Council perhaps helped build a sense of political partnership aimed at pursuing a better future for the island.

Reducing troop numbers

It was clear to London by late May that factors including APU training and the potential for further unrest in Anguilla caused by political uncertainty necessitated the retention of high troop levels on the island. Nevertheless, there was continued eagerness to reduce this number when possible. In the middle months of 1969, the APU were gradually revising their approach. On the one hand, they continued to pursue their methods of building the trust of islanders, partly in the hope that this would deter future violence. Enhancing this process, between 26 May and 30 June four houses were rented at Road Bay, Sandy Harbour, Island Harbour and Lower South Hill to establish more permanent police stations away from the rather centralised British administration in The Valley. Each station was occupied by an APU detachment who, according to its commander, 'patrol on foot in the surrounding villages getting to know the local inhabitants; dealing with petty disputes between neighbours and, in the almost complete absence of crime, fulfilling a welfare and public relations role'.[54] Adding to this decentralised approach, on 30 June the APU deployment was organised into three divisions – Central, Eastern and Western – each under the command of an Inspector.

Remnant of the Metropolitan Police, to train his force in colonial policing tactics. Henry A.A. Hankey of the FCO claimed in early-July that 'Commander Remnant is still wholly opposed to proposals for building up an effective riot control squad trained on traditional Colonial Service lines and instructed in how to charge and break up a mob using shields, batons, etc.' Instead, Hankey continued, the cultivation of 'good relations' with islanders was hoped to create a situation in which 'demonstration and riot leaders would find it much harder than on previous occasions to secure general cooperation'. Remnant, therefore, 'insisted that in his view the traditional methods used by the police in London, which he summarised as turning the other cheek, would be equally effective in Anguilla'.[56]

The APU approach was, nevertheless, gradually changing. 2PARA's historical record notes that, prior to completing their Anguilla tour in May, Lieutenant Martin and Sergeant Miller of D Company 'helped train a police baton squad to a standard of rare precision and skill'.[57] Moreover, Hankey noted that Remnant had recently visited the Royal Police Force of Antigua who, with only 300 officers 'in a troubled island and no likelihood of early reinforcements in the event of serious difficulty' had established 'a very effective riot control organisation on typical British colonial lines'. According to Hankey, 'Remnant had been much impressed and although it horrified him, I think it may have altered his views slightly'.[58] Whether due to persuasion, pressure or necessity, it was evident that Remnant soon accepted riot training for the APU, Lt. Colonel Giles reporting on 9 July that 'the Chief of Police has accepted the commitment of maintaining a baton and shield squad of 20 strong'. The Commander of Force Anguilla, however, added the caveat that 'the concept of a colonial type police force which is trained in riot drills is contrary to the training and tradition of the Metropolitan Police and is hard for them to accept'. Giles therefore warned that, in the event of particularly serious unrest, the APU

An APU officer. Note the adaptation of the Metropolitan Police uniform for tropical conditions. Whilst the light blue shirt and police cap were retained, the blue serge tunic was discarded, and khaki trousers adopted. (Albert Grandolini collection)

might have needed to hand over riot control to the British Army earlier than would have been the case with a normal colonial police force.[59]

The trend towards pursuing colonial policing methods in Anguilla was advanced further with the arrival of Superintendent Thomas Crennell, formerly of the Malayan Police, in late August 1969. According to Sinclair, 'Crennell became responsible for organising the training of the 'new' Anguilla Police, which initially recruited officers locally to work alongside expatriates as 'police messengers".[60] In time, these local police recruits would eventually constitute the majority of Anguilla's police force, taking over from the British police officers whose tenure amounted to only three months at a time and were replaced periodically by 16 fresh personnel from the UK. The establishment of this local force, however, was anticipated to take considerable time and face significant challenges. Brigadier Martin's

report of late April outlined that the 'long term proposal' was to create a 25-strong Anguillian force but recognised that it would 'be difficult to recruit this force and to organise their training outside the island'. Indeed, he acknowledged that 'even these problems will have to wait until Mr Bradshaw is prepared to agree the establishment of this force'.[61] Whilst Crennell's appointment constituted an advance towards British objectives of delegating security responsibility to a local force, Hankey highlighted in July that the training of this unit 'cannot be regarded as a factor in the security situation until at the earliest the end of this year'.[62]

On 25 July John Cumber resigned as HM Commissioner for Anguilla, barely more than three months after taking over from Tony Lee. Despite his short tenure, Cumber had made a significant contribution to stabilising the island and had worked generally well with the Council. He was replaced by Willoughby H. 'Tommy' Thompson who had previously worked as Acting Administrator of the British Virgin Islands and Administrator of the Falkland Islands. Before his departure, however, Cumber was asked to report on the security situation and troop levels in light of the impending completion of B Company 2PARA's tour in September and the possible need for their replacement. His analysis of 19 July concluded that the APU 'should be strong enough to cope with any disturbances which are likely to occur in Anguilla between September and the publication of the [Wooding] Commission's Report'. This assessment was perhaps partly based on the relatively quiet security situation that had prevailed since April in which police dependency on the military had dropped considerably. Moreover, Cumber may have recognised that APU capability would increase now that the unit had accepted the need for riot training. The main pillar of 2PARA's Hearts and Minds campaign – foot patrols – were also being reduced at the time of Cumber's report, the HM Commissioner recognising that '[these] patrols have proved very successful, but it is generally conceded that their object has been achieved and, in order to avoid the possibility of familiarity breeding public contempt, they have been reduced for the time being'.[63]

If violence once again broke out in Anguilla that the APU could not handle alone, Cumber believed that the half squadron of 33 Field Squadron REs 'should be able to provide adequate support in an internal security role'.[64] This meant that the British Army sappers, who would maintain a presence after the potential Para withdrawal, could leave their building projects and take up arms to quell unrest.

A line of APU officers lift supplies from the loading ramp of an RAF Andover at Anguilla's airfield. (Albert Grandolini collection)

A Para poses with his L1A1 SLR. (Albert Grandolini collection)

Consequently, Cumber concluded that the 'replacement of the Paratroop Company by a company of Infantry in September 1969 is unnecessary'. He added the caveat, however, that London might very well have to send an infantry company back to the island at short notice should the Wooding Commission recommend a political solution in its eventual report that was unacceptable to the Anguillians.[65]

Commander Remnant's own report from the APU perspective came to similar conclusions, underlining that his force could deal with any demonstrations whilst also being reduced in strength by 11 percent to 84 officers. He also recommended the use of the REs, who were a 'trained, disciplined military force with a strong internal security capability', in situations where military assistance was required by the APU.[66] Indeed, Remnant saw the 'distinct psychological advantage' of the sappers undertaking this dual role, claiming that:

Were a situation to arise whereby it is necessary to alert the Royal Engineers for possible aid to the civil power, work on the engineering projects would cease forthwith. As the projects upon which they are engaged are for the benefit of the Anguillan people as a whole, the diversion of the Royal Engineers to I.S. duties would demonstrate most clearly that those causing disorder have much to lose by their conduct, and would demonstrably be "cutting off their nose to spite their face".[67]

Having evaluated APU capability and the support available from the REs, Remnant also recommended the withdrawal of the Paras in September without replacement. Lt. Colonel Giles of Force Anguilla, however, notably disagreed with Cumber and Remnant about infantry withdrawal, arguing instead '[that] an infantry company be retained in Anguilla after September 1969 until the political future of the island has been satisfactorily resolved.' Whilst he agreed that the REs could be feasibly used in the security role envisaged by

the APU commander and HM Commissioner, he underlined the undesirability and counter-productivity of distracting the REs from their development projects. Rather than valuing the psychological advantages of downing tools, Giles noted that the sappers would, if called upon in dangerous unrest, have to 'maintain a degree of readiness…probably for lengthy periods' and that a portion of RE strength would potentially need to be allocated to guard duties. Ultimately, therefore, Giles concluded that '[if] this situation came about, it is considered that to use Sappers in this role would completely defeat the object of their work on the Island.'[68]

Therefore, a key point of disagreement about infantry withdrawal facing Whitehall decisionmakers lay with the role of the REs and, ultimately, the interaction between the Hearts and Minds campaign and security. The MoD consequently wanted to reassure the FCO that 'it is quite proper for RE units doing civil development work to have a stand-by IS role'.[69] Whilst it was acknowledged that heavy reliance on the REs would be detrimental and, in this case, other infantry would be required, if reliance on the sappers was infrequent then the dual role would be acceptable. Indeed, the MoD analysis drew attention to a recent instance in the British Virgin Islands 'where there were no troops other than RE and supporting services. On three occasions, they drew weapons and stood by to support the police, and each time the threat of disorder subsided.' Moreover, the report continued, the Administrator of the British Virgin Islands – possibly Tommy Thompson who was in the process of becoming HM Commissioner for Anguilla – had reportedly considered the RE presence 'generally sufficient' to deter unrest. Indeed, 'the same reason was put forward by the Administrator of St Vincent in support of his request for RE to build Bequia Airstrip'.[70] Clearly, there was a trend amongst Caribbean colonial administrators to rely on REs in both an infrastructural development and internal security role during this period.

Ultimately, the MoD, FCO, HO and SNOWI each considered the implications of withdrawing regular infantry from Anguilla and all decided in favour of withdrawal without replacement. There were many factors which may have influenced the final decision. Apart from the sufficient capacity of the remaining security forces to deal with unrest, the withdrawal also conformed to the aims of the Caradon Declaration and hence would, according to an FCO official, 'be desirable, both in removing an Anguillan grievance, and as reflecting the restoration of settled conditions in the island'.[71] Whitehall agreed to infantry withdrawal, however, on the proviso that '[should] the situation in Anguilla deteriorate to the point where IS duties interfere severely with the primary tasks of the Royal Engineers, SNOWI could despatch one or both West Indies Frigates to the Island. If further reinforcement were required a tactical battalion HQ and the leading company of the Spearhead Battalion could reinforce Anguilla.'[72] The Spearhead Company, operating through the Army Strategic Command, was estimated to reach Anguilla within 68 hours.[73]

On 14 September 1969, therefore, the 120 men of B Company 2PARA boarded RAF transports and departed Anguilla. Other military personnel including 82 REs, 36 support personnel in Anguilla and another 13 in Antigua would also leave in the same month, whilst a replacement force of 123 personnel from the REs, signals and other support units arrived in Anguilla.[74] Lt. Colonel Giles did not, however, hand over command of Force Anguilla to Lt. Colonel John Waymark of the REs until 12 October. The MoD was clearly eager for the Para withdrawal to receive sufficient media coverage, sending a public relations team to Anguilla who would travel with journalists from the BBC, ITV and the British press.

B Company 2PARA leave Anguilla for Britain on an Andover aircraft. Despite the tropical appeal of Anguilla, Paras expressed their relief to be leaving a fairly inactive posting. (Airborne Assault Museum)

The FCO, meanwhile, asserted that they were 'less enthusiastic about extensive publicity for this occasion, because of the possibility of further offence to Mr. Bradshaw'.[75] According to T.R.M. Sewell a 'lack of security among the troops on Anguilla' had meant that the timing of a public announcement about the Para withdrawal had to be brought forward. This meant, in turn, that Bradshaw received only one day's notice before the announcement thus resulting, according to Sewell, in Bradshaw expressing 'his resentment'.[76]

There was, nevertheless, satisfaction in Whitehall at British media coverage of the withdrawal. A.C. Watson of the FCO watched both the BBC and ITV coverage and concluded that '[both] were friendly and sympathetic, emphasising the relaxed nature

A British Para says goodbye to a Metropolitan Police officer at airfield. The relationship between the Paras and APU had been a positive one, soldiers expressing surprise that they could ever be so popular with the British bobby. (Airborne Assault Museum)

of the departure. Perhaps reflecting upon the barrage of ridicule with which the British media had previously covered the initial intervention in March, Watson recollected that 'I could scarcely believe my ears when I heard the BBC commentator referring to "a minor triumph for British diplomacy…"', the journalist having just noted Webster's attendance at a farewell cocktail party held for B Company 2PARA.[77] Webster was interviewed by this same BBC journalist, John Bierman, prior to the troop departure and was asked how he felt about these soldiers. He responded that '[they] were no trouble to us from the beginning…If they'd wanted to use brutal force on Anguillans, well then the world would have looked on them to be criminals.' Subsequently asked whether he would be glad or sorry to see the soldiers leave, Webster replied that 'we won't miss them. We won't miss them absolutely.'[78]

The Paras also seemed pleased to leave. Ian Ball of the *Daily Telegraph* observed that the soldiers 'most in their early 20s, will be happy to leave. The "send us home" grumbling started the day after the invasion and has not abated, despite the endless sunshine, the sugar-white beaches, the ripping coconut palms and rum at one quarter the United Kingdom price.'[79] Indeed, one Para reflected this eagerness to leave, telling Ball that Anguilla 'is simply the end of the earth, particularly if you are young, unmarried and have already seen a lot of the action in the outside world'.[80] As the Paras boarded their RAF transports at the airstrip they may have noticed the nearby wire-enclosed area prepared by the REs and labelled 'Waving base' at which Anguillians could bid farewell to them.[81] They may also have been aware of the message of thanks sent by the Foreign Secretary to mark the departure of the Parachute Regiment and other units, which stated briefly that:

> You have had a difficult task; to establish and maintain law and order, to give a helping hand with development work in the island, and above all to restore the confidence of the people of Anguilla in the friendship towards them of the British people. This called for a very high standard of discipline, and impeccable conduct, often in trying conditions. You have succeeded magnificently; and I want you to know that it is very much to your credit that the relations between Britain and Anguilla today are so much better than they were six months ago.[82]

The sappers of 33 Field Squadron, who had replaced the outgoing military force in September, had a tour of six months ahead of them and were themselves due to leave Anguilla in March 1970. Already, in the month following their arrival, discussion amongst decisionmakers had turned to the continuation of an RE presence on the island after this tour was completed. HM Commissioner Thompson wrote to the FCO on 3 October 1969 stating that the 'idea of a possibility of withdrawing any troops in March must be positively discouraged'.[83] He then included an analysis drafted by his colleague Richard Posnett, who was Acting Commissioner whilst Thompson was on leave, as to why a military presence was needed beyond this month. Crucially, there were security implications to military withdrawal at this point. The political situation would remain uncertain and tense until at least the publication of the Wooding Report and its immediate aftermath. Posnett anticipated various possible situations, writing that:

> One can assume that, if all goes well, the Constitutional Commission will have visited Anguilla before then [March 1970], and may indeed have started writing their report, but it seems safe to assume that the report will not have been published

before then. My own assessment (with which Colonel Giles and Waymark and Chief Superintendent Anning agree) is that the time immediately following publication of the report may be a critical one for security and that it will not be possible to advise removal of the remaining Army force prior to that. If on the other hand things do not go according to plan with the Commission, there is little reason to hope that the situation next March will have improved in a way which would permit the withdrawal of the troops.[84]

As the political situation was predicted to remain uncertain after the end of the current RE tour, therefore, a continued military presence beyond March 1970 was regarded as necessary. Furthermore, building work undertaken by the sappers was not expected to be completed by the end of their current posting. A key project embarked upon by the squadron was a primary school for 600 pupils and this building had indeed been largely completed by early September. Construction of a 220ft long deepwater jetty capable of catering for cargo vessels of up to one thousand tons had then been started at Road Bay. According to Posnett, Lt. Colonel Waymark assessed that this project would be incomplete by the end of the tour and accordingly requested an additional 25 sappers be added to his force to meet the deadline. Posnett regarded this request as problematic partly as 'to increase the strength of the force now would run counter to our policy of maintaining a steady level and of reducing the strength whenever circumstances allow'.[85] Therefore, he recognised the detrimental political messaging of increasing the size of Force Anguilla at a time when the British were aiming to reduce the number of troops on the island.

Posnett also recognised that there would be numerous potential development projects that Anguilla needed after the jetty was completed, listing 'more school buildings to be erected, more roads to be built, the airstrip to be improved and a good deal of work on water resources'. However, no local works unit could be trained quickly enough to continue the development effort after March. Ultimately, therefore, he concluded that 'my own view based on the outlook here (with which Giles, Waymark and Anning agree) is that it would be wiser to plan on the basis of extending the Sappers' stay for a further six months, although this would mean a change around for personnel next March'. Considering the political presentation of this proposed troop replacement, Posnett also assessed that if the jetty was still incomplete by the end of the current RE tour then 'this would provide a perfect ostensible reason for a normal rotation of Sappers in March, and this would make easier the political presentation of a decision in that sense'.[86]

The FCO subsequently raised the issue of a continued RE presence after March 1970 with the MoD. The FCO's John Vaughan summarised that at a subsequent meeting with the Treasury he had stated that 'the M.O.D. had indicated their willingness to agree; that for operational reasons it was desirable to plan for an extension of six months until September 1970 but that if political circumstances permitted, an earlier withdrawal might be possible'.[87] By early December 1969, however, agreement had not yet been obtained from the Treasury for another RE six-month tour. R.H.J. Steel of this ministry, perhaps indicating the cause of the delayed decision, later wrote that 'we have as you already know, been very disturbed for some time now at the way the situation has been developing. The likely date when we might be able to withdraw seems to get further away every time we discuss Anguilla and in addition there now seems to be a certain amount of slippage on the date when the Commission may be expected to report.' The Treasury, nevertheless,

Sappers of 33 Field Squadron Royal Engineers arrive on an RAF Vickers VC10. (Albert Grandolini collection)

reluctantly agreed to an RE presence in Anguilla until September 1970, whilst stating conditions to their support, including that the FCO do their 'utmost to ensure that our forces and commissioner are withdrawn by September 1970 at the latest'.[88] Funding this seemingly unending military operation may indeed have been anxiety inducing in Whitehall. In April 1970 it was reported that the cost of Britain's peacekeeping force had thus far amounted to around £1,500,000.[89] This is equivalent to around £21,125,400 in modern currency.[90]

The Anguilla Crisis (almost) ends

Anguilla entered the new decade without incident. When a British government minister was asked questions about Anguilla in Parliament on 2 February 1970, he responded that '[there] is at this moment no hostility against the police being there [Anguilla], and, in our judgement, it is desirable that they should be there'.[91] The minister also responded that he had nothing to add to a reply which he had given the previous October, where he had highlighted that Anguilla's future 'is a matter for the Commission' and that he predicted a 'satisfactory settlement'.[92] Ultimately, therefore, neither the political or security situation had changed very much since the appointment of the Wooding Commission and withdrawal of 2PARA. Indeed, this state of affairs would remain fairly constant throughout 1970 until the publication of the Wooding Report.

The Constitutional Commission had been slow to form, having been announced in May 1969 and its chairman appointed in November. It had then spent spring 1970 carrying out its consultation investigation and had been due to publish its findings in August, although a delay pushed the Wooding Report's release to 6 November 1970.[93] Rather predictably, considering the commission's terms of

reference established in mid-1969, the report's recommendations were dependent on Anguilla remaining inside the Associated State of St Kitts-Nevis-Anguilla. The document stated that:

> … the most satisfactory way of resolving the situation would be by a substantial devolution to the Anguillans of power to manage their own affairs. We recommend accordingly. But in so doing we must add that we see this as part of a package the other part of which comprises the completion of the programme of development already begun which will enable Anguilla to achieve within a relatively short period an infrastructure comparable to that of the other units constituting the state.[94]

Anguilla's greater share of power within the Associated State would be established through an island Council with wide-ranging powers; through a new Co-ordinating Council in which St Kitts, Nevis and Anguilla would have equal representation and, additionally, through increased Anguillian representation in the State's House of Assembly and in both the Public and Police Service Commissions.[95]

The reaction of Anguillians to the Wooding Report was predictable opposition and rejection. An editorial in *The Beacon* stated that '[it] is with a feeling of utter disbelief and a sense of having been badly let down that Anguillans at long last receive the news of the Commission report'. It went on to conclude that the 'recommendations by the Wooding Commission are neither durable nor lasting. In terms of providing a practicable and acceptable solution to the problem, it is clearly a "total waste"'.[96] However, the anticipated sense of Anguillian outrage which the British had been forced to consider in their internal security planning for 1970 was nevertheless somewhat muted. This perhaps indicates how far continued British assurances about Anguilla's political future had generated a relatively trusting relationship. Indeed, this trend had continued despite a change of British government in London from Labour under Harold Wilson to Conservative under Edward Heath in June 1970.

According to a statement by Webster, published in the same edition of *The Beacon* noted above, the new Minister of State for the FCO – Joseph Godber – had visited Anguilla in September and informed the Council that 'any settlement in Anguilla would have to be acceptable to the people of Anguilla, because a solution is only going to be permanent and lasting if it is accepted by us, the people of Anguilla'. Webster was thus confident enough about the meaninglessness of the Wooding Report to assure islanders that 'these proposals are nothing to worry about! We've been assured that the British Government are not going to force us to accept any administration we do not want.' Accordingly, he requested that Anguillians 'be calm, do not get excited'.[97] Bradshaw, meanwhile, largely accepted the recommendations of the Wooding Report. In early December he again visited London for talks, although these soon stalled. The day after he left London the *Daily Telegraph*, perhaps sensing the way the political winds were blowing, stated that 'Anguilla appears now to have won her case, if not independence, as the world's smallest island republic, then at least permanent separation from the detested government of St. Kitts.' The newspaper pointed to Britain's public pledge that it would never force Anguilla to live under an unwanted administration as the 'crucial element' in the island's victory.[98]

Having failed to act on the recommendations of the Wooding Report, the Heath government evidently chose to embark upon a new more unilateral approach to solving the Anguilla quagmire.

In June 1971 Godber travelled to both St Kitts and Anguilla with new proposals that, according to Westlake, 'in effect altered the legal status of Anguilla to a Crown Colony of Great Britain without ever quite using that terminology'.[99] With Anguilla accepting the proposals and Bradshaw's government rejecting them, the British government nevertheless proceeded with drawing up the Anguilla Act 1971 in July. This legislation stated that 'Her Majesty may by Order in Council make such provision as Her Majesty thinks fit for securing peace, order and good government in Anguilla'. It outlined that a British Commissioner could be appointed to govern Anguilla, exercising powers conferred through an Order in Council. Moreover, in

Edward Heath is seen here greeting US President Richard Nixon in the early 1970s. Heath's Conservative government won an election against Wilson's Labour Party in 1970 and in doing so inherited the situation in Anguilla. (Open source)

a situation whereby the Associated State government declared total independence from the UK, London could 'by an Order in Council…direct that Anguilla shall not any longer form part of the territory of that state' and could also subsequently 'by Order in Council provide a constitution for Anguilla'.[100]

Although Anguilla would remain officially part of the Associated State alongside St Kitts and Nevis, it would do so essentially in name only. The island would instead form a direct colonial relationship with the UK, the Commissioner governing in consultation with the island's Council, whilst new courts of law could also be established and local policemen trained. Summarising the British government's approach to the new political arrangements under the Anguilla Act and Order in Council, the *Daily Telegraph* stated that:

The Government's intention was to provide an effective administration for a period of years to allow tempers to cool. The position would be reconsidered after the new arrangements had been working for three years. If the Anguilla people at a later stage wished to revert to their links with St Kitts that could be done. If, on the other hand, they wished to continue on the lines the Government were now establishing that also could be done.[101]

Webster responded to the temporary nature of this political arrangement by observing that '[the] talk about a three-year period and then a referendum on the island's future we regard as a joke… We are thinking of 10, 15, 20, even 25 years of this arrangement'.[102] Webster's joy over the new relationship, shared by many islanders, was reflected in *The Beacon*'s editorial, which estimated that '[it] should not be long now, when Anguillans will enjoy good government and government of their choice, therefore reaping the rewards of their struggles since 1967'.[103]

The new Anguilla Police Force, facilitated by the 1971 settlement, was established in January 1972 to replace the APU and would eventually consist of 80 officers, most of whom were Anguillian although some were recruited from St Vincent.[104] The unit was commanded by a Chief of Police, a post ably filled between 1972 and 1976 by Lt. Colonel Claudius Roberts. Roberts, an Anguillian from a family of policemen, brought considerable experience to the role in a crucial period when the unit was developing. Having joined the Leeward Islands Police Force in 1932, he had ascended to the role of Commissioner of Police in Grenada during 1967, a position from which he retired in 1969. When command of the new Anguilla Police Force became available in 1972, however, he left retirement to serve his home island once more. According to *The Anguillian* newspaper, Roberts was known for 'his emphasis on discipline, a huge appetite for work, the ability to communicate with people on all levels and a phenomenal memory'. Moreover, 'he believed that it was crucially important to communicate with his Officers in a straightforward, honest way'.[105]

With policing being handed to a local unit, the remaining British security forces could finally withdraw from Anguilla. Indeed, this process had already begun even prior to the 1971 settlement, with the Heath government announcing in February the halving of troop and APU numbers on the island. In mid-March, the Royal Engineers would be reduced from around 120 to 60 troops whilst police numbers would drop from 80 to around 30.[106] Soon after the implementation of the Anguilla Act and Anguilla (Administration) Order, Foreign Secretary Alec Douglas-Home was able to conclude that the 'situation in Anguilla is peaceful' and that, although Commonwealth Caribbean governments had 'criticised' the settlement, they 'now show signs of accepting the position'. Furthermore, Douglas-Home noted that he had been 'advised that there is very little likelihood of any Commonwealth Caribbean governments, either singly or together, taking action which would threaten our presence in Anguilla'. Ultimately, therefore, both the Foreign and Defence Secretaries agreed to the complete withdrawal of the remaining Royal Engineers, to take place in mid-September 1971.[107]

The men of 33 Field Squadron Royal Engineers had made a significant contribution to improving Anguilla's infrastructure by the time of their withdrawal. Not only had the sappers helped to construct school buildings and the Road Bay jetty, they had also improved Anguilla's roads and airfield, plus repairing generators at the hospital and at pumping stations. With their departure, Force Anguilla's long presence on the island beginning in March 1969 came to an end. What had been hoped could be a quick military intervention followed by a quick exit had become a very expensive long-term Hearts and Minds campaign lasting for 30 months. The British occupation had cost around £3,000,000 by September 1971, approximately translating to £42,250,800 in modern currency.[108] In the interests of safety, it was arranged that a Royal Navy frigate would be available near Anguilla for five weeks after the Royal Engineers had left the island.[109] The APU, meanwhile, was reduced by half to 15 officers in October and then again reduced to four when the new Anguilla Police Force took over policing duties on the island in early 1972. These final British bobbies stayed for a short while longer, tasked with supervising the new locally recruited force.[110]

Aftermath

Whilst the main tensions that had driven the Anguilla crisis since 1967 had been somewhat settled by the time of British military withdrawal from the island in 1971, the political journey of Anguilla would continue to be rocky. This was partly caused by the ambiguity of Anguilla's status, being administered like a British colony but officially still part of the Associated State. Webster continued to lobby the British government for greater constitutional clarity throughout the early 1970s and the ensuing lack of progress eventually provoked him into leading the Council in non-cooperation with the British administration. Eventually, a new constitution helped to overcome the impasse, being implemented in February 1976 under the Anguilla (Constitution) Order. A ministerial system of government was thus established consisting of an Executive Council, in which sat a Chief Minister and six other ministers, and a 13-strong Legislative Assembly. Webster's People's Progressive Party subsequently won the election of March 1976 and he was accordingly made the island's first Chief Minister.

Anguilla would, however, briefly enter another period of instability in the wake of Webster's subsequent removal from office in early 1977. A land dispute led to a motion of no confidence and Webster's replacement as Chief Minister by Emile Gumbs, who was appointed by the British Commissioner. Unrest broke out at the swearing in ceremony, with Gumbs later informing the *Daily Telegraph* that Webster had led a group of supporters to disrupt the event and that these supporters had been dispersed by police using tear gas.[111] Indeed, the unrest was serious enough for the Commissioner to summon a Royal Navy frigate, HMS *Tartar*, to the area. Although the ship carried a Royal Marine detachment, only *Tartar*'s captain went ashore to investigate. Nevertheless, the military presence appeared to calm the situation.[112]

The late 1970s would prove important years for resolving the remaining grievances of the Anguilla crisis. The death of Premier Robert Bradshaw in May 1978 constituted a significant milestone. As a memorandum by Foreign Secretary Lord Carrington later noted, '[until] 1978 the major obstacle to separation was the opposition of the former Premier of St Kitts, Mr Bradshaw. Had Anguilla been separated without his agreement, he would undoubtedly have sought to isolate the island politically and economically'. The memorandum went on to highlight that '[after] his death in May 1978…negotiations became possible with his successors, who accepted the principle of separation'.[113] Furthermore, in March 1979 an Anguillian delegation was invited to London for talks following

the Associated State's request to pursue its own total independence from Britain. Anguilla's ambiguous constitutional status thus needed resolving. By December, the Associated State's premier, Lee Moore, had agreed with the new British government of Prime Minister Margaret Thatcher to start the constitutional process of separating Anguilla from St Kitts-Nevis through a consent motion in the Associated State's legislature. However, Moore's Labour government fell in February 1980 and his successor, Dr Kennedy Simmonds, declined to introduce the consent motion due to political dynamics in the Associated State. Nevertheless, Simmonds committed not to oppose Anguillian separation.[114]

The British government itself, therefore, undertook the task of legally separating Anguilla from St Kitts-Nevis through the UK Parliament. Whilst this would be a simple legislative task for the British government to complete, Carrington's memorandum noted that there was 'a degree of urgency' in the securing of Anguilla's separation.[115] The document went on to explain that:

> To fail to honour at this stage our commitment to Anguilla could have dangerous consequences. An election is due in Anguilla by the end of May. If Mr Gumbs (the present Chief Minister) is obliged in his campaign to go back on his promise to his people of formal separation this year there would be a very real threat of unrest. Mr Webster, the former Chief Minister, would have no compunction in resorting to violence again if he thought it would restore him to power. Any further delay in separating Anguilla would be his strongest card.[116]

The Cabinet Secretary, Robert Armstrong, subsequently informed Thatcher that 'I do not believe that any members of OD [Defence and Oversea Policy Committee] will disagree with the Foreign and Commonwealth Secretary's proposal' of quickly introducing legislation to separate Anguilla.[117] Subsequently, despite Parliament's crowded programme, the Anguilla Act 1980 was pushed through and received royal assent on 16 December. Under this new act, Her Majesty could make provisions by Order in Council for Anguilla to achieve 'fully responsible status' or, if needed, 'the establishment of Anguilla as an independent republic'.[118]

At last Anguilla had achieved what it had been fighting for since its absorption into the Associated Statehood project in the 1960s. Its ties with St Kitts-Nevis had been officially severed and it had obtained a direct colonial relationship with the UK, changing its official categorisation from Crown Colony to British Dependent Territory in 1983. The Anguilla Act 1980 was a cause of much rejoicing on the island. Webster recollected that '[we] had a big celebration in Anguilla when formal detachment was declared. People went all out to express themselves on that joyous occasion. We had marches, we had dancing, speeches and all kinds of events. People from East to West were truly united.'[119] Webster won the election of May 1980 and, returning as Chief Minister, served until March 1984. The Associated State, meanwhile, pursued its own independence from Britain and accordingly became the Federation of St Kitts and Nevis in September 1983.

CONCLUSION

Indifference and misunderstanding may be regarded as the two key failings that led to Operation Sheepskin in March 1969. Indifference can perhaps be detected in the serious long-term underdevelopment of Anguilla. Poor infrastructure and living standards generated deep-rooted grievances that would fuel the Anguilla crisis. The prioritisation of economic and security concerns over local self-determination through Britain's Associated State project perhaps reveals more evidence of indifference. Fearing fragmentation of the Anglophone Caribbean and assessing that small islands could never thrive economically, London fused Anguilla into an unwanted political arrangement. Indeed, this decision would also influence the duration of the Anguilla crisis; initially, through Britain's refusal to contemplate an Anguillian future outside the Associated State and, in the longer-term, by restricting London's ability to act, in deference to the Associate State government. Unwillingness, therefore, to accept Anguillian self-determination thus drove the crisis, with all its accompanying demonstrations against government authority, referendums and declarations of independence.

The neglect that Anguilla experienced may, in turn, have impacted upon the misunderstanding that also fuelled the crisis. The British had a very limited intelligence-gathering capability on the island – as in much of the Caribbean – and accordingly decided to launch Operation Sheepskin based on a very limited understanding of the Anguillian security situation. This poor decision-making was not helped by British diplomats who were inclined to believe the more fantastical rumours about Webster's willingness to accommodate American gangster interests. Moreover, the security picture was distorted by Webster's tactic of sabre-rattling, claiming to possess a large and dangerous arsenal that British troops would have to face when they hit the beaches. Whitlock's dramatic ejection from the island gave British concerns a thin layer of credibility. The scale of the assumed security threat in Anguilla therefore influenced the size of Britain's military intervention. The reality of the situation which confronted British troops upon landing – little trace of gangster influence, very few weapons and no Anguillian armed resistance – therefore came as an embarrassing surprise to both Whitehall and Force Anguilla. The British had come prepared for a different kind of military campaign and it took time to adjust to the sort of Hearts and Minds campaign that would address the real situation.

Finally, British misunderstanding was perhaps also reflected in the length of the military occupation. What was initially intended to be a quick action by teeth-arm troops turned into months of relative inactivity by one of Britain's most elite regiments, 2PARA. Even after 2PARA's departure in September 1969, British troops were compelled to stay in Anguilla until September 1971 partly due to the belief that the APU would be unable to cope with potential unrest. Had the British understood the nature of the Anguillian security situation, particularly when planning Operation Sheepskin, they might have avoided the large and long-term military commitment that transpired.

Having assessed an international crisis defined by indifference and misunderstanding, it must be considered whether Operation Sheepskin truly lives up to its reputation for miscalculation and farce. Certainly, the British government's conviction that military force was justified appears with hindsight to constitute a miscalculation. Whitehall's willingness to trust unfounded rumours about gangster influence in Anguilla proved a mistake

and, indeed, Labour government ministers were embarrassed by this error once the reality of the situation became clear. London's decision to intervene so quickly after Whitlock's ejection suggests either a reactionary impulse based on the afront to British dignity or, alternatively, that Whitehall – tired of a deteriorating situation – was looking for a justification to act and the Whitlock affair fitted the bill. In either case, Operation Sheepskin was planned, approved and implemented very quickly and this haste perhaps contributed to miscalculation, particularly in terms of military overreaction. Had the British, through better and more patient intelligence-gathering, known the reality of the security threat then – if a military response was deemed necessary – they could perhaps have just deployed Royal Marine detachments from the two frigates available to SNOWI, rather than calling upon the Army Strategic Command Spearhead Unit intended for major worldwide emergencies. Whitehall had used this approach in 1967 and appeared prepared to do so again in 1977. Other miscalculations included the use of transportation routes through the Canadian Gander airbase without seeking Ottawa's permission, an oversight that might have been partly caused by hasty planning. Assessed from these perspectives, therefore, Operation Sheepskin's reputation for miscalculation can be regarded as justified.

However, had the British not intervened militarily, it is questionable whether the Anguilla crisis would have been resolved so peacefully. In the quickly deteriorating political context on the island after the end of the Interim Agreement, the British or any other reconciling power needed a strong presence in isolated Anguilla to understand the situation accurately. This presence could have been provided by a multinational Caribbean peacekeeping force, but this had failed to materialise in 1967. London, unenthusiastic about UN involvement in an area of British responsibility, was unlikely to agree to a UN peacekeeping force. Consequently, unilateral British action was the most feasible approach in early 1969. Whilst the British military landings were unopposed, had London decided to only deploy its Metropolitan Police contingent, it is perhaps foreseeable that Anguillians might have resisted the invasion. Use of overwhelming British military strength therefore possibly prevented bloodshed. Had the British not invaded in early 1969, then Anguilla's isolation and the growing political divisions between its people could have deepened the crisis further. More decisive action earlier in the crisis by Britain may, nevertheless, have prevented the situation from developing to the point where military action was deemed necessary in March 1969.

The farcical reputation gained by Operation Sheepskin was certainly justified to an extent. The sight of British paratroopers landing by sea and air on an island devoid of active opposition and tasked with hunting down gangsters and weapons caches of doubtful existence would inevitably attract satirical media coverage. Following closely on from Britain's withdrawal from East of Suez, Sheepskin appeared to epitomise a diminished Britain that pursued petty and outdated imperialism out of step with modern times. Perhaps the more farcical element of Sheepskin – in terms of its absurdity rather than comedy – lay in the leakage of plans to the media prior to the troop landings. Although the impact of this leak was subsequently assessed to have been minimal, it caused the Wilson government considerable concern. This episode ultimately added to the farcical reputation that engulfed the military intervention.

The operation's embarrassing nature perhaps also somewhat explains why it has been so easily forgotten outside of Anguilla itself. Mawby highlights the 'prevailing coyness' amongst British Cabinet ministers about Anguilla, Barbara Castle deciding not to include Anguilla in her published diaries; James Callaghan failing to mention the crisis at all in his memoirs; Denis Healey referring to it only briefly and Harold Wilson, according to Mawby, showing 'a level of ambivalence bordering on incomprehensibility in his analysis'.[1] This desire to forget a humiliating moment in British colonial history – possibly shared with the public – may partly account for the amnesia surrounding Operation Sheepskin. The timing of the military intervention may also explain this memory loss, sandwiched as the Anguilla crisis was between the series of late-imperial counterinsurgencies ending with Aden in 1967 and the long war in Northern Ireland starting in August 1969 which would dominate public consciousness for decades to come. In this timeline, Anguilla could be regarded as an anomaly of little military importance worth remembering. However, the military occupation of Anguilla is indeed significant for a number of reasons and can, accordingly, be viewed somewhat positively.

Firstly, British military strategy soon adapted to the realities of the Anguillian security situation after Force Anguilla's initial arrival. The early communications problems identified by the military in conveying British messages to the islanders was somewhat addressed by the creation of a makeshift, and later more permanent, radio station. Nevertheless, Britain's efforts in this regard arguably never totally triumphed over Webster's own communications and was hindered for a significant period by the mixed messaging caused by Britain's attempt to placate both Anguilla and Basseterre. Communications were, however, greatly improved by the British Army's Hearts and Minds campaign. Considering the Anguillian suspicion that existed when Force Anguilla arrived, the level of friendliness that existed towards 2PARA when it departed suggested that military efforts to win the trust of islanders were fairly successful. 'Grassroots' patrols helped soldiers to better understand Anguillian society, whilst sporting events, children's parties, cinema screenings and the Toys for Anguilla scheme all encouraged Anguillian trust in the military. Perhaps the most important Hearts and Minds initiative, however, was the Royal Engineer building programme between 1969–71 which notably improved the island's infrastructure: a key grievance for Anguillians.

Whilst the Malayan Emergency is often identified as the highpoint of British Hearts and Minds strategy, the Anguilla military intervention could also arguably be recognised as a small-scale but successful manifestation of this approach. On 9 July 1970, Lt. Colonel Dawnay was awarded the Wilkinson Sword of Peace for 1969 on behalf of 2PARA by Field Marshal Sir Gerald Templer at Cutlers' Hall in London. Established by Wilkinson Sword Limited in 1966 and awarded annually to one unit each from the army, navy and air force for 'acts of humanity and kindness overseas', the army award was given to 2PARA for the Anguilla deployment.[2] A letter from General H.J. Mogg of Army Strategic Command to the MoD recommending the award in March 1970 praised 2PARA's performance, noting that:

> From the moment that it became known that the Islanders were unarmed, the British Press launched attack after attack on their own Government and on their own soldiers who were conducting the operation, and the soldiers found that their every action was criticised, condemned, and laughed at. This would have been daunting enough for even the most phlegmatic infantryman.

It was a particularly hard pill for the high-spirited and battle-trained men of 2 Para to swallow, but by a combination of high discipline, good humour, patience and tolerance they eventually turned the tables on their detractors.[3]

Linked to hearts and minds, Anguilla could also generally be regarded as a triumph of minimum force strategy. After the initial military operation, the Army consistently acted in support of the APU and were only deployed in a riot control capacity where the police were unable to cope with unrest. The relative calm established on Anguilla after the invasion must, however, be attributed primarily to the efforts of the APU. Largely resisting suggestions that they adopt a colonial policing approach, these London police were at the forefront of confronting unrest on the island and built successfully a relationship of trust with Anguillians. The confidence of islanders in the APU became particularly strong when the unit adopted a decentralised deployment based at police stations across Anguilla. The mostly quiet and calm course of the military occupation is therefore worthy of note, attributable to police, soldiers and the generally peaceful Anguillian people.

When the final soldiers of Force Anguilla left the island in September 1971 the Foreign Secretary, Alec Douglas-Home, wrote that the British military 'have left behind them a valuable legacy of goodwill and friendly relations with the inhabitants which will be helpful to the work of H.M. Commissioner during the coming years'.[4] The friendship between Anguillians and Britons remains strong and enduring over half a century later.

BIBLIOGRAPHY

Digital Sources

1st Battalion The Argyll and Sutherland Highlanders History from 1945 to 1971. http://argylls1945to1971.co.uk/

Airborne Assault ParaData. https://www.paradata.org.uk/

Anguilla Library Service: The Beacon Newspaper. https://www.axalibrary.ai/thebeacon.php

Caricom Caribbean Community. https://caricom.org/

Gale Primary Sources: Daily Mail Historical Archive; Declassified Documents Online: Twentieth-Century British Intelligence; Mirror Historical Archive, 1903–2000; The Sunday Times Historical Archive; The Telegraph Historical Archive; The Times Digital Archive. https://link.gale.com/apps/menu?userGroupName=leedsuni

Historic Hansard. https://api.parliament.uk/historic-hansard/index.html

Legislation.gov.uk. https://www.legislation.gov.uk/

Margaret Thatcher Foundation. https://www.margaretthatcher.org/

Navy News Archive. https://www.royalnavy.mod.uk/news-and-latest-activity/navy-news/archive

ProQuest Historical Newspapers: ProQuest Historical Newspapers: Chicago Tribune; ProQuest Historical Newspapers: Los Angeles Times; ProQuest Historical Newspapers: The Guardian and The Observer; ProQuest Historical Newspapers: The New York Times; ProQuest Historical Newspapers: The Washington Post. https://www.proquest.com/

The Anguillian. https://theanguillian.com/

The Guardian. https://www.theguardian.com/uk

The National Archives. https://www.nationalarchives.gov.uk/

The National Archives Currency converter: 1270–2017. https://www.nationalarchives.gov.uk/currency-converter/

The New York Times. https://www.nytimes.com/

United Nations Archive. https://archives.un.org/

vLexJustis. https://vlex.co.uk/

Manuscript and Archival Sources

Duxford, *Airborne Assault Museum*, 'Anguilla. 1969 Reports, Photos' Etc', 3.A.5. 2/32/1

Duxford, *Airborne Assault Museum*, Pegasus: Journal of The Parachute Regiment & Airborne Forces AAL-091-1970

London, *The National Archives*, Foreign and Commonwealth Office: North American and Caribbean Department and Caribbean Department: Registered Files (AN Series), FCO 63.

London, *The National Archives*, Foreign Office and Foreign and Commonwealth Office: Defence Department and successors: Registered Files (ZD, DP and DT Series), FCO 46.

London, *The National Archives*, Ministry of Defence: Chiefs of Staff Committee: Registered Files, DEFE 11.

London, *The National Archives*, Prime Minister's Office: Correspondence and Papers, 1964–1970, PREM 13.

Secondary Sources

Abbott, George C., 'Political Distintegration: The Lessons of Anguilla', *Government and Opposition*, 6 (1971), 58–74

Andrade, John, *World Police & Paramilitary Forces* (Basingstoke: Palgrave Macmillan, 2016)

Beckles, Hilary, and Verene Shepherd, eds., *Caribbean Freedom: Economy and Society from Emancipation to the Present* (London: James Currey Publishers, 1996)

Brown, Steve, *By Fire and Bayonet: Grey's West Indies Campaign of 1794* (Solihull: Helion & Company, 2018)

Browne, Whitman, 'Overt Militarism and Covert Politics in St Kitts-Nevis', in *Conflict, Peace and Development in the Caribbean*, eds. by Jorge Rodriguez Beruff, J. Peter Figueroa and J. Edward Greene (Basingstoke: Palgrave Macmillan, 1991), 175–193

Carty, Brenda, and Colville Petty, *Anguilla: Tranquil Isle of the Caribbean* (Basingstoke: Macmillan Education Ltd, 1997)

Charters, David A., 'Intelligence and Psychological Warfare Operations in Northern Ireland', *The RUSI Journal*, 122 (1977), 22–27

Clarke, Colin G., 'Political fragmentation in the Caribbean: the case of Anguilla', *Canadian Geographer/Le Géographe canadien*, 15 (1971), 13–29

Cox-Alomar, Rafael, 'An Anglo-Barbadian dialogue: the negotiations leading to Barbados' independence, 1965–66', *The Roundtable: The Commonwealth Journal of International Affairs*, 93 (2004), 671–690

Cox-Alomar, Rafael, 'Britain's withdrawal from the Eastern Caribbean 1965–67: A reappraisal', *The Journal of Imperial and Commonwealth History*, 31 (2003), 74–106

Cox-Alomar, Rafael, 'Revisiting the Transatlantic Triangle: The Decolonisation of the British Caribbean in Light of the Anglo-American Special Relationship', *Diplomacy and Statecraft*, 15 (2004), 353–373

Dyde, Brian, *Out of the Crowded Vagueness: A history of the islands of St. Kitts, Nevis and Anguilla* (Oxford: Macmillan Education, 2005)

French, David, *Army, Empire and Cold War: The British Army and Military Policy 1945–1971* (Oxford: Oxford University Press, 2012)

French, David, *The British Way in Counter-Insurgency, 1945–1967* (Oxford: Oxford University Press, 2011)

Harclerode, Peter, *PARA! Fifty Years of the Parachute Regiment* (London: Brockhampton Press, 1992)

Hart, Richard, 'Labour Rebellions of the 1930s', in *Caribbean Freedom: Economy and Society from Emancipation to the Present*, eds. by Hilary Beckles and Verene Shepherd (London: James Currey Publishers, 1996), 370–375

Healey, Denis, *The Time of My Life* (London: Michael Joseph, 1989)

Howard, Martin R., *Death Before Glory! The British Soldier in the West Indies in the French Revolutionary and Napoleonic Wars 1793–1815* (Barnsley: Pen and Sword, 2015)

Mawby, Spencer, *Ordering Independence: The End of Empire in the Anglophone Caribbean 1947-69* (Basingstoke: Palgrave Macmillan, 2012)

Mawby, Spencer, 'Overwhelmed in a Very Small Place: The Wilson Government and the Crisis Over Anguilla', *Twentieth Century British History*, 23 (2012), 246–274

Meeks, Brian, *Caribbean Revolutions and Revolutionary Theory: An Assessment of Cuba, Nicaragua and Grenada* (Kingston: University of the West Indies Press, 2001)

Metzgen, Humphrey, and John Graham, *Caribbean Wars Untold: A Salute to the West Indies* (Kingston: University of the West Indies Press, 2007)

Moran, Christopher, *Classified: Secrecy and the State in Modern Britain* (Cambridge: Cambridge University Press, 2013)

Ovendale, Ritchie, ed., *Documents in Contemporary History: British defence policy since 1945* (Manchester: Manchester University Press, 1994)

Palmer, Colin A., *Cheddi Jagan and the Politics of Power: British Guiana's Struggle for Independence* (Chapel Hill: University of North Carolina Press, 2010)

Phillips, D.E., 'Barbados and the Militarization of the Eastern Caribbean, 1979–1985', *Latin American Perspectives*, 17 (1990), 73–85

Posnett, Richard, *The Scent of Eucalyptus: A Journal of Colonial and Foreign Service* (London: The Radcliffe Press, 2001)

Puri, S., and L. Putman, eds., *Caribbean Military Encounters* (New York: Palgrave Macmillan, 2017)

Ramakrishna, Kumar, *Emergency Propaganda: The Winning of Malayan Hearts and Minds 1948–1958* (Abingdon: Routledge, 2002)

'Report of the Commission of Inquiry appointed by the Governments of the United Kingdom and St. Christopher-Nevis-Anguilla to examine the Anguilla Problem', Miscellaneous No. 23 (1970)

Rodriguez Beruff, Jorge, J. Peter Figueroa and J. Edward Greene, eds., *Conflict, Peace and Development in the Caribbean* (Basingstoke: Palgrave Macmillan, 1991)

Schwartz, Heather E., *Gangsters, Bootleggers, and Bandits* (Minneapolis: Lerner Publications Company, 2013)

Sinclair, Georgina, *At the end of the line: Colonial policing and the imperial endgame 1945–80* (Manchester: Manchester University Press, 2006)

Speller, Ian, *The Role of Amphibious Warfare in British Defence Policy, 1945–56* (Basingstoke: Palgrave, 2001)

Thomson, Calum, 'Ripples from the South Atlantic: Examining the Wider Significance of the Falklands War for the British Overseas Territories' (unpublished masters thesis, Universiteit Leiden, 2018)

Walicek, Don E., 'The Anguilla Revolution and Operation Sheepskin', in *Caribbean Military Encounters*, eds. by S. Puri and L. Putman (New York: Palgrave Macmillan, 2017), pp. 147–170.

Watt, D.C., 'Britain's Caribbean Interests', *Military Review*, 43 (1963), 74–80

Watts, Carl, 'Killing Kith and Kin: The Viability of British Military Intervention in Rhodesia, 1964–5', *Twentieth Century British History*, 16 (2005), 382–415

Webster, J. Ronald, *Revolutionary Leadership: Reflections on Life, Leadership, Politics* (Denver; Outskirts Press, Inc., 2011)

Webster, Ronald, *Scrap Book of Anguilla's Revolution* (The Valley: Seabreakers (Anguilla) Ltd, 1987)

Westlake, Donald E., *Under an English Heaven* (London: Hodder & Stoughton, 1973)

Wilson, Harold, *The Labour Government 1964–1970: A Personal Record* (London: Weidenfeld and Nicolson and Michael Joseph, 1971)

Winder, Simon, *The Man Who Saved Britain* (London: Pan MacMillan, 2006), Google ebook

NOTES

Introduction

1 Charles Douglas-Home, 'How the Army planned Operation Sheepskin', *The Times*, 20 March 1969, p. 10, *The Times Digital Archive* <link.gale.com/apps/doc/CS168390772/TTDA?u=leedsuni&sid=bookmark-TTDA&xid=4fbe62a7.> [accessed 28/07/22].

2 'Sledgehammer on Anguilla', *The Guardian*, 20 March 1969, p. 12, *ProQuest Historical Newspapers: The Guardian and The Observer* <https://go.openathens.net/redirector/leeds.ac.uk?url=https://www.proquest.com/historical-newspapers/sledgehammer-on-anguilla/docview/185333281/se-2> [accessed 18/09/23].

3 Walter Terry, 'Is this Wilson's Bay of Piglets?', *Daily Mail*, 19 March 1969, p. 1, *Daily Mail Historical Archive* <link.gale.com/apps/doc/EE1864323693/DMHA?u=leedsuni&sid=bookmark-DMHA&xid=907fec8f.> [accessed 06/07/22].

4 'It's not funny', *The Washington Post, Times Herald*, 20 March 1969, p. 24, *ProQuest Historical Newspapers: The Washington Post* <https://go.openathens.net/redirector/leeds.ac.uk?url=https://www.proquest.com/historical-newspapers/not-funny/docview/143539607/se-2> [accessed 18/09/23]; ''Twas a famous victory', *Chicago Tribune*, 20 March 1969, p. 22, *ProQuest Historical Newspapers: Chicago Tribune* <https://go.openathens.net/redirector/leeds.ac.uk?url=https://www.proquest.com/historical-newspapers/twas-famous-victory/docview/168856986/se-2> [accessed 18/09/23].

5 Early academic studies included, George C. Abbott, 'Political Distintegration: The Lessons of Anguilla', *Government and Opposition*, 6 (1971), 58–74; Colin G. Clarke, 'Political fragmentation in the Caribbean: the case of Anguilla', *Canadian Geographer/Le Géographe canadien*, 15 (1971), 13–29

6 Donald E. Westlake, *Under an English Heaven* (London: Hodder & Stoughton, 1973), p. 11.

7 Spencer Mawby, 'Overwhelmed in a Very Small Place: The Wilson Government and the Crisis Over Anguilla', *Twentieth Century British History*, 23 (2012), 246–274 (pp. 273–274).

8 Don E. Walicek, 'The Anguilla Revolution and Operation Sheepskin', in *Caribbean Military Encounters*, eds. by S. Puri and L. Putman (New York: Palgrave Macmillan, 2017), pp. 147–170 (p. 165).

9 Ronald Webster, *Scrap Book of Anguilla's Revolution* (The Valley: Seabreakers (Anguilla) Ltd, 1987). J. Ronald Webster, *Revolutionary Leadership: Reflections on Life, Leadership, Politics* (Denver: Outskirts Press, Inc., 2011).

10 Mawby, 'Overwhelmed', pp. 265–266.

11 Most recent studies focus on operations during the Eighteenth Century. Steve Brown, *By Fire and Bayonet: Grey's West Indies Campaign of 1794* (Solihull: Helion & Company, 2018). Martin R. Howard, *Death Before Glory! The British Soldier in the West Indies in the French Revolutionary and Napoleonic Wars 1793–1815* (Barnsley: Pen and Sword, 2015).

12 Rafael Cox-Alomar, 'Britain's withdrawal from the Eastern Caribbean 1965–67: A reappraisal', *The Journal of Imperial and Commonwealth History*, 31 (2003), 74–106 (p. 78).

13 Rafael Cox-Alomar, 'An Anglo-Barbadian dialogue: the negotiations leading to Barbados' independence, 1965–66', *The Roundtable: The Commonwealth Journal of International Affairs*, 93 (2004), 671–690 (p. 686).

14 Spencer Mawby, *Ordering Independence: The End of Empire in the Anglophone Caribbean 1947–69* (Basingstoke: Palgrave Macmillan, 2012), p. 20, 216.

15 Ibid, p. 255. It should be noted that islanders will be referred to as 'Anguillians' rather than the more historical 'Anguillans', reflecting more recent debates about their national identity, although contemporary sources often use the latter word. See Walicek, p. 163. When using quotations, the original word may be retained.

16 Simon Winder, *The Man Who Saved Britain* (London: Pan MacMillan, 2006), Chapter 7. Google ebook.

Chapter 1

1 Richard Hart, 'Labour Rebellions of the 1930s', in *Caribbean Freedom: Economy and Society from Emancipation to the Present*, eds. by Hilary

Beckles and Verene Shepherd (London: James Currey Publishers, 1996), 370–375 (p. 372).

2   Brian Dyde, *Out of the Crowded Vagueness: A history of the islands of St. Kitts, Nevis and Anguilla* (Oxford: Macmillan Education, 2005), pp. 249–250.

3   Mawby, *Ordering Independence*, p. 227.

4   Ibid, p. 234.

5   Hart, p. 371.

6   Mawby, *Ordering Independence*, p. 22.

7   Ibid.

8   Brian Meeks, *Caribbean Revolutions and Revolutionary Theory: An Assessment of Cuba, Nicaragua and Grenada* (Kingston: University of the West Indies Press, 2001), p. 133.

9   Colin A. Palmer, *Cheddi Jagan and the Politics of Power: British Guiana's Struggle for Independence* (Chapel Hill: University of North Carolina Press, 2010), p. 51.

10 '1st Battalion The Argyll and Sutherland Highlanders: British Guiana 1953–1954', *1st Battalion The Argyll and Sutherland Highlanders History from 1945 to 1971* <http://argylls1945to1971.co.uk/AandSH_BG1953to54.htm> [accessed 09/08/22].

11 David French, *The British Way in Counter-Insurgency, 1945–1967* (Oxford: Oxford University Press, 2011), pp. 45–46.

12 Ibid, p. 46.

13 Mawby, *Ordering Independence*, p. 90.

14 D.C. Watt, 'Britain's Caribbean Interests', *Military Review*, 43 (1963), 74–80 (pp. 78–79).

15 'The Caribbean Scene', *Naval Intelligence Report (NIR)*, No. 17, Summer 1968, July 1–31, 1968, p. 20. TS Ministry of Defence: DEFE 63: Defence Intelligence Staff: Directorate of Service Intelligence, later Deputy Directorate of Intelligence (Warsaw Pact) and Deputy Directorate of Intelligence (Rest of the World): Intelligence Assessments, Reports and Studies DEFE 63/34. The National Archives (Kew, United Kingdom). *Declassified Documents Online: Twentieth-Century British Intelligence* <link.gale.com/apps/doc/HXCUEB532503195/TCBI?u=leedsuni&sid=bookmark-TCBI&xid=2fcdb789&pg=11.> [accessed 18/07/22].

16 Rafael Cox-Alomar, 'Revisiting the Transatlantic Triangle: The Decolonisation of the British Caribbean in Light of the Anglo-American Special Relationship', *Diplomacy and Statecraft*, 15 (2004), 353–373 (pp. 353, 365).

17 Watt, pp. 75, 78.

18 Ibid, p. 77.

19 'The Caribbean Scene', p. 21.

20 Mawby, *Ordering Independence*, p. 122.

21 'The Caribbean Scene', p. 19.

22 Watt, p. 75.

23 Ibid, p. 77.

24 'War Office: Headquarters British Forces Caribbean Area: Files', *The National Archives* <https://discovery.nationalarchives.gov.uk/details/r/C14540> [accessed 08/08/22].

25 'The Caribbean Scene', p. 24.

26 'British move paratroops to Caribbean', *Chicago Tribune*, 18 March 1969, p. 1, *ProQuest Historical Newspapers: Chicago Tribune* <https://go.openathens.net/redirector/leeds.ac.uk?url=https://www.proquest.com/historical-newspapers/british-move-paratroops-caribbean/docview/168855370/se-2> [accessed 20/09/23].

27 Humphrey Metzgen and John Graham, *Caribbean Wars Untold: A Salute to the West Indies* (Kingston: University of the West Indies Press, 2007), p. 217.

28 Dyde, pp. 199–200.

29 'The West Indies Federation', *Caricom Caribbean Community* <https://caricom.org/the-west-indies-federation/#:~:text=The%20Federation%20was%20established%20by,political%20union%20among%20its%20members.&text=The%20Governor%20General%20was%20Lord,located%20in%20Trinidad%20and%20Tobago.> [accessed 10/08/22].

30 Alvin Shuster, 'Anguilla: A Slap for the Mouse That Roared', *New York Times*, 23 March 1969, p. E2, *ProQuest Historical Newspapers: The New York Times* <https://go.openathens.net/redirector/leeds.ac.uk?url=https://www.proquest.com/historical-newspapers/anguilla/docview/118622094/se-2> [accessed 20/09/23].

31 Mawby, *Ordering Independence*, p. 25.

32 Ibid, p. 124.

33 Cox-Alomar, 'Revisiting the Transatlantic Triangle', p. 363.

34 Ibid, p. 364.

35 Cox-Alomar, 'Britain's withdrawal', p. 74.

36 Cox-Alomar, 'An Anglo-Barbadian dialogue', pp. 675, 686.

37 Westlake, p. 29.

38 Cox-Alomar, 'Britain's withdrawal', pp. 85–86.

39 Westlake, p. 29.

40 Cox-Alomar, 'Britain's withdrawal', p. 86.

41 Clarke, p. 14.

42 Ibid. Mawby, *Ordering Independence*, p. 6. Brenda Carty and Colville Petty, *Anguilla: Tranquil Isle of the Caribbean* (Basingstoke: Macmillan Education Ltd, 1997), p. 27.

43 Carty and Petty, p. 7.

44 Abbott, p. 62.

45 Westlake, p. 28.

46 Ibid, pp. 27–28.

47 'Robert Bradshaw, Premier in St. Kitts for 11 Years, Dies', *New York Times*, 25 May 1978, p. 22, *The New York Times* <https://www.nytimes.com/1978/05/25/archives/robert-bradshaw-premier-in-st-kitts-for-11-years-dies.html> [accessed 16/08/22].

48 Mawby, *Ordering Independence*, p. 55.

49 Dyde, p. 286.

50 Robert Llewellyn Bradshaw, quoted in Westlake, p. 27.

51 Westlake, pp. 26–27.

52 'Report of the Commission of Inquiry appointed by the Governments of the United Kingdom and St. Christopher-Nevis-Anguilla to examine the Anguilla Problem', Miscellaneous No. 23 (1970), p. 48 [henceforward known as the 'Wooding Report'].

53 Mawby, 'Overwhelmed', p. 256.

54 Westlake, p. 30.

55 Cox-Alomar, 'Britain's withdrawal', p. 91.

56 Dyde, pp. 263–264.

57 Westlake, p. 30.

58 Webster, *Revolutionary Leader*, p. 11.

59 Ibid, p. 12.

60 Ibid, p. 6.

61 Webster, *Scrap Book*, p. 7.

62 Webster, *Revolutionary Leader*, p. 26.

63 Westlake, p. 36.

64 Colin Rickards, 'Mr Lee genuinely welcomed back by islanders', *The Times*, 20 March 1969, p. 10, *The Times Digital Archive* <link.gale.com/apps/doc/CS168128628/TTDA?u=leedsuni&sid=bookmark-TTDA&xid=efc4eb1b.> [accessed 30/06/22].

65 Westlake, p. 37.

66 London, *The National Archives* [henceforth *TNA*], DEFE 11/885, Commander Metropolitan Police, Anguilla Police Unit, 'Anguilla Police Unit. An Appreciation of the Police Position at 0800 hrs, 10th July, 1969', Annex C to 1/10/1 dated 19th July 1969.

67 Webster, *Revolutionary Leader*, p. 8.

68 Ibid.

Chapter 2

1   Clarke, p. 19.

2   Webster, *Scrap Book*, p. 9.

3   Dyde, p. 264.

4   Webster, *Scrap Book*, p. 10.

5   'Brute Farce and Ignorance', *Sunday Times*, 23 March 1969, p. 13, *The Sunday Times Historical Archive* <link.gale.com/apps/doc/FP1800360838/STHA?u=leedsuni&sid=bookmark-STHA&xid=2d2b71e2.> [accessed 07/07/22].

6   Webster, *Scrap Book*, p. 10. Our Commonwealth Staff, 'Police landed on Anguilla by frigate', *The Times*, 18 February 1967, p. 1, *The Times Digital Archive* <link.gale.com/apps/doc/CS19360850/TTDA?u=leedsuni&sid=bookmark-TTDA&xid=8197eb30.> [accessed 23/08/22]. 'Brute Farce and Ignorance', p. 13.

7   'Brute Farce and Ignorance', p. 13.

8   Ibid.

9   Westlake, p. 30.

10 Wooding Report, p. 18.

11 Webster, *Scrap Book*, p. 9.

12 Westlake, p. 50.

13 Webster, *Revolutionary Leader*, p. 40.

14 Webster, *Scrap Book*, p. 12.

15 Wooding Report, p. 23.

16 Webster, *Scrap Book*, p. 12.

17 Webster, *Revolutionary Leader*, p. 42.

18 Ibid. Our Own Correspondent, 'Island asks for British troops', *The Times*, 2 June 1967, p. 1, *The Times Digital Archive* <link.gale.com/apps/doc/CS17525954/TTDA?u=leedsuni&sid=bookmark-TTDA&xid=09d3d64a.> [accessed 02/09/22].

19 'The British View of Rebellion', in Webster, *Scrap Book*, p. 14.

20 See mention of foreign arms purchases in 'The British View of Rebellion', in Webster, *Scrap Book*, p. 14.

21 Webster, *Revolutionary Leader*, p. 43.

22 Westlake, pp. 56–57.

23 Webster, *Revolutionary Leader*, p. 43.

24 'Island asks for British troops', p. 1.

25 Ian Mather, 'Island revolts after beauty row', *Daily Mail*, 2 June 1967, p. 2, *Daily Mail Historical Archive* <link.gale.com/apps/doc/EE1864552851/DMHA?u=leedsuni&sid=bookmark-DMHA&xid=f550930b.> [accessed 02/09/22]. David Wright, 'Isle's Police Flee in Revolt', *Daily Mirror*, 2

June 1967, p. 28, *Mirror Historical Archive, 1903–2000* <link.gale.com/apps/doc/GODJEP958229441/DMIR?u=leedsuni&sid=bookmark-DMIR&xid=2cd900c4.> [accessed 02/09/22].

26 'Anguilla cuts ties with new Caribbean unit: Hoist Union Jack, oust St. Kitts Police', *Chicago Tribune*, 1 June 1967, p. A7, *ProQuest Historical Newspapers: Chicago Tribune* <https://go.openathens.net/redirector/leeds.ac.uk?url=https://www.proquest.com/historical-newspapers/anguilla-cuts-ties-with-new-garribean-unit/docview/179235963/se-2> [accessed 25/09/23].

27 Webster, *Revolutionary Leader*, p. 45.

28 Clarke, p. 21.

29 Walicek, p. 159.

30 Carty and Petty, p. 59.

31 Ibid, pp. 59–60.

32 Dyde, pp. 199–200.

33 Webster, *Scrap Book*, p. 21.

34 Westlake, p. 65.

35 Webster, *Scrap Book*, p. 21.

36 Ibid.

37 Westlake, p. 64. Dyde, p. 270.

38 Whitman Browne, 'Overt Militarism and Covert Politics in St Kitts-Nevis', in *Conflict, Peace and Development in the Caribbean*, edited by Jorge Rodriguez Beruff, J. Peter Figueroa and J. Edward Greene (Basingstoke: Palgrave Macmillan, 1991), pp. 175–193 (p. 178).

39 Westlake, p. 64.

40 Diana Prior-Palmer quoted in 'The British View of Rebellion', in Webster, *Scrap Book*, p. 14.

41 Webster, *Scrap Book*, p. 21.

42 Bradshaw, quoted in Dyde, p. 269.

43 Browne, p. 178.

44 Dyde, pp. 269–70.

45 Westlake, p. 65.

46 Ibid, p. 66.

47 Dyde, p. 270.

48 D.E. Phillips, 'Barbados and the Militarization of the Eastern Caribbean, 1979–1985', *Latin American Perspectives*, 17 (1990), 73–85 (p. 77).

49 Browne, p. 175.

50 Ibid, p. 183.

51 Ibid.

52 Ibid, p. 185.

53 Westlake, p. 67. Browne, p. 185.

54 Westlake, p. 66.

55 Webster, *Revolutionary Leader*, p. 51.

56 Ibid.

57 'Voters of Anguilla confirm independence action: West Indian islanders greet formal step -- Five oppose breach with St. Kitts', *New York Times*, 13 July 1967, p. 10, *ProQuest Historical Newspapers* <https://go.openathens.net/redirector/leeds.ac.uk?url=https://www.proquest.com/historical-newspapers/voters-anguilla-confirm-independence-action/docview/117607965/se-2> [accessed 07/09/22].

58 Westlake, pp. 77–78.

59 Ibid, pp. 79–80.

60 Ibid, p. 71.

61 Michael Knipe, 'Anguilla hopes of Mr Gumbs', *The Times*, 22 April 1969, p. 5, *The Times Digital Archive* <link.gale.com/apps/doc/CS84897942/TTDA?u=leedsuni&sid=bookmark-TTDA&xid=fbfd4383.> [accessed 05/07/22].

62 Webster, *Scrap Book*, pp. 28, 33.

63 Colin Rickards, 'Mr Lee genuinely welcomed back by islanders', *The Times*, 20 March 1969, p. 10, *The Times Digital Archive* <link.gale.com/apps/doc/CS168128628/TTDA?u=leedsuni&sid=bookmark-TTDA&xid=efc4eb1b.> [accessed 30/06/22]. Westlake, p. 70.

64 Webster, *Scrap Book*, p. 28.

65 'Tributes to the Late Lord Shepherd', HL Deb 09 April 2001 vol 624 cc981-5, *Historic Hansard* <https://api.parliament.uk/historic-hansard/lords/2001/apr/09/tributes-to-the-late-lord-shepherd> [accessed 07/09/22].

66 London, *TNA*, PREM 13/2517, FCO to Certain Missions and Dependent Territories, 'St. Kitts, Nevis and Anguilla', 18 August 1967.

67 Ibid.

68 Webster, *Revolutionary Leader*, p. 54.

69 Ibid.

70 Dyde, p. 271.

71 'St. Kitts, Nevis and Anguilla', 18 August 1967.

72 Ibid.

73 *TNA*, PREM 13/2517, Secretary [unknown] to Commonwealth Secretary to Defence Secretary, 'St. Kitts/Nevis/Anguilla', 6 August 1967.

74 Ibid.

75 Mr Bennett to Foreign Office, 2 August 1967.

76 Ibid.

77 'St Kitts/Nevis/Anguilla', 6 August 1967.

78 C.H. Godden to A.M. Palliser, 14 August 1967.

79 Secretary of State for Commonwealth Affairs George Thomson to Prime Minister Harold Wilson, 'Anguilla', 14 September 1967.

80 R.M. Hastie-Smith to Oliver G. Forster, 'St Kitts/Nevis/Anguilla', 14 August 1967.

81 'Anguilla's rebellion is over but antipathies remain', *The Times*, 2 August 1967, p. 6, *The Times Digital Archive* <link.gale.com/apps/doc/CS101149954/TTDA?u=leedsuni&sid=bookmark-TTDA&xid=3be63735.> [accessed 28/09/22].

82 Our Commonwealth Staff, "Gunmen control Anguilla", *The Times*, 2 September 1967, p. 4, *The Times Digital Archive* <link.gale.com/apps/doc/CS68644130/TTDA?u=leedsuni&sid=bookmark-TTDA&xid=03cb3d15.> [accessed 28/09/22]. Douglas Williams, 'Deadlock over Anguilla Dispute', *Sunday Telegraph*, 20 August 1967, p. 24, *The Telegraph Historical Archive* <link.gale.com/apps/doc/IO0709114079/TGRH?u=leedsuni&sid=bookmark-TGRH&xid=49888d58.> [accessed 28/09/22].

83 Donald McLachlan, 'Rag-tag republic digs in for the invaders', *Daily Mail*, 11 August 1967, p. 2, *Daily Mail Historical Archive* <link.gale.com/apps/doc/EE1864562254/DMHA?u=leedsuni&sid=bookmark-DMHA&xid=9ad2ed97.> [accessed 28/09/22].

84 Terence Prittie, 'Anguilla peace force stays put', *The Guardian*, 15 August 1967, p. 7, *ProQuest Historical Newspapers: The Guardian and The Observer* <https://go.openathens.net/redirector/leeds.ac.uk?url=https://www.proquest.com/historical-newspapers/anguilla-peace-force-stays-put/docview/185200410/se-2> [accessed 28/09/22].

85 Henry Giniger, 'Ambiguity in Anguilla: Caribbean island wants independence but knows it must depend on others', *New York Times*, 19 August 1967, p. 3, *ProQuest Historical Newspaper: The New York Times* <https://go.openathens.net/redirector/leeds.ac.uk?url=https://www.proquest.com/historical-newspapers/ambiguity-anguilla/docview/118069666/se-2> [accessed 28/09/22].

86 Juan de Onis, 'Britain decries U.N.'s consideration of Anguilla', *New York Times*, 16 August 1967, p. 20, *ProQuest Historical Newspapers: The New York Times* <https://go.openathens.net/redirector/leeds.ac.uk?url=https://www.proquest.com/historical-newspapers/britain-decries-u-n-s-consideration-anguilla/docview/118070288/se-2> [accessed 30/09/22].

87 Commonwealth Affairs Correspondent, 'Gamblers in Caribbean Disturbances', *Daily Telegraph*, 4 August 1967, p. 21, *The Telegraph Historical Archive* <link.gale.com/apps/doc/IO0702909975/TGRH?u=leedsuni&sid=bookmark-TGRH&xid=3671bb1e.> [accessed 29/09/22].

88 Terence Prittie, 'Anguilla 'back in the fold'', *The Guardian*, 4 August 1967, p. 9, *ProQuest Historical Newspapers: The Guardian and The Observer* <https://go.openathens.net/redirector/leeds.ac.uk?url=https://www.proquest.com/historical-newspapers/anguilla-back-fold/docview/185241859/se-2> [accessed 30/09/22].

89 Henry Giniger, 'Anguillan leader seeks visitors and hotels: Disputes ad saying island will attempt to block tourism', *New York Times*, 18 August 1967, p. 3, *ProQuest Historical Newspapers: The New York Times* <https://go.openathens.net/redirector/leeds.ac.uk?url=https://www.proquest.com/historical-newspapers/anguillan-leader-seeks-visitors-hotels/docview/117746929/se-2> [accessed 06/10/22].

90 Commonwealth Affairs Correspondent, 'Anguilla 'Open to Strong-Arm Influences'', *Daily Telegraph*, 23 August 1967, p. 20, *The Telegraph Historical Archive* <link.gale.com/apps/doc/IO0703787790/TGRH?u=leedsuni&sid=bookmark-TGRH&xid=fac4646f.> [accessed 29/09/22].

91 Westlake, p. 111.

92 Prime Minister Eric Williams, quoted in Westlake, p. 112.

93 Webster, *Scrap Book*, p. 44.

94 Webster, *Revolutionary Leader*, p. 59.

95 Alistair Cooke, 'Anguilla carries war to UN', *The Guardian*, 7 August 1967, p. 7, *ProQuest Historical Newspapers: The Guardian and The Observer* <https://go.openathens.net/redirector/leeds.ac.uk?url=https://www.proquest.com/historical-newspapers/anguilla-carries-war-un/docview/185106892/se-2> [accessed 05/10/22].

96 Webster, *Scrap Book*, p. 52.

97 Ibid, p. 48.

98 Display ad 93 -- no title, *New York Times*, 14 August 1967, p. 25, *ProQuest Historical Newspapers: The New York Times* <https://go.openathens.net/redirector/leeds.ac.uk?url=https://www.proquest.com/historical-newspapers/display-ad-93-no-title/docview/118057092/se-2> [accessed 24/10/23].

99 Webster, *Scrap Book*, p. 52.

100 Westlake, p. 133.

101 Ibid, pp. 133–34.

102 'Anguillan leader seeks visitors and hotels', p. 3.

103 Webster, *Scrap Book*, p. 48.

104 *TNA*, PREM 13/2517, George Thomson to Prime Minister Harold Wilson, 'Anguilla', 14 September 1967.

105 Ibid.
106 Colville L. Petty, 'He Lives Within Our Hearts', *The Anguillian*, 6 February 2017 <https://theanguillian.com/2017/02/he-lives-within-our-hearts-by-colville-l-petty/> [accessed 27/10/22].
107 Atlin Harrigan, 'Editorial: A Word to Anguillans', *The Beacon*, 27 September 1967, p. 1, *Anguilla Library Service* <https://www.axalibrary.ai/the%20beacon/Volume%201/Beacon%20Vol%201%20Issue%2001.pdf> [accessed 27/10/22].
108 'A Message to Britain', *The Beacon*, September 1967, p. 2, *Anguilla Library Service* <https://www.axalibrary.ai/the%20beacon/Volume%201/Beacon%20Vol%201%20Issue%2001.pdf> [accessed 27/10/22].
109 Westlake, p. 149.
110 'Premier's request of 20 December, 1967, to the British Government for a cooling-off period in Anguilla', quoted from The Wooding Report, p. 32.
111 'The Anguilla People's request of 18 December, 1967 to the British Government for a cooling-off period', quoted in The Wooding Report, p. 33.

Chapter 3

1 Colin Rickards, 'Mr Lee genuinely welcomed back by islanders', *The Times*, 20 March 1969, p. 10, *The Times Digital Archive* <link.gale.com/apps/doc/CS168128628/TTDA?u=leedsuni&sid=bookmark-TTDA&xid=efc4eb1b.> [accessed 30/06/22].
2 Atlin Harrigan, 'Editorial', *The Beacon*, 13 January 1968, p. 1, *Anguilla Library Service* <https://www.axalibrary.ai/the%20beacon/Volume%201/Beacon%20Vol%201%20Issue%2017.pdf> [accessed 10/11/22].
3 Webster, *Revolutionary Leader*, p. 67.
4 Webster, *Scrap Book*, p. 73.
5 Webster, *Revolutionary Leader*, p. 75.
6 Letter from Webster to William Whitlock, 15 July 1968, in Webster, *Revolutionary Leader*, p. 75.
7 Ibid.
8 Webster, *Scrap Book*, p. 73.
9 Westlake, p. 160.
10 Mawby, 'Overwhelmed', p. 252.
11 Westlake, p. 160.
12 Atlin Harrigan, 'Editorial: An open letter to Lord Shepherd', *The Beacon*, 24 February 1968, p. 1, *Anguilla Library Service* <https://www.axalibrary.ai/the%20beacon/Volume%201/Beacon%20Vol%201%20Issue%2023.pdf> [accessed 11/11/22].
13 Lord Lambton, 'The Jekyll and Hyde of St Kitts', *London Evening Standard*, 22 February 1968, reprinted in *The Beacon*, 9 March 1968, p. 2, *Anguilla Library Service* <https://www.axalibrary.ai/the%20beacon/Volume%201/Beacon%20Vol%201%20Issue%2025.pdf> [accessed 15/11/22].
14 Clarke, p. 26.
15 Carty and Petty, p. 96.
16 Clarke, p. 26.
17 Browne, pp. 183–84.
18 London, *TNA*, DEFE 11/885, Detective Inspector R.F. Williams, 'A Report on the Facts Elicited from Enquiries into the Anguillan Situation', Appendix 'A' to Annex A to 1/10/1 dated 19th July 1969.
19 Ibid.
20 Ibid.
21 Walicek, pp. 158–59.
22 Wooding Report, p. 36.
23 Westlake, p. 168.
24 Ibid, p. 222.
25 Walicek, p. 158.
26 Andrew Roth, 'Obituary: William Whitlock', *The Guardian*, 7 November 2001 <https://www.theguardian.com/news/2001/nov/07/guardianobituaries.obituaries> [accessed 29/12/21].
27 London, *TNA*, FCO 63/180, W.C. Whitlock to Secretary of State for Foreign and Commonwealth Affairs, 6 February 1969.
28 'Webster in UK for talks on Anguilla', 12 October 1968 [newspaper cutting], in Webster, *Scrap Book*, p. 83.
29 'Statement issued by Mr Ronald Webster at end of London Talks', *The Beacon*, 2 November 1968, p. 2, *Anguilla Library Service* <https://www.axalibrary.ai/the%20beacon/Volume%202/Beacon%20Vol%202%20Issue%2058.pdf> [accessed 02/12/22].
30 Webster, *Revolutionary Leader*, p. 79.
31 Webster, *Scrap Book*, p. 82.
32 'Statement issued by Mr Ronald Webster', pp. 2–3.
33 Bradshaw, quoted in Webster, *Revolutionary Leader*, pp. 79–80.
34 Atlin Harrigan, 'Editorial', *The Beacon*, 26 October 1968, p. 1, *Anguilla Library Service* <https://www.axalibrary.ai/the%20beacon/Volume%202/Beacon%20Vol%202%20Issue%2057.pdf> [accessed 02/12/22].
35 Letter from Clive C. Smith, 'Congratulations to Mr Ronald Webster', *The Beacon*, 2 November 1968, p. 4, *Anguilla Library Service* <https://www.axalibrary.ai/the%20beacon/Volume%202/Beacon%20Vol%202%20Issue%2058.pdf> [accessed 02/12/22].
36 Letter from 'Anguillan', 'What is the next move? Independence?', *The Beacon*, 2 November 1968, p. 3, *Anguilla Library Service* <https://www.

37 Webster, *Revolutionary Leader*, p. 83.
38 Ronald Webster to Lord Chalfont, 'The Government of Anguilla, British West Indies', 30 December 1968, reproduced in The Wooding Report, pp. 95–96.
39 Calum Thomson, 'Ripples from the South Atlantic: Examining the Wider Significance of the Falklands War for the British Overseas Territories' (unpublished masters thesis, Universiteit Leiden, 2018), p. 18.
40 Secretary of State for Foreign and Commonwealth Affairs, Michael Stewart, 'Anguilla', HC Deb 19 March 1969 vol 780 cc493-506 [495], *Historic Hansard* <https://api.parliament.uk/historic-hansard/commons/1969/mar/19/anguilla> [accessed 15/12/22].
41 Homer Bigart, 'Anguillan leaders have big plans for their tiny Caribbean island republic', *New York Times*, 18 March 1969, p. 16, *ProQuest Historical Newspapers: The New York Times* <https://go.openathens.net/redirector/leeds.ac.uk?url=https://www.proquest.com/historical-newspapers/anguillan-leaders-have-big-plans-their-tiny/docview/118601085/se-2> [accessed 14/12/22].
42 Westlake, p. 166.
43 Ibid.
44 Special to The New York Times, 'Holcomb a frequent visitor', *New York Times*, 18 March 1969, p. 16, *ProQuest Historical Newspapers: The New York Times* <https://go.openathens.net/redirector/leeds.ac.uk?url=https://www.proquest.com/historical-newspapers/holcomb-frequent-visitor/docview/118573197/se-2> [accessed 14/12/22].
45 Charles Hillinger, 'Anguilla factory owner wants U.S. to step in: American resident and adviser to native government hopes for ouster of British', *Los Angeles Times*, 26 March 1969, p. A8, *ProQuest Historical Newspapers: Lost Angeles Times* <https://go.openathens.net/redirector/leeds.ac.uk?url=https://www.proquest.com/historical-newspapers/anguilla-factory-owner-wants-u-s-step/docview/156112185/se-2> [accessed 15/12/22].
46 Ibid.
47 Westlake, pp. 165–66.
48 Atlin Harrigan, 'Editorial', *The Beacon*, 14 December 1968, p. 1, *Anguilla Library Service* <https://www.axalibrary.ai/the%20beacon/Volume%202/Beacon%20Vol%202%20Issue%2064.pdf> [accessed 08/12/22].
49 Atlin Harrigan, 'Editorial', *The Beacon*, 28 December 1968, p. 1, *Anguilla Library Service* <https://www.axalibrary.ai/the%20beacon/Volume%202/Beacon%20Vol%202%20Issue%2065.pdf> [accessed 08/12/22].
50 Webster, *Scrap Book*, p. 66.
51 Webster, *Revolutionary Leader*, p. 93.
52 Ibid.
53 Ibid, pp. 93, 95.
54 London, *TNA*, PREM 13/2517, The Anguillan Declaration of Independence, reported in Lee to FCO, 7 February 1969.
55 Ibid.
56 London, *TNA*, FCO 63/180, Lee to T.R.M. Sewell, 6 February 1969.
57 Ibid.
58 'Anguilla vote to break the old ties', *The Times*, 8 February 1969, p. 6, *The Times Digital Archive* <link.gale.com/apps/doc/CS101544008/TTDA?u=leedsuni&sid=bookmark-TTDA&xid=219b1493.> [accessed 16/12/22]. UPI, 'Anguilla Votes to Cut Ties', *Daily Telegraph*, 8 February 1969, p. 22, *The Telegraph Historical Archive* <link.gale.com/apps/doc/IO0704098360/TGRH?u=leedsuni&sid=bookmark-TGRH&xid=412fbf17.> [accessed 16/12/22].
59 Colin Rickards, 'Caribbean Quiet UDI', *Daily Telegraph*, 11 February 1969, p. 19, *The Telegraph Historical Archive* <link.gale.com/apps/doc/IO0703268396/TGRH?u=leedsuni&sid=bookmark-TGRH&xid=ee5baa50.> [accessed 16/12/22].
60 'The inside Page', *Daily Mirror*, 7 February 1969, p. 11, *Mirror Historical Archive, 1903–2000* <link.gale.com/apps/doc/REDQZJ864896450/DMIR?u=leedsuni&sid=bookmark-DMIR&xid=62087770.> [accessed 16/12/22].
61 'Home rule calypso', *The Guardian*, 12 February 1969, p. 9, *ProQuest Historical Newspapers: The Guardian and The Observer* <https://go.openathens.net/redirector/leeds.ac.uk?url=https://www.proquest.com/historical-newspapers/home-rule-calypso/docview/185421268/se-2> [accessed 15/12/22].
62 TNA, FCO 63/180, Whitlock to Secretary of State for Foreign and Commonwealth Affairs, 6 February 1969.
63 Lee to FCO, 13 February 1969.
64 Westlake, pp. 187–88. *Private Eye*, quoted in Westlake, p. 188.
65 Heather E. Schwartz, *Gangsters, Bootleggers, and Bandits* (Minneapolis: Lerner Publications Company, 2013), pp. 14–15.
66 *Private Eye*, quoted in Westlake, p. 188.
67 TNA, FCO 63/180, Foreign Office Note, 28 January 1969.
68 J.M. Stewart to Washington, 31 January 1969.
69 Lee to T.R.M. Sewell, 13 February 1969.
70 Ibid.

71 Communique from Fifth Heads of Government Conference held at the Hilton Hotel, 3–6 February 1969, attached to G.P. Hampshire to Sewell, 'Commonwealth Caribbean Heads of Government's Conference', 13 February 1969.

72 Hampshire to Sewell, 'Commonwealth', 13 February 1969.

73 Mr Murray to FCO, 24 February 1969.

74 Stewart to Kingston, 21 February 1969.

75 Our Naval Correspondent, 'Anguilla airlift likely', *Sunday Telegraph*, 16 February 1969, p. 2, *The Telegraph Historical Archive* <link.gale.com/apps/doc/IO0709203606/TGRH?u=leedsuni&sid=bookmark-TGRH&xid=293f6325.> [accessed 08/01/23].

76 *TNA*, FCO 63/180, Stewart to St. Lucia, 21 February 1969.

77 Lee to Sewell, 6 February 1969.

78 Lee to FCO, 6 February 1969.

79 Kerr to FCO, 7 February 1969.

80 Lord Caradon to FCO, 14 February 1969.

81 T.R.M. Sewell to R.C.C. Hunt, 'Sir Alan Burns, G.C.M.G., and Lt. Col. M.R. Robinson, D.S.O.', 20 February 1969.

82 Kerr to FCO, 20 February 1969.

83 Record of Meeting on 13 February 1969 between Mr. Whitlock and members of the C.P.A. delegation to the Leeward and Windward Islands.

84 Record of a meeting held in Mr. Whitlock's room at 11 a.m. on 11 February [1969].

85 Westlake, pp. 176–77.

86 *TNA*, FCO 63/180, Kerr to FCO, 20 February 1969.

87 Sewell to Hunt, 'Anguilla', 19 February 1969.

88 Hunt to Whitlock, 'The question of a meeting with Mr. Webster', 19 February 1969.

89 *TNA*, PREM 13/2517, Whitlock to FCO, 11 March 1969.

90 Webster to Stewart, 12 March 1969.

91 Westlake, pp. 178–84.

92 *TNA*, PREM 13/2517, Webster to Stewart, 12 March 1969.

93 Webster, *Revolutionary Leader*, p. 106.

94 Webster, *Scrap Book*, p. 98. Webster, *Revolutionary Leader*, p. 106.

95 *TNA*, PREM 13/2517, Whitlock to FCO, 11 March 1969.

96 Ibid.

97 Westlake, pp. 184–85.

98 *TNA*, PREM 13/2517, Whitlock to FCO, 11 March 1969.

99 *TNA*, FCO 63/180, Record of a meeting held in Mr. Whitlock's room at 11 a.m. on 11 February.

100 Stewart to St Lucia, 18 February 1969.

101 'Anguillans 'ruled by fear'', *The Times*, 13 March 1969, p. 1, *The Times Digital Archive* <link.gale.com/apps/doc/CS17133677/TTDA?u=leedsuni&sid=bookmark-TTDA&xid=ae2c2510.> [accessed 17/01/23].

102 Our Commonwealth Staff, 'Anguillans 'dominated by gangsters'', *The Times*, 14 March 1969, p. 5, *The Times Digital Archive* <link.gale.com/apps/doc/CS84242542/TTDA?u=leedsuni&sid=bookmark-TTDA&xid=c1344f4a.> [accessed 17/01/23].

103 Ian Ball, et al., 'Mafia Gangs 'Rule Island by Fear'', *Daily Telegraph*, 13 March 1969, p. 1, *The Telegraph Historical Archive* <link.gale.com/apps/doc/IO0702166907/TGRH?u=leedsuni&sid=bookmark-TGRH&xid=4e900d32.> [accessed 17/01/23].

104 Reuter, 'Island gunmen kick out Minister', *Daily Mail*, 13 March 1969, p. 2, *Daily Mail Historical Archive* <link.gale.com/apps/doc/EE1864052290/DMHA?u=leedsuni&sid=bookmark-DMHA&xid=0ebff668.> [accessed 17/01/23]. David Smithers, 'Why the Bullets Fly in Paradise', *Daily Mirror*, 14 March 1969, p. 9, *Mirror Historical Archive, 1903–2000* <link.gale.com/apps/doc/HTLEVF274422836/DMIR?u=leedsuni&sid=bookmark-DMIR&xid=d3a0b04f.> [accessed 17/01/23].

105 Our Foreign Staff, 'Hostile crowd ejects envoy from Anguilla', *The Guardian*, 13 March 1969, p. 2, *ProQuest Historical Newspapers: The Guardian and The Observer* <https://go.openathens.net/redirector/leeds.ac.uk?url=https://www.proquest.com/historical-newspapers/hostile-crowd-ejects-envoy-anguilla/docview/185413040/se-2> [accessed 17/01/23].

106 *TNA*, PREM 13/2517, Note by A.M. Palliser, March 1969.

107 Barbara Castle, quoted in Mawby, 'Overwhelmed', p. 266.

108 *TNA*, PREM 13/2517, Sir Burke Trend to Prime Minister, 'Anguilla', 13 March 1969.

109 Denis Healey, quoted in Mawby, 'Overwhelmed', p. 266.

110 Mawby, 'Overwhelmed', p. 266.

111 Michael Stewart, quoted in Ibid.

112 Mawby, 'Overwhelmed', p. 266.

Chapter 4

1 Ian Speller, *The Role of Amphibious Warfare in British Defence Policy, 1945–56* (Basingstoke: Palgrave, 2001), p. 204.

2 David French, *Army, Empire and Cold War: The British Army and Military Policy 1945–1971* (Oxford: Oxford University Press, 2012), pp. 245–46, 249.

3 'East of Suez strategy', in *Documents in Contemporary History: British defence policy since 1945*, ed. by Ritchie Ovendale (Manchester: Manchester University Press, 1994), pp. 136–141 (p. 138).

4 'British withdrawal from the Far East and the Persian Gulf', in Ovendale, pp. 144–145 (p. 144).

5 French, *Army, Empire and Cold War*, pp. 290–91.

6 Ibid.

7 'Police fire on rioters in Antigua', *The Times*, 21 March 1968, p. 6, *The Times Digital Archive* <link.gale.com/apps/doc/CS102985333/TTDA?u=leedsuni&sid=bookmark-TTDA&xid=ffe2ce4b.> [accessed 07/02/23].

8 *TNA*, PREM 13/2517, Mr Roberts to Commonwealth Office, 22 March 1968.

9 Air Vice Marshal Peter Le Cheminant to Prime Minister Harold Wilson, 22 March 1968.

10 French, *Army, Empire and Cold War*, pp. 250, 264–65.

11 Ibid, p. 257.

12 Ibid, p. 282.

13 *TNA*, FCO 46/356, Major General Tony Deane-Drummond, 'Meeting of the Defence Operations Executive Held at 1415 on Friday 14th March 1969', 14 March 1969.

14 'Significant dates around operations in Anguilla', p. 5, *Airborne Assault ParaData* <https://www.paradata.org.uk/media/405> [accessed 22/03/22].

15 Duxford, *Airborne Assault Museum* [henceforth *AAM*], 3.A.5. 2/32/1, 'Regimental record', p. 39.

16 3.A.5. 2/32/1, Lieutenant-Colonel R.W. Dawnay, 'Anguilla 1969', *The Infantryman*, No. 86, November 1970, 33–37 (p. 33).

17 Paul Rees, quoted in 'Brigadier Richard W Dawnay OBE', *Airborne Assault ParaData* <https://www.paradata.org.uk/people/richard-w-dawnay> [accessed 11/02/23].

18 'Brigadier Richard W Dawnay OBE', *Airborne Assault ParaData* <https://www.paradata.org.uk/people/richard-w-dawnay> [accessed 11/02/23].

19 *TNA*, FCO 46/356, 'Operation Sheepskin – Narrative of Events', Annex B to the Senior Naval Officer West Indies' letter 226/5, 25 April 1969.

20 *AAM*, 3.A.5. 2/32/1, Dawnay, 'Anguilla 1969', p. 33.

21 *TNA*, DEFE 11/885, 'Defence and Internal Security' [Annex A], in Memorandum by the Secretary of State for Foreign and Commonwealth Affairs, 'Cabinet Defence and Overseas Policy Committee: British Policy in the Commonwealth Caribbean', 21 July 1969.

22 FCO 46/356, Reports on Operation Sheepskin by the Senior Naval Officer, West Indies and GSO1(Psyops), Joint Warfare Establishment (Preliminary Draft), Date Unknown.

23 'Operation Sheepskin – Intelligence Report', Annex D to the Senior Naval Officer West Indies' letter 226/5, 25 April 1969.

24 *AAM*, 3.A.5. 2/32/1, Dawnay, 'Anguilla 1969', p. 33.

25 Webster, quoted in Ian Ball, 'Rebels in Anguilla 'ready for Navy'', *Daily Telegraph*, 14 March 1969, p. 1, *The Telegraph Historical Archive* <link.gale.com/apps/doc/IO0702390126/TGRH?u=leedsuni&sid=bookmark-TGRH&xid=1f1176a8.> [accessed 09/03/23].

26 *TNA*, FCO 63/180, 'President of Anguilla talks tough', 13 February 1969.

27 *TNA*, PREM 13/2517, Note by officials, 'Anguilla', 16 March 1969.

28 *TNA*, DEFE 11/885, Williams, 'A Report on the Facts'.

29 *TNA*, FCO 46/357, 'Reports on "Operation Sheepskin" and Psychological Operations in Anguilla, March/April 1969', 23 July 1969.

30 *TNA*, FCO 46/356, Report by Lt. Colonel B.R. Johnston, 'Psychological Operations Support in Anguilla 1969 (JTP 61)', 6 June 1969, Annex A to Joint Warfare Establishment Letter JWE/s1815/3, 9 June 1969.

31 'Joint Theatre Plan 61: Comments and Recommendations', Annex A to the Senior Naval Officer West Indies' letter 226/5, 25 April 1969.

32 *TNA*, FCO 46/356, Johnston, 'Psychological Operations Support'.

33 *TNA*, FCO 46/357, 'Report on "Operation Sheepskin" in Anguilla, March/April 1969', Annex A to COS 54/69, attached to Note by the Secretary (MoD Chiefs of Staff Committee), 'Report on "Operation Sheepskin" in Anguilla March/April 1969', 29 August 1969.

34 'Reports on "Operation Sheepskin"', 23 July 1969.

35 *TNA*, FCO 46/356, 'Operation Sheepskin – Psyops Report', Annex E to the Senior Naval Officer West Indies' letter 226/5, 25 April 1969.

36 Peter Harclerode, *PARA! Fifty Years of the Parachute Regiment* (London: Brockhampton Press, 1992), p. 279.

37 *TNA*, FCO 46/356, A.C. Watson to Mr Campbell, 'Anguilla: Defence Report by Defence Operations Staff', 10 July 1969.

38 Commodore M.N. Lucey to Chief of Defence Staff, 25 April 1969, Annex A to COS 1316/14/5/69.

39 'Reports on Operation Sheepskin by the Senior Naval Officer, West Indies and GSO1(Psyops), Joint Warfare Establishment', Date Unknown, [Annex A to DOP 521/69 (Preliminary Draft)].

40 Ibid.

41 *AAM*, 3.A.5. 2/32/1, Dawnay, 'Anguilla 1969', p. 33.

42 Our Crime Correspondent, 'Yard's Deputy Chief Retires next Month', *Daily Telegraph*, 28 November 1969, p. 19, *The Telegraph Historical Archive* <link.

43 Georgina Sinclair, *At the end of the line: Colonial policing and the imperial endgame 1945–80* (Manchester: Manchester University Press, 2006), pp. 99–100. Ellis Plaice and Tom Tullett, 'The Men Who Are Set for Action', *Daily Mirror*, 18 March 1969, p. 1, *Mirror Historical Archive, 1903–2000* <link.gale.com/apps/doc/MQSOPO015953785/DMIR?u=leedsuni&sid=bookmark-DMIR&xid=70348a6e.> [accessed 16/03/23].

44 *TNA*, FCO 46/357, 'Report on "Operation Sheepskin" in Anguilla, March/April 1969', Annex A to COS 54/69, attached to Note by the Secretary (MoD Chiefs of Staff Committee), 'Report on "Operation Sheepskin" in Anguilla March/April 1969', 29 August 1969.

45 *TNA*, PREM 13/2517, Note to the Prime Minister, 'Anguilla', 16 March 1969.

46 Note by officials, 'Anguilla', 16 March 1969.

47 Ibid.

48 Clarke, p. 14. Carty and Petty, p. 27.

49 *TNA*, FCO 46/356, 'Operation Sheepskin – Narrative of Events', Annex B to the Senior Naval Officer West Indies' letter 226/5, 25 April 1969.

50 Ibid.

51 Commodore P.J. Bayne, 'Anguilla', 17 March 1969.

52 *TNA*, PREM 13/2517, 'Draft Confidential Directive to H.M. Commissioner for Anguilla', Appendix A(i) to Note by officials, 'Anguilla', 16 March 1969.

53 Ibid.

54 Note by officials, 'Anguilla', 16 March 1969.

55 'Draft Signal from the Chiefs of the Defence Staff to the Senior Naval Officer West Indies; Political Directive', Appendix A(ii) to Note by officials, 'Anguilla', 16 March 1969.

56 Ibid.

57 *TNA*, FCO 46/356, 'Operation Sheepskin – Intelligence Report'.

58 *TNA*, PREM 13/2517, 'Draft Confidential Directive to H.M. Commissioner for Anguilla', Appendix A(i).

59 Sinclair, p. 99.

60 *TNA*, FCO 46/356, Major General A.J. Deane Drummond, 'Meeting of the Defence Operations Executive Held at 1100 on Monday 17th March 1969 – Anguilla', 17 March 1969.

61 Ibid.

62 Ibid.

63 *TNA*, PREM 13/2517, FCO message to certain missions, 'Anguilla', 19 March 1969.

64 Note by officials, 'Anguilla', 16 March 1969.

65 'Juridical Basis of Proposed Order in Council for Anguilla', Appendix C to Note by officials, 'Anguilla', 16 March 1969.

66 'U.N. Aspects', Appendix F to Note by officials, 'Anguilla', 16 March 1969.

67 Carl Watts, 'Killing Kith and Kin: The Viability of British Military Intervention in Rhodesia, 1964–5', *Twentieth Century British History*, 16 (2005), 382–415 (p. 383).

68 *TNA*, PREM 13/2517, 'U.N. Aspects'.

69 Note by officials, 'Anguilla', 16 March 1969.

70 Stewart to Washington, 17 March 1969.

71 Ibid.

72 'Timetable for informing other Governments and Posts', Appendix E to Note by officials, 'Anguilla', 16 March 1969.

73 Lee to FCO (Telegram No. 50), 16 March 1969.

74 Ibid.

75 Lee to FCO, 16 March 1969.

76 P.T. Hayman to Private Secretary, 'Mr. Lee', 16 March 1969.

77 'Publicity and Presentation', Appendix D(i) to Note by officials, 'Anguilla', 16 March 1969.

78 Ibid.

79 *TNA*, PREM 13/2927, 'Note for the record: Anguilla', 18 March 1969.

80 'Inter-departmental Leak Procedure', 29 April 1969.

81 Cabinet Office Note of Meeting, 'Anguilla: Leakage of Information', 20 March 1969.

82 Robert Carvel, 'Rebel Isle – Skymen Alert', *Evening Standard*, 17 March 1969, p. 1 [newspaper cutting].

83 Christopher Moran, *Classified: Secrecy and the State in Modern Britain* (Cambridge: Cambridge University Press, 2013), p. 136.

84 Lady Falkender, quoted in Moran, p. 136.

85 *TNA*, PREM 13/2927, 'Anguilla: Leakage of Information', 20 March 1969.

86 'Note of a Meeting at No. 10 Downing Street at 11 p.m. on Monday, March 17, 1969', 18 March 1969.

87 Ibid.

88 Ibid.

89 Ibid.

90 Moran, p. 137.

91 *TNA*, PREM 13/2927, 'Note of a Meeting at No. 10'.

92 Ibid.

93 'Anguilla: Leakage of Information', 20 March 1969.

94 'Note for the record: Anguilla'.

95 'Police Special Patrol Group', *Daily Mail*, 18 March 1969, p. 1, *Daily Mail Historical Archive* <link.gale.com/apps/doc/EE1864052675/DMHA?u=leedsuni&sid=bookmark-DMHA&xid=765ee99b.> [accessed 21/04/23].

96 *TNA*, PREM 13/2927, 'Inter-departmental Leak Procedure', 29 April 1969.

97 Ibid.

98 Ibid.

99 Armstrong to Halls, 8 May 1969.

100 Ian Ball, 'Anguilla Tests its Defences', *Sunday Telegraph*, 16 March 1969, p. 2, *The Telegraph Historical Archive* <link.gale.com/apps/doc/IO0709172703/TGRH?u=leedsuni&sid=bookmark-TGRH&xid=4ab6e702.> [accessed 07/07/22].

101 Ibid.

102 Letter from Webster to Canon Guy Carleton, 15 March 1969, quoted in Webster, *Revolutionary Leader*, p. 109.

103 Gumbs quoted in Kathleen Teltsch, 'Anguilla seeking an inquiry by U.N.: Disputes Briton's charge of control by gangsters', *New York Times*, 15 March 1969, p. 11, *ProQuest Historical Newspapers: The New York Times* <https://go.openathens.net/redirector/leeds.ac.uk?url=https://www.proquest.com/historical-newspapers/anguilla-seeking-inquiry-u-n/docview/118468583/se-2> [accessed 07/07/22].

104 Charles Douglas-Home, 'Troops and police stand by for Anguilla', *The Times*, 18 March 1969, p. 1, *The Times Digital Archive* <link.gale.com/apps/doc/CS18051186/TTDA?u=leedsuni&sid=bookmark-TTDA&xid=bed5a968.> [accessed 03/10/23].

105 Gumbs to Ambassador Mahmoud Mestiri (Chairman of the Special Committee of 24), 'Petition from Mr. Jeremiah Gumbs concerning St. Kitts-Nevis-Anguilla', 18 March 1969, *United Nations Archive* S-0504-0096-0014-00001: 'St. Kitts-Nevis-Anguilla – Jeremiah Gumbs – A/AC.109/ PET.1044 & Add.1 – Comms.#1935(H), 1938' <https://search.archives.un.org/ uploads/r/united-nations-archives/f/3/8/ f38a60d14445b8f8375ad9a6054aeb2040014c7 c2ff7cec3b727895941dc47a2/S-0504-0096-0014-00001.PDF> [accessed 28/03/22].

106 *TNA*, PREM 13/2517, Cypher from UK Mission New York to FCO, 17 March 1969.

107 'U.N. Aspects'.

108 Dolores and Lawrence Landry to U Thant, 'Petition from Mrs. Dolores Landry and Mr. Lawrence Landry concerning St. Kitts-Nevis-Anguilla', 18 March 1969, *United Nations Archive* S-0504-0097-0018-00001: ST.KITTS-NEVIS-ANGUILLA – Dolores & Lawrence Landry – A/AC.109/PET.1062 – COMM.#1942 <https://search.archives.un.org/st-kitts-nevis-anguilla-dolores-lawrence-landry-a-ac-109-pet-1062-comm-1942-2> [accessed 27/03/22].

109 *TNA*, PREM 13/2927, 'Note for the record: Anguilla'.

110 'Significant dates around operations in Anguilla', *Airborne Assault ParaData* <https://www.paradata.org.uk/media/405> [accessed 22/03/22].

111 Richard Cox, 'Troops Ready for Airlift', *Daily Telegraph*, 18 March 1969, p. 1, *The Telegraph Historical Archive* <link.gale.com/apps/doc/IO0703503598/TGRH?u=leedsuni&sid=bookmark-TGRH&xid=1580a3fd.> [accessed 07/07/22].

112 *AAM*, 3.A.5. 2/32/1, Dawnay, 'Anguilla 1969', p. 34.

113 Geoffrey Wakeford, 'Police set to invade pirate isle', *Daily Mail*, 18 March 1969, p. 1, *Daily Mail Historical Archive* <link.gale.com/apps/doc/EE1864052665/DMHA?u=leedsuni&sid=bookmark-DMHA&xid=ac48870d.> [accessed 28/04/23].

114 *AAM*, 3.A.5. 2/32/1, Dawnay, 'Anguilla 1969', p. 33.

115 Ibid, pp. 33–34.

116 Westlake, p. 203.

117 *TNA*, FCO 46/356, 'Operation Sheepskin – Narrative of Events', Annex B to the Senior Naval Officer West Indies' letter 226/5, 25 April 1969.

118 Westlake, p. 203.

119 Webster, *Scrap Book*, p. 104.

120 See French, *Army, Empire and Cold War*, p. 257.

121 *TNA*, PREM 13/2517, Sir Colin Crowe to FCO, (Telegram Number 256), 18 March 1969.

122 Sir Colin Crowe to FCO, (Telegram Number 259), 18 March 1969.

123 Ibid.

124 Stewart to Ottawa, (Telegram Number 138), 19 March 1969.

125 Stewart to Ottawa, (Telegram Number 139), 19 March 1969.

Chapter 5

1 *TNA*, FCO 46/356, 'Operation Sheepskin – Narrative of Events', Annex B to the Senior Naval Officer West Indies' letter 226/5, 25 April 1969.

2 Webster, *Scrap Book*, p. 104.

3 *AAM*, 3.A.5. 2/32/1, Dawnay, 'Anguilla 1969', p. 34.

4 Ibid.

5 *TNA*, FCO 46/356, 'Operation Sheepskin – Narrative of Events'.

6 Westlake, p. 205.

7 Webster, *Scrap Book*, p. 104.

8 'Significant dates around operations in Anguilla', *Airborne Assault ParaData* <https://www.paradata.org.uk/media/405> [accessed 22/03/22].

9 *TNA*, FCO 46/356, 'Operation Sheepskin – Narrative of Events'.

10 'Captain Mick Cotton describes beach landing at Anguilla', *Airborne Assault ParaData* <https://www.paradata.org.uk/media/11611> [accessed 21/03/22].

11 Westlake, p. 205.

12 *AAM*, 3.A.5. 2/32/1, Lt. Colonel Dawnay, quoted in Regimental history – Chapter 24, 'Anguilla 1969'.

13 Dawnay, 'Anguilla 1969', p. 34.

14 'Captain Mick Cotton describes beach landing at Anguilla', *Airborne Assault ParaData* <https://www.paradata.org.uk/media/11611> [accessed 21/03/22].

15 Webster, *Scrap Book*, p. 104.

16 *TNA*, FCO 46/356, 'Operation Sheepskin – Narrative of Events'.

17 'Anguilla delight – Not for the R.N.', *Navy News*, No. 178, 15 April 1969, p. 1, *Navy News Archive* <https://www.royalnavy.mod.uk/-/media/royal-navy-responsive/images/navynews/archivepdfs/1960s/1969/navy-news-april-1969-issue-178.pdf?rev=83be5b87e2c2450a8af4540a8dd70223> [accessed 09/08/22].

18 Laurence Stern, 'Anguilla conquered quietly: Anguilla submits quietly to British', *The Washington Post,* 20 March 1969, p. 1, *ProQuest Historical Newspapers: The Washington Post* <https://go.openathens.net/redirector/leeds.ac.uk?url=https://www.proquest.com/historical-newspapers/anguilla-conquered-quietly/docview/143648541/se-2> [accessed 06/10/23].

19 'Significant dates around operations in Anguilla'.

20 Ibid.

21 Ibid.

22 *TNA*, FCO 46/356, 'Operation Sheepskin – Narrative of Events'.

23 Ibid.

24 Westlake, p. 206.

25 Webster, *Scrap Book,* p. 104.

26 *TNA*, FCO 46/356, 'Operation Sheepskin – Narrative of Events'.

27 *AAM*, 3.A.5. 2/32/1, Dawnay, 'Anguilla 1969', p. 34.

28 *TNA*, PREM 13/2517, 'Text of Leaflet: Message to the People of Anguilla from the British Government', Appendix D(ii) to Note by officials, 'Anguilla', 16 March 1969.

29 *TNA*, FCO 46/356, Johnston, 'Psychological Operations Support'.

30 'Operation Sheepskin – Psyops Report'.

31 Johnston, 'Psychological Operations Support'.

32 Ibid. FCO 46/357, 'Reports on "Operation Sheepskin" and Psychological Operations in Anguilla, March/April 1969', 23 July 1969.

33 FCO 46/356, Report to Mr Curson, 'Anguilla: The Information Aspect', [date unknown], attached to Campbell to Mr A. Watson, 'Anguilla: Snowi's Report', 9 July 1969.

34 Johnston, 'Psychological Operations Support'.

35 Ibid.

36 Kumar Ramakrishna, *Emergency Propaganda: The Winning of Malayan Hearts and Minds 1948–1958* (Abingdon: Routledge, 2002), p. 215.

37 Anguilla's only domestically printed newspaper, *The Beacon*, had had its roller broken meaning that the British could not use this printing outlet upon arriving on the island.

38 David A. Charters, 'Intelligence and Psychological Warfare Operations in Northern Ireland', *The RUSI Journal*, 122 (1977), 22–27 (p. 26).

39 *TNA*, FCO 46/356, 'Operation Sheepskin – Communications Report', Annex C to the Senior Naval Officer West Indies' letter 226/5, 25 April 1969. M.B. Eaden to A. Routledge, 'Operation Sheepskin – Communication Report Comments by Communications Department', 25 June 1969.

40 Eaden to Routledge, 25 June 1969.

41 'Operation Sheepskin – Communications Report', Annex C.

42 Eaden to Routledge, 25 June 1969.

43 'Operation Sheepskin – Communications Report', Annex C.

44 Eaden to Routledge, 25 June 1969.

45 Ibid.

46 'Operation Sheepskin – Communications Report', Annex C.

47 Ibid.

48 Webster, *Revolutionary Leader*, p. 111.

49 Westlake, p. 207.

50 Douglas-Home, 'How the Army'.

51 Ian Ball, et al, 'Rebel home guard waits', *Daily Telegraph*, 19 March 1969, pp. 1 and 32, *The Telegraph Historical Archive* <link.gale.com/apps/doc/IO0702391075/TGRH?u=leedsuni&sid=bookmark-TGRH&xid=7fcc3b66.> [accessed 07/07/22].

52 *AAM*, 3.A.5. 2/32/1, '2nd Battalion The Parachute Regiment: Anguilla', *Pegasus: The Journal of Airborne Forces*, XXV:1 (January 1970), p. 43.

53 'Brute Farce and Ignorance', *Sunday Times*, 23 March 1969, p. 13, *The Sunday Times Historical Archive* <link.gale.com/apps/doc/FP1800360838/STHA?u=leedsuni&sid=bookmark-STHA&xid=2d2b71e2.> [accessed 07/07/22].

54 Westlake, p. 209.

55 *TNA*, FCO 46/356, 'Operation Sheepskin – Narrative of Events'.

56 Our Military Correspondent, 'Cross-Roads Key Point in Landing', *Daily Telegraph*, 20 March 1969, p. 36, *The Telegraph Historical Archive* <link.gale.com/apps/doc/IO0702391767/TGRH?u=leedsuni&sid=bookmark-TGRH&xid=5f2dc64f.> [accessed 11/07/22].

57 Ian Ball, 'Bloodless Victory for Paratroops', *Daily Telegraph*, 20 March 1969, p. 1, *The Telegraph Historical Archive* <link.gale.com/apps/doc/IO0702391415/TGRH?u=leedsuni&sid=bookmark-TGRH&xid=9cab45f0.> [accessed 11/07/22].

58 Ibid.

59 Ibid.

60 Ibid.

61 Ibid.

62 Olive Rogers, quoted in Walicek, p. 161.

63 'British land more troops on Anguilla: Angry natives hail rebel leader', *Chicago Tribune*, 21 March 1969, p. C11, *ProQuest Historical Newspapers: Chicago Tribune* <https://go.openathens.net/redirector/leeds.ac.uk?url=https://www.proquest.com/historical-newspapers/british-land-more-troops-on-anguilla/docview/168915423/se-2> [accessed 19/07/22].

64 Lt. Jeff Robinson, quoted in A. Raphael, 'After the invasion, police ask a few questions on Anguilla', *The Guardian*, 20 March 1969, p. 1, *ProQuest Historical Newspapers: The Guardian* <https://go.openathens.net/redirector/leeds.ac.uk?url=https://www.proquest.com/historical-newspapers/after-invasion-police-ask-few-questions-on/docview/185341423/se-2> [accessed 02/06/23].

65 A. Raphael, 'Anguilla: The smiles fade', *The Guardian*, 24 March 1969, p. 13, *ProQuest Historical Newspapers: The Guardian* <https://go.openathens.net/redirector/leeds.ac.uk?url=https://www.proquest.com/historical-newspapers/anguilla-smiles-fade/docview/185336314/se-2> [accessed 02/06/23].

66 Tony Hobbs, 'Anguilla woke – all smiling', *Navy News*, No. 178 15 April 1969, p. 12, *Navy News Archive* <https://www.royalnavy.mod.uk/-/media/royal-navy-responsive/images/navynews/archivepdfs/1960s/1969/navy-news-april-1969-issue-178.pdf?rev=83be5b87e2c2450a8af4540a8dd70223> [accessed 09/08/22].

67 Charlie Gumbs, quoted in Laurence Stern, 'Londoner's dream fulfilled: Caribbean oliday on Anguuia: Deprived of cricket low crime rate islanders skeptical signs show frustration time for a tour', *The Washington Post*, 23 March 1969, p. 14, *ProQuest Historical Newspapers: The Washington Post* <https://go.openathens.net/redirector/leeds.ac.uk?url=https://www.proquest.com/historical-newspapers/londoners-dream-fulfilled-caribbean-oliday-on/docview/147710046/se-2> [accessed 03/06/23].

68 Walicek, p. 162.

69 Ball, 'Bloodless Victory for Paratroops'.

70 Ibid.

71 Freeman Goodge, quoted in Laurence Stern, 'Anguillans tell British to get out', *The Washington Post*, 21 March 1969, p. A1, *ProQuest Historical Newspapers: The Washington Post* <https://go.openathens.net/redirector/leeds.ac.uk?url=https://www.proquest.com/historical-newspapers/anguillans-tell-british-get-out/docview/147690432/se-2> [accessed 03/06/23].

72 Stern, 'Anguillans tell British to get out'.

73 Ian Ball, "Racist' feeling grows', *Daily Telegraph*, 21 March 1969, pp. 1 and 36, *The Telegraph Historical Archive* <link.gale.com/apps/doc/IO0702391773/TGRH?u=leedsuni&sid=bookmark-TGRH&xid=bdb02d94.> [accessed 11/07/22].

74 Way, quoted in A. Raphael, 'Anguilla haul: One rifle and no gangsters', *The Guardian*, 21 March 1969, p. 1, *ProQuest Historical Newspapers: The Guardian and The Observer* <https://go.openathens.net/redirector/leeds.ac.uk?url=https://www.proquest.com/historical-newspapers/anguilla-haul-one-rifle-no-gangsters/docview/185340514/se-2> [accessed 03/06/23].

75 Webster, *Scrap Book*, p. 104.

76 *TNA*, FCO 46/356, 'Operation Sheepskin – Narrative of Events'.

77 Webster, *Scrap Book*, p. 104.

78 Douglas-Home, 'How the Army'.

79 Westlake, p. 207.

80 Ball, 'Bloodless Victory for Paratroops'.

81 Chief Petty Officer Stuart Bowen, quoted in Hobbs, 'Anguilla woke – all smiling'.

82 Michael Stewart, 'Anguilla', HC Deb 19 March 1969 vol 780 cc493-506, col. 495, *Historic Hansard* <https://api.parliament.uk/historic-hansard/commons/1969/mar/19/anguilla> [accessed 06/06/23].

83 Ibid, col. 495–496.

84 Ibid, col. 496.

85 Reginald Maudling, 'Anguilla', HC Deb 19 March 1969 vol 780 cc493-506, col. 496-497, *Historic Hansard* <https://api.parliament.uk/historic-hansard/commons/1969/mar/19/anguilla> [accessed 06/06/23].

86 George Brown, 'Anguilla', HC Deb 19 March 1969 vol 780 cc493-506, col. 500, *Historic Hansard* <https://api.parliament.uk/historic-hansard/commons/1969/mar/19/anguilla> [accessed 06/06/23].

87 Ibid, col. 504.

88 Edward Heath, 'Anguilla', HC Deb 19 March 1969 vol 780 cc493-506, col. 502, *Historic Hansard* <https://api.parliament.uk/historic-hansard/commons/1969/mar/19/anguilla> [accessed 06/06/23].

89 H.B. Boyne, 'Stewart Disarms MP Critics', *Daily Telegraph*, 20 March 1969, p. 1, *The Telegraph Historical Archive* <link.gale.com/apps/doc/IO0702391417/TGRH?u=leedsuni&sid=bookmark-TGRH&xid=219751f0.> [accessed 11/07/22].

90 R.F. Wright (letter to editor), 'The Difference of Anguilla', *Daily Telegraph*, 20 March 1969, p. 18, *The Telegraph Historical Archive* <link.gale.com/apps/doc/IO0702391592/TGRH?u=leedsuni&sid=bookmark-TGRH&xid=a96afb08.> [accessed 11/07/22].

91 Douglas-Home, 'How the Army'.

92 Hugh Noyes, 'Relief and anxiety in Commons', *The Times*, 20 March 1969, p. 1, *The Times Digital Archive* <link.gale.com/apps/doc/CS17133684/TTDA?u=leedsuni&sid=bookmark-TTDA&xid=3a7539b9.> [accessed 07/06/23].

93 Walter Terry, 'Is this Wilson's Bay of Piglets?', *Daily Mail*, 19 March 1969, p. 1, *Daily Mail Historical Archive* <link.gale.com/apps/doc/EE1864323693/DMHA?u=leedsuni&sid=bookmark-DMHA&xid=907fec8f.> [accessed 07/06/23].

94 George Murray, 'Why doesn't Wilson let the people know?', *Daily Mail*, 21 March 1969, p. 10, *Daily Mail Historical Archive* <link.gale.com/apps/doc/EE1864324162/DMHA?u=leedsuni&sid=bookmark-DMHA&xid=c9618965.> [accessed 06/07/22].

95 'Sledgehammer on Anguilla', *The Guardian*, 20 March 1969, p. 12, *ProQuest Historical Newspapers: The Guardian* <https://go.openathens.net/redirector/leeds.ac.uk?url=https://www.proquest.com/historical-newspapers/sledgehammer-on-anguilla/docview/185333281/se-2> [accessed 07/06/23].

96 Reverend Douglas O. Field (letter to editor), 'Tragic intervention in Anguilla', *The Guardian*, 20 March 1969, p. 12, *ProQuest Historical Newspapers: The Guardian and The Observer* <https://go.openathens.net/redirector/leeds.ac.uk?url=https://www.proquest.com/historical-newspapers/tragic-intervention-anguilla/docview/185341108/se-2> [accessed 07/06/23].

97 D.E. Maxwell (letter to the editor), 'Tragic intervention in Anguilla', *The Guardian*, 20 March 1969, p. 12, *ProQuest Historical Newspapers: The Guardian and The Observer* <https://go.openathens.net/redirector/leeds.ac.uk?url=https://www.proquest.com/historical-newspapers/tragic-intervention-anguilla/docview/185341108/se-2> [accessed 07/06/23].

98 Alvin Shuster, 'Anguilla: A slap for the mouse that roared', *New York Times*, 23 March 1969, p. E2, *ProQuest Historical Newspapers: The New York Times* <https://go.openathens.net/redirector/leeds.ac.uk?url=https://www.proquest.com/historical-newspapers/anguilla/docview/118622094/se-2> [accessed 07/06/23].

99 'Twas a famous victory', *Chicago Tribune*, 20 March 1969, p. 22, *ProQuest Historical Newspapers: Chicago Tribune* <https://go.openathens.net/redirector/leeds.ac.uk?url=https://www.proquest.com/historical-newspapers/twas-famous-victory/docview/168856986/se-2> [accessed 07/06/23].

100 'Anguilla invaded by British troops; new chief installed: Incomplete source', *Los Angeles Times*, 20 March 1969, p. 1, *ProQuest Historical Newspapers: Los Angeles Times* <https://go.openathens.net/redirector/leeds.ac.uk?url=https://www.proquest.com/historical-newspapers/anguilla-invaded-british-troops-new-chief/docview/156202232/se-2> [accessed 07/06/23]. 'It's not funny', *The Washington Post*, 20 March 1969, p. 24, *ProQuest Historical Newspapers: The Washington Post* <https://go.openathens.net/redirector/leeds.ac.uk?url=https://www.proquest.com/historical-newspapers/not-funny/docview/143539607/se-2> [accessed 07/06/23].

101 *TNA*, PREM 13/2517, Stewart to Washington, 17 March 1969.

102 Richard Beeston, "On the Fence' Reaction by America', *Daily Telegraph*, 19 March 1969, p. 32, *The Telegraph Historical Archive* <link.gale.com/apps/doc/IO0702391409/TGRH?u=leedsuni&sid=bookmark-TGRH&xid=945f7c20.> [accessed 07/07/22].

103 Our Diplomatic Staff, 'World-wide ridicule of Britain's new 'finest hour'', *Daily Telegraph*, 21 March 1969, p. 26, *The Telegraph Historical Archive* <link.gale.com/apps/doc/IO0702392020/TGRH?u=leedsuni&sid=bookmark-TGRH&xid=b342da8d.> [accessed 13/07/22].

104 *TNA*, DEFE 11/885, Memorandum by the Secretary of State for Foreign and Commonwealth Affairs, 'Cabinet Defence and Overseas Policy Committee: British Policy in the Commonwealth Caribbean', 21 July 1969.

105 Tim Hector to Thant, 'Petition from Mr. Tim Hector, Chairman, Antigua Opposition Party Concerning St. Kitts-Nevis-Anguilla', 19 March 1969, S-0504-0097-0021-00001: 'ST.KITTS-NEVIS-ANGUILLA – T. Hector, Antigua Opposition Party – A/AC.109/PET.1065 – COMM.#1945',

United Nations Archive <https://search.archives.un.org/uploads/r/united-nations-archives/ a/b/2/ab27c6fab131e162bd35c8aec1c985dbed61f7 a35fc274b9c91f14bdc8ed74bdS-0504-0097-0021-00001. PDF> [accessed 28/03/22].

106 Charles Kindle (African Affairs United Negro Protest Committee) to Thant, 'Petition from Mr. Charles Kindle, African Affairs United Negro Protest Committee concerning St. Kitts-Nevis-Anguilla', 30 March 1969, S-0504-0098-0002-00001: 'ST. KITTS-NEVIS-ANGUILLA – C. Kindle, African Affairs United Negro Protest Committee – A/AC.109/PET.1071 – COMM.#1951', *United Nations Archive* <https://search.archives.un.org/uploads/r/ united-nations-archives/b/4/5/b451459fce884187aa12dac199beb1294e6e3cdf6564e35f8cbfaaa c5b13394 a/S-0504-0098-0002-00001.PDF> [accessed 29/03/22]. President Students Guild to United Nations Commission on Colonialism, 20 March 1969, S-0504-0097-0023-00001: ST.KITTS-NEVIS-ANGUILLA – Pres. Students' Guild. U. of W. Indies – A/AC.109/PET.1067 – COM.#1941, *United Nations Archive* <https://search.archives.un.org/uploads/r/united-nations-archives/1/b/4/1b42ca4bdb4fc07e9500adff6a2f6de782966c0da86f48f9b274 412bc8bf9c84/S-0504-0097-0023-00001.PDF> [accessed 28/03/22].

107 Dr. F.W. Boon to The United Nations Commission on Colonialism, 23 March 1969, S-0504-0098-0001-00001: ST. KITTS-NEVIS-ANGUILLA – F. W. Boon – A/AC.109/PET.1070 – COMM.#1939, *United Nations Archive* <https://search.archives.un.org/st-kitts-nevis-anguilla-f-w-boon-a-ac-109-pet-1070-comm-1939-2> [accessed 27/03/22].

108 Consensus concerning St. Kitts-Nevis-Anguilla adopted by the Special Committee at its 663rd meeting, on 21 March 1969, S-0443-0091-0001-00001: Non-Self-Governing Territories, *United Nations Archive* <https://search.archives.un.org/uploads/r/united-nations-archives/f/9/0/ f90d0661af746f0994aa85fa4fe71c2e6e160f76fbd 2b44276ddd058b1e34be9/S-0443-0091-0001-00001.PDF> [accessed 29/03/22].

109 Charles Hargrove, in Innis Macbeath, 'World ridicule and criticism for British invasion', *The Times*, 21 March 1969, p. 10, *The Times Digital Archive* <link.gale.com/apps/doc/CS167997557/TTDA?u=leedsuni&sid=bookmark-TTDA&xid=6caac8d7.> [accessed 15/06/23].

110 Eduard Baskakov, in Macbeath, 'World ridicule'.

111 Macbeath, 'World ridicule'.

112 *Algemeen Dagblad*, quoted in Macbeath, 'World ridicule'.

113 *TNA*, FCO 46/356, Andro Gabelić, 'Military-Political Comment – The Example of Anguilla', BORBA – Belgrave, 29 March 1969.

114 Sir Terence Garvey to R.A. Sykes, 12 April 1969.

115 *TNA*, PREM 13/2517, Palliser to D.J.D. Maitland, 'Visit of the Prime Minister of Trinidad and Tobago', 19 March 1969.

116 Minute to Prime Minister, 'Foreign and Commonwealth Secretary's Lunch with Dr. Williams', 19 March 1969.

117 *TNA*, FCO 46/356, Commodore M.N. Lucey to Chief of Defence Staff Sir Charles Elworthy, 25 April 1969, Annex A to COS 1316/14/5/69.

118 'Operation Sheepskin – Intelligence Report'.

119 'Operation Sheepskin – Narrative of Events'.

120 Webster, *Scrap Book*, p. 114.

121 Ibid.

122 'Operation Sheepskin – Intelligence Report'.

123 Westlake, p. 206.

124 *TNA*, FCO 46/356, 'Operation Sheepskin – Intelligence Report'.

125 *TNA*, DEFE 11/885, Williams, 'A Report on the Facts'.

126 *TNA*, FCO 46/356, Lucey to Elworthy, 25 April 1969.

127 'Anguilla (Previous Reference: COS 13th Meeting/69, Minute 1)', Part I to COS 14th Meeting/69, 21 March 1969.

128 Brigadier Peter L. de C. Martin, 'Report on visit to Anguilla by Brigadier Martin 19–22 April 69', attached to DMO to SECCOS, 'Visit of Brigadier P.L. de C. Martin OBE, Brig A/Q HQ Army Strategic Command, to Anguilla', 24 April 1969.

129 *TNA*, DEFE 11/885, Williams, 'A Report on the Facts'.

130 J.A. Cumber, 'Anguilla – Appreciation of the Situation', 19 July 1969, Annex A to 1/10/1, 19 July 1969.

131 Mawby, 'Overwhelmed', p. 268.

132 Richard Crossman, quoted in Mawby, 'Overwhelmed', p. 268.

133 Mawby, 'Overwhelmed', p. 269.

134 Castle, quoted in Mawby, 'Overwhelmed', p. 269.

135 Denis Healey, *The Time of My Life* (London: Michael Joseph, 1989), p. 323.

136 Harold Wilson, *The Labour Government 1964–1970: A Personal Record* (London: Weidenfeld and Nicolson and Michael Joseph, 1971), p. 626.

137 *TNA*, FCO 46/356, 'Operation Sheepskin – Narrative of Events'.

138 Ibid.

139 Johnston, 'Psychological Operations Support'.

140 *AAM*, 3.A.5. 2/32/1, '2nd Battalion The Parachute Regiment: Anguilla', p. 42.

141 Regimental history – Chapter 24, 'Anguilla 1969', p. 170.

142 '2nd Battalion The Parachute Regiment: Anguilla', p. 42.

143 Ibid.

144 Dawnay, 'Anguilla 1969', p. 35.

145 *AAM*, AAL-091-1970, CSM Knowles, 'Toys for Anguilla: Two Ways Public Relations', *Pegasus: The Journal of Airborne Forces*, XXV:2 (April 1970), 10–12 (p. 10).

146 Ibid, p. 11.

147 Ibid.

148 Ibid, p. 12.

149 Ibid.

150 Major F.B. Mayes, RAMC, 'Medical Report, Anguilla 1969', *Airborne Assault ParaData* <https://www.paradata.org.uk/media/404> [accessed 21/03/22].

151 'Medical News', *The Beacon*, 31 March 1969, p. 8, *Anguilla Library Service* <https://www.axalibrary.ai/the%20beacon/Volume%202/Beacon%20Vol%202%20Issue%2077.pdf> [accessed 13/07/23].

152 Mayes, 'Medical Report'.

153 *TNA*, FCO 46/356, 'Operation Sheepskin – Psyops Report', Annex E to the Senior Naval Officer West Indies' letter 226/5, 25 April 1969. *TNA*, FCO 46/357, 'GS01(Psyops) Report on Psychological Operations Support in Anguilla 1969', Appendix 1 to Annex A to COS 54/69, attached to Note by the Secretary (MoD Chiefs of Staff Committee), 'Report on "Operation Sheepskin" in Anguilla March/April 1969', 29 August 1969.

154 *TNA*, FCO 46/356, 'Anguilla (Previous Reference: COS 13th Meeting/69, Minute 1)', Part I to COS 14th Meeting/69, 21 March 1969.

155 E.A.F. Seaman to Sykes, 'Anguilla: Brigadier Martin's report', 24 April 1969.

156 'Anguilla: British police in battle with shouting mob crowd chases Tony Lee away from his office', *The Observer*, 23 March 1969, p. 1, *ProQuest Historical Newspapers: The Guardian and The Observer* <https://go.openathens.net/redirector/leeds.ac.uk?url=https://www.proquest.com/historical-newspapers/anguilla/docview/475978673/se-2> [accessed 04/07/23].

157 Henry Giniger, 'Hundreds of angry Anguillans scuffle with British occupiers: British scuffle with Anguillans', *New York Times*, 23 March 1969, pp. 1 and 26, *ProQuest Historical Newspapers: The New York Times* <https://go.openathens.net/redirector/leeds.ac.uk?url=https://www.proquest.com/historical-newspapers/hundreds-angry-anguillans-scuffle-with-british/docview/118707686/se-2> [accessed 04/07/23].

158 Cal McCrystal, 'Webster flying back after Anguillan riot', *Sunday Times*, 23 March 1969, p. 1, *The Sunday Times Historical Archive* <link.gale.com/apps/doc/FP1800360749/STHA?u=leedsuni&sid=bookmark-STHA&xid=9fbb1c7d.> [accessed 07/07/22].

159 Giniger, 'Hundreds', p. 26.

160 McCrystal, p. 1.

161 Sergeant Edward Cook, quoted in Giniger, 'Hundreds', p. 26.

162 Ian Ball, 'Island remains tense', *Daily Telegraph*, 24 March 1969, p. 1, *The Telegraph Historical Archive* <link.gale.com/apps/doc/IO0703269813/TGRH?u=leedsuni&sid=bookmark-TGRH&xid=b8f4ea9e.> [accessed 13/07/22].

163 'Anguilla: British police in battle', p. 1.

164 McCrystal, p. 1. Giniger, 'Hundreds', p. 26.

165 Johnston, quoted in 'Anguilla: British police in battle', p. 1.

166 Raphael, 'Anguilla: The smiles fade', p. 13.

167 Lee, quoted in McCrystal, p. 1.

168 *TNA*, FCO 46/356, 'Operation Sheepskin – Narrative of Events'.

169 Ibid.

170 Dr Davidson Nicol, 'Lord Caradon', *The Times*, 14 September 1990, p. 16, *The Times Digital Archive* <link.gale.com/apps/doc/IF0501829496/TTDA?u=leedsuni&sid=bookmark-TTDA&xid=79aa5b8f.> [accessed 06/07/23].

171 Ibid.

172 *TNA*, FCO 46/356, 'Operation Sheepskin – Narrative of Events'.

173 'Report on visit to Anguilla by Brigadier Martin 19–22 April 69', attached to DMO to SECCOS, 'Visit of Brigadier P.L. de C. Martin OBE, Brig A/Q HQ Army Strategic Command, to Anguilla', 24 April 1969.

174 Caradon Declaration, quoted in Wooding Report, pp. 41–42.

175 *TNA*, FCO 46/356, 'Operation Sheepskin – Narrative of Events'.

176 Webster, *Revolutionary Leader*, p. 119.

177 *TNA*, FCO 46/356, 'Operation Sheepskin – Narrative of Events'.

178 Bradshaw, quoted in 'Bradshaw flouts pact with Anguilla', *The Times*, 2 April 1969, p. 4, *The Times Digital Archive* <link.gale.com/apps/doc/CS68251778/TTDA?u=leedsuni&sid=bookmark-TTDA&xid=25d46023.> [accessed 11/07/23].

179 Nicholas Harman, 'Problems remain after Anguilla agreement', *The Times*, 1 April 1969, p. 1, *The Times Digital Archive* <link.gale.com/apps/doc/CS17264769/TTDA?u=leedsuni&sid=bookmark-TTDA&xid=ce2bee23.> [accessed 11/07/23].

180 Andrew McEwen, 'Caradon wins over the rebels', *Daily Mail*, 1 April 1969, p. 2, *Daily Mail Historical Archive* <link.gale.com/apps/doc/EE1863628320/DMHA?u=leedsuni&sid=bookmark-DMHA&xid=e051a36e.> [accessed 11/07/23].

Chapter 6

1 'Anguilla Temporary Provision Order 1969', *The Beacon*, 31 March 1969, p. 3, *Anguilla Library Service* <https://www.axalibrary.ai/the%20beacon/Volume%202/Beacon%20Vol%202%20Issue%2077.pdf> [accessed 19/07/23].

2 Westlake, p. 234.

3 Ibid. Wooding Report, p. 42.

4 FCO Statement, quoted in Our Commonwealth Correspondent, 'Accusations by Anguilla scorned', *Daily Telegraph*, 8 April 1969, p. 22, *The Telegraph Historical Archive* <link.gale.com/apps/doc/IO0704651668/TGRH?u=leedsuni&sid=bookmark-TGRH&xid=27edbef7.> [accessed 20/07/23].

5 Henry Miller, 'Lee Sees '50-50 Chance' of New Man in Anguilla', *Daily Telegraph*, 10 April 1969, p. 32, *The Telegraph Historical Archive* <link.gale.com/apps/doc/IO0703271209/TGRH?u=leedsuni&sid=bookmark-TGRH&xid=48958371.> [accessed 20/07/23].

6 Lee, quoted in Miller, 'Lee Sees '50-50 Chance', p. 32.

7 Henry Miller, 'Bayonets guard Lee from Anguilla mob', *Daily Telegraph*, 12 April 1969, p. 1, *The Telegraph Historical Archive* <link.gale.com/apps/doc/IO0705134651/TGRH?u=leedsuni&sid=bookmark-TGRH&xid=0847520d.> [accessed 20/07/23].

8 Henry Miller, 'Lee is quitting Anguilla', *Sunday Telegraph*, 13 April 1969, pp. 1 and 30, *The Telegraph Historical Archive* <link.gale.com/apps/doc/IO0709584396/TGRH?u=leedsuni&sid=bookmark-TGRH&xid=fcb5f5d7.> [accessed 20/07/23].

9 Miller, 'Bayonets guard', p. 1.

10 Miller, 'Lee is quitting Anguilla', p. 30.

11 Wooding Report, p. 43.

12 Lord Caradon, quoted in Miller, 'Lee is quitting Anguilla', p. 1.

13 Our Parliamentary Staff, 'Stewart Denies Anguilla Dismissal of Lee', *Daily Telegraph*, 15 April 1969, p. 26, *The Telegraph Historical Archive* <link.gale.com/apps/doc/IO0702911682/TGRH?u=leedsuni&sid=bookmark-TGRH&xid=8a24434f.> [accessed 22/07/23].

14 Henry Miller, 'Lee is whisked from Anguilla in secrecy', *Daily Telegraph*, 21 April 1969, p. 1, *The Telegraph Historical Archive* <link.gale.com/apps/doc/IO0703360711/TGRH?u=leedsuni&sid=bookmark-TGRH&xid=8edcb55f.> [accessed 23/07/23].

15 'Sir John Cumber', *The Times*, 20 May 1991, p. 16, *The Times Digital Archive* <link.gale.com/apps/doc/IF0500342351/TTDA?u=leedsuni&sid=bookmark-TTDA&xid=7add49ff.> [accessed 23/07/23].

16 Westlake, p. 246.

17 *TNA*, FCO 63/235, Lord Caradon to H.A.A. Hankey, 29 June 1969.

18 *TNA*, FCO 46/356, Lucey to Chief of Defence Staff, 25 April 1969, Annex A to COS 1316/14/5/69.

19 *AAM*, 3.A.5. 2/32/1, '2nd Battalion The Parachute Regiment: Anguilla', p. 41.

20 *TNA*, FCO 46/356, 'Report on visit to Anguilla'.

21 Ibid.

22 Sinclair, p. 100.

23 Ibid.

24 *TNA*, FCO 46/356, 'Report on visit to Anguilla'.

25 Ibid.

26 *AAM*, 3.A.5. 2/32/1, '2nd Battalion The Parachute Regiment: Anguilla', p. 41.

27 Ibid, pp. 41–42.

28 *TNA*, FCO 46/356, 'Report on visit to Anguilla'.

29 Ibid.

30 Ibid.

31 *TNA*, FCO 63/235, Draft Minute from Secretary of State to Secretary of State for Defence, 'Anguilla', [undated].

32 Ibid.

33 *TNA*, FCO 46/356, 'Report on visit to Anguilla'.

34 *TNA*, FCO 63/235, Caradon to Hankey, 29 June 1969.

35 *AAM*, 3.A.5. 2/32/1, '2nd Battalion The Parachute Regiment: Anguilla', p. 42.

36 Richard Posnett, *The Scent of Eucalyptus: A Journal of Colonial and Foreign Service* (London: The Radcliffe Press, 2001), p. 130.

37 Ibid.

38 *AAM*, 3.A.5. 2/32/1, '2nd Battalion The Parachute Regiment: Anguilla', p. 42.

39 Ibid.

40 Ibid, p. 43.

41 'Aberdeen Para on Guard in Anguilla', *Aberdeen Evening Express*, 23 April 1969 [newspaper cutting].

42 '2nd Battalion The Parachute Regiment: Anguilla', p. 43.

43 Ibid.

44 Llewellyn Chanter, 'St Kitts Premier to fight Anguilla breakaway', *Daily Telegraph*, 8 May 1969, p. 27, *The Telegraph Historical Archive* <link.gale.com/apps/doc/IO0701617902/TGRH?u=leedsuni&sid=bookmark-TGRH&xid=ee54ac90.> [accessed 01/08/23].

45 Bradshaw, quoted in Chanter, p. 27.
46 Chanter, p. 27.
47 Caradon Declaration, quoted in Wooding Report, p. 42.
48 'Text of Statement made in Parliament on 23 May, 1969, by the British Secretary of State for Foreign and Commonwealth Affairs on conclusion of his talks in London with the Premier of St. Kitts, Nevis and Anguilla', Annex 12 in Wooding Report, p. 116.
49 Anguillan, 'Britain blows hot and cold', *The Beacon*, 7 June 1969, p. 2, *Anguilla Library Service* <https://www.axalibrary.ai/the%20beacon/Volume%202/Beacon%20Vol%202%20Issue%2086.pdf> [accessed 01/08/23].
50 J.A. Cumber, 'Letter to the Editor', *The Beacon*, 21 June 1969, p. 2, *Anguilla Library Service* <https://www.axalibrary.ai/the%20beacon/Volume%202/Beacon%20Vol%202%20issue%2088.pdf> [accessed 01/08/23].
51 Westlake, p. 252.
52 *TNA*, FCO 63/235, Caradon to Hankey, 29 June 1969.
53 *TNA*, DEFE 11/885, Report by Cumber, 'Anguilla – Appreciation of the Situation', 19 July 1969, Annex A to 1/10/1, 19 July 1969.
54 'Anguilla Police Unit. An Appreciation of the Police Position'.
55 Ibid.
56 *TNA*, FCO 63/235, Hankey to Sewell, 'Anguilla: Security', 4 July 1969.
57 *AAM*, 3.A.5. 2/32/1, Historical Record of 2nd Battalion, The Parachute Regiment 1 April 1969 – 31 March 1970.
58 *TNA*, FCO 63/235, Hankey to Sewell, 'Anguilla: Security', 4 July 1969.
59 *TNA*, DEFE 11/885, Lt Col. J.E.N. Giles to Acting Commissioner Anguilla, 'Force Levels in Anguilla', 9 July 1969, Annex B to 1/10/1, 19 July 1969.
60 Sinclair, p. 101.
61 *TNA*, FCO 46/356, 'Report on visit to Anguilla'.
62 *TNA*, FCO 63/235, Hankey to Sir Edward Peck, 17 July 1969.
63 *TNA*, DEFE 11/885, 'Anguilla – Appreciation of the Situation'.
64 Ibid.
65 Ibid.
66 'Anguilla Police Unit. An Appreciation of the Police Position'.
67 Ibid.
68 Ibid.
69 Colonel GS (MO2) to DS6, 'Employment of Royal Engineers on IS Duties', 25 July 1969.
70 Ibid.
71 Draft report from Sewell to J.C. Morgan, 12 August 1969.
72 Acting Chief of the Defence Staff to Secretary of State, 'Anguilla – Future Force Levels', 13 August 1969.
73 Sewell to Morgan, 12 August 1969.
74 'Anguilla – Future Force Levels'.
75 *TNA*, FCO 63/235, Sewell to Sir L. Monson, 'Anguilla: Proposed Message from the Secretary of State on the departure of the Parachute Company', 10 September 1969.
76 Ibid.
77 A.C. Watson to R.N. Posnett, 19 September 1969.
78 Webster, quoted in 'Insert for T.V. News 2050 Bierman/Webster', 15 September 1969.
79 Ian Ball, 'Troops to Leave Anguilla', *Daily Telegraph*, 28 August 1969, pp. 1 and 32, *The Telegraph Historical Archive* <link.gale.com/apps/doc/IO0704101221/TGRH?u=leedsuni&sid=bookmark-TGRH&xid=4279cfa6.> [accessed 10/08/23].
80 Soldier, quoted in Ball, 'Troops to leave', p. 32.
81 Ball, 'Troops to leave', p. 32.
82 *TNA*, FCO 63/235, Draft Message from the Foreign and Commonwealth Secretary.
83 W.H. Thompson to Sewell, 'Royal Engineers', 3 October 1969.
84 Richard N. Posnett, quoted in Thompson to Sewell, 3 October 1969.
85 Ibid.
86 Ibid.
87 J.H.H. Vaughan to D.A. Truman, 'Anguilla: Royal Engineers', 29 October 1969.
88 R.H.J. Steel to Sewell, 'Anguilla', 16 December 1969.
89 Our Political Staff, 'Anguilla Cost £1½m', *Daily Telegraph*, 24 April 1970, p. 36, *The Telegraph Historical Archive* <link.gale.com/apps/doc/IO0702857277/TGRH?u=leedsuni&sid=bookmark-TGRH&xid=03659181.> [accessed 14/08/23].
90 The National Archives Currency converter: 1270–2017 <https://www.nationalarchives.gov.uk/currency-converter/> [accessed 16/08/23].
91 Maurice Foley, 'Anguilla', HC Deb 02 February 1970 vol 795 cc7-8, *Historic Hansard* <https://api.parliament.uk/historic-hansard/commons/1970/feb/02/anguilla> [accessed 16/08/23].
92 Ibid. Maurice Foley, 'Anguilla', HC Deb 13 October 1969 vol 788 cc16-7, *Historic Hansard* <https://api.parliament.uk/historic-hansard/commons/1969/oct/13/anguilla> [accessed 16/08/23].
93 Westlake, pp. 252–53.
94 Wooding Report, p. 62.
95 Ibid.

96 'Editorial: Wooding Report – 'A Waste'', *The Beacon*, 7 November 1970, p. 4, *Anguilla Library Service* <https://www.axalibrary.ai/the%20beacon/Volume%204/Beacon%20Vol%204%20Issue%2004.pdf> [accessed 17/08/23].
97 Ronald Webster, 'Statement issued by Mr. Ronald Webster, on the release of the Wooding Report', *The Beacon*, 7 November 1970, p. 1, *Anguilla Library Service* <https://www.axalibrary.ai/the%20beacon/Volume%204/Beacon%20Vol%204%20Issue%2004.pdf> [accessed 17/08/23].
98 Ian Ball, 'Anguilla sees a future free of St. Kitts', *Sunday Telegraph*, 13 December 1970, p. 2, *The Telegraph Historical Archive* <link.gale.com/apps/doc/IO0709217579/TGRH?u=leedsuni&sid=bookmark-TGRH&xid=6404581f.> [accessed 17/08/23].
99 Westlake, p. 259.
100 Anguilla Act 1971 c. 63 Section 1, *vLexJustis* <https://vlex.co.uk/vid/anguilla-act-1971-808284461> [accessed 30/10/23].
101 Our Parliamentary Staff, 'Anguilla to train own police during 3-year 'cooling-off' period', *Daily Telegraph*, 17 July 1971, p. 2, *The Telegraph Historical Archive* <link.gale.com/apps/doc/IO0704573430/TGRH?u=leedsuni&sid=bookmark-TGRH&xid=6ef7762e.> [accessed 28/08/23].
102 Webster, quoted in Ian Ball, 'Anguillan rebellion wins new period of colonialism', *Daily Telegraph*, 25 August 1971, p. 4, *The Telegraph Historical Archive* <link.gale.com/apps/doc/IO0704769052/TGRH?u=leedsuni&sid=bookmark-TGRH&xid=6ae7a849.> [accessed 28/08/23].
103 'Editorial', *The Beacon*, 10 July 1971, p. 4, *Anguilla Library Service* <https://www.axalibrary.ai/the%20beacon/Volume%204/Beacon%20Vol%204%20Issue%2018.pdf> [accessed 28/08/23].
104 John Andrade, *World Police & Paramilitary Forces* (Basingstoke: Palgrave Macmillan, 2016), p. 6.
105 Sharon Roberts-Hodge, 'Lt.Col. Claudius Matthias Roberts, MBE., CPM', *The Anguillian*, 30 November 2012 <https://theanguillian.com/2012/11/lt-col-claudius-matthias-roberts-mbe-cpm-by-sharon-roberts-hodge/> [accessed 29/08/23].
106 Our Diplomatic Staff, 'Britain to Cut Anguilla Force by Half', *Daily Telegraph*, 18 February 1971, p. 30, *The Telegraph Historical Archive* <link.gale.com/apps/doc/IO0705554397/TGRH?u=leedsuni&sid=bookmark-TGRH&xid=07f0e42d.> [accessed 28/08/23].
107 *TNA*, FCO 63/785, Draft Memorandum by the Secretary of State for Foreign and Commonwealth Affairs, 'Anguilla', August 1971.
108 Our Diplomatic Correspondent, 'Police and Army to Quit Anguilla', *Daily Telegraph*, 2 September 1971, p. 1, *The Telegraph Historical Archive* <link.gale.com/apps/doc/IO0704575989/TGRH?u=leedsuni&sid=bookmark-TGRH&xid=175c5133.> [accessed 03/09/23]. The National Archives Currency converter: 1270–2017 <https://www.nationalarchives.gov.uk/currency-converter/> [accessed 03/09/23].
109 *TNA*, FCO 63/785, Memorandum by the Secretary of State for Foreign and Commonwealth Affairs, 'Anguilla', August 1971.
110 Ibid.
111 Henry Miller, 'Briton Invades Anguilla', *Daily Telegraph*, 12 February 1977, p. 1, *The Telegraph Historical Archive* <link.gale.com/apps/doc/IO0704452002/TGRH?u=leedsuni&sid=bookmark-TGRH&xid=36d8fa34.> [accessed 08/09/23].
112 Ibid.
113 'Cabinet: Carrington memo circulated to OD Committee – OD(80) 32 (Bill for the Separation of Anguilla from St Kitts-Nevis) [declassified 2010]', *Margaret Thatcher Foundation* <https://c59574e9047e61130f13-3f71d0fe2b653c4f00f32175760e96e7.ssl.cf1.rackcdn.com/98192BD8BBF34E7394303E67B6142A2B.pdf> [accessed 29/03/22].
114 Webster, *Revolutionary Leader*, pp. 176–77.
115 'Cabinet: Carrington memo circulated to OD Committee'.
116 Ibid.
117 'Anguilla: Armstrong briefing for MT ("Bill for the Separation of Anguilla from St. Kitts-Nevis (OD(80) 32)") [declassified 2010]', *Margaret Thatcher Foundation* <https://c59574e9047e61130f13-3f71d0fe2b653c4f00f32175760e96e7.ssl.cf1.rackcdn.com/46792470BD294222B3FF42C01F7A7FFC.pdf> [accessed 29/03/22].
118 'Anguilla Act 1980', *legislation.gov.uk* <https://www.legislation.gov.uk/ukpga/1980/67> [accessed 12/09/23].
119 Webster, *Scrap Book*, p. 152.

Conclusion

1 Mawby, 'Overwhelmed', pp. 265–66.
2 *AAM*, AAL-091-1970, Wilkinson Sword of Peace criteria, quoted in '2nd Battalion: The Wilkinson Sword of Peace Award, 1969', *Pegasus: Journal of The Parachute Regiment & Airborne Forces*, XXV:4 (October 1970), p. 5.
3 General H.J. Mogg to MoD, 'The Wilkinson Award', 13 March 1970, in *Pegasus: Journal of The Parachute Regiment & Airborne Forces*, XXV:4 (October 1970), p. 7.
4 'Letter of gratitude to 2 PARA and Royal Engineers from Alec Douglas-Home' [20 September 1971], *Airborne Assault ParaData* <https://www.paradata.org.uk/media/1279> [accessed 24/03/22].

ABOUT THE AUTHOR

Matthew J. Lord (PhD) has lectured in military history, political science and international relations at Aberystwyth University, the University of Leeds and the University of Central Lancashire. Specialising in British military culture, low intensity conflict and counterinsurgency after 1945, he is the author of *British Concepts of Heroic 'Gallantry' and the Sixties Transition: The Politics of Medals* (2021) and co-editor of *Redcoats to Tommies: The Experience of the British Soldier from the Eighteenth Century* (2021).